EXPLORING ANIMALS

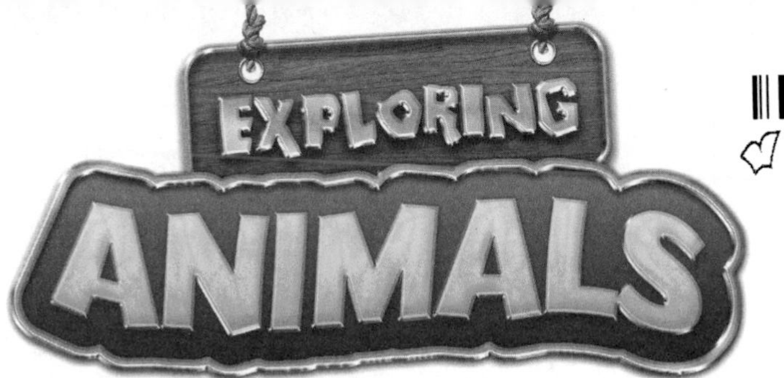

GRADES 2–3

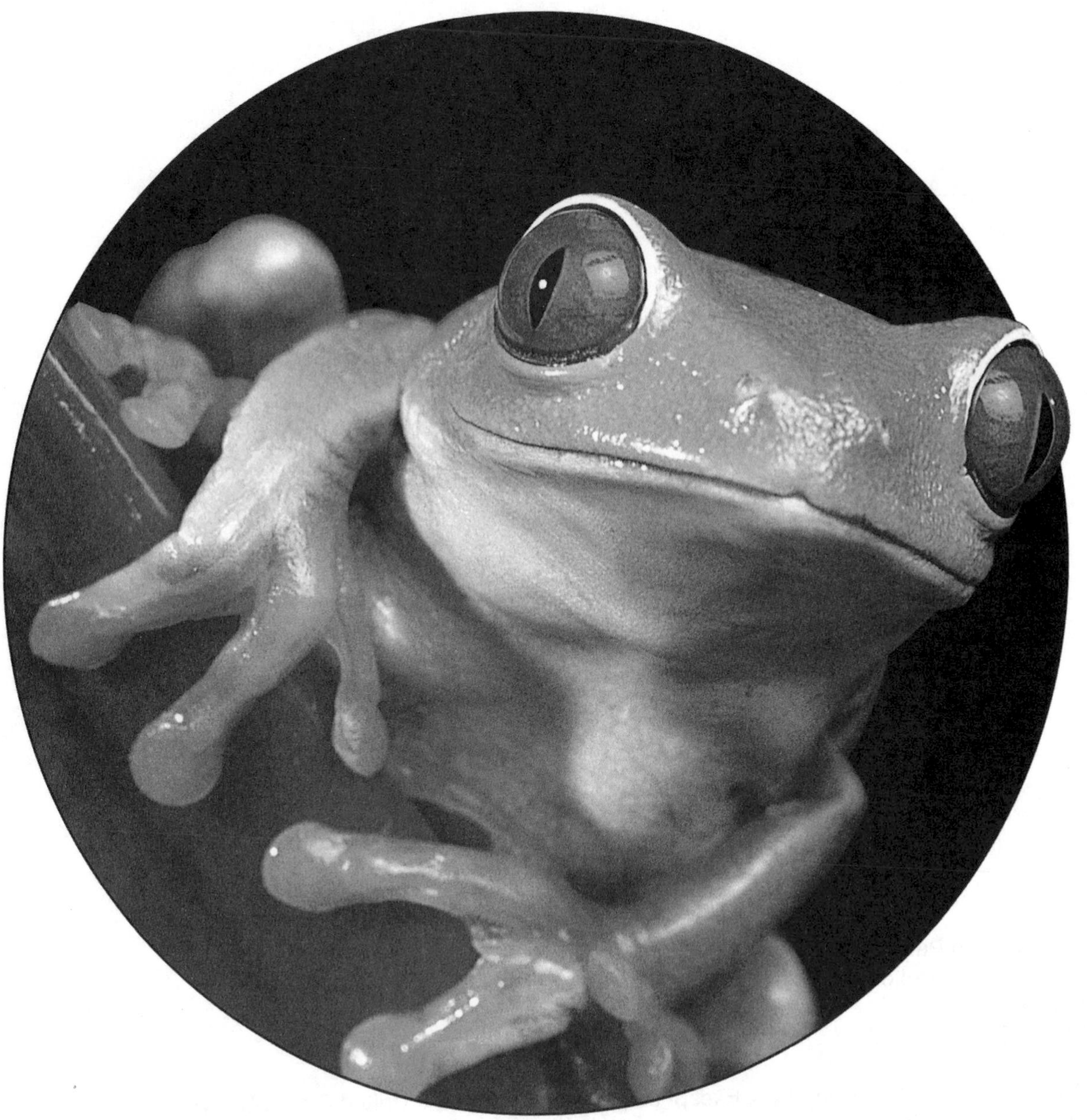

AMERICAN EDUCATION PUBLISHING™
An imprint of Carson-Dellosa Publishing
Greensboro, NC

American Education Publishing™
An imprint of Carson-Dellosa Publishing LLC
P.O. Box 35665
Greensboro, NC 27425 USA

ISBN 978-1-60996-785-7

02-244127811

TABLE OF CONTENTS

Arctic and Antarctic Land and Sea Animals
Caribou....8
Ermine....9
Lemming....10
Musk Ox....11
Orca (Killer Whale)....12
Pull-Out Storybook: Penguins....13–20
Color-Your-Own Picture: Penguins....21
Polar Bear....23
Seal....24
Predator and Prey....25
Snowy Owl....26
Walrus....27
Wolverine....28

North American Animals
Bald Eagle....30
Beaver....31
Gray Wolf....32
Pull-Out Storybook: Wolves....33–40
Color-Your-Own Picture: Wolf....41
Grizzly Bear....43
Moose....44
Otter....45
Wild Turkey....46
Porcupine....47
Striped Skunk....48
White-Tailed Deer....49
Pronghorn....50

Asian Animals
Chevrotain....52
Giant Panda....53
A Vanishing Act....54
Gibbon....55
Malayan Tapir....56
Orangutan....57
Sloth Bear....58
Snow Leopard....59
Tiger....60
Water Buffalo....61
Wild Boar....62

Central and South American Animals
Chinchilla....64
Giant Anteater....65
Giant Armadillo....66
Jaguar....67
Llama....68
Macaw....69
Spider Monkey....70
Spider Monkey Dot-to-Dot....71
Toucan....72
Two-Toed Sloth....73
Woolly Monkey....74

Australian Animals
Dingo....76
Dugong....77
Echidna....78
Giant Gray Kangaroo....79
Australian Animal Scramble....80
Koala....81
Kookaburra....82
Platypus....83
Tasmanian Devil....84

TABLE OF CONTENTS

Wallaby 85
Wombat 86

African Animals

African Elephant 88
Pull-Out Storybook: Elephants 89–96
Color-Your-Own Picture: Elephants 97
Giraffe 99
Chimpanzee 100
Gorilla 101
Apes and Monkeys 102
Hippopotamus 103
Lion 104
Ostrich 105
Black Rhinoceros 106
Vulture 107
Zebra 108

Insects

Ant 110
Ant Colonies 111
Bee 112
Honeybees 113
Beetle 114
Butterfly 115
Cricket 116
Fly 117
Grasshopper 118
Mosquito 119
Moth 120

Reptiles

Tuatara 122
Crocodile 123
Alligator 124
Compare and Contrast 125
Lizard 126
Chameleon 127
Snake 128
Garter Snake 129
Rattlesnake 130
Turtle 131
Sea Turtle 132

Animals That Live in the Water

Crab 134
Dolphin 135
Dolphin Dot-to-Dot 136
Pull-Out Storybook: Dolphins .. 137–144
Color-Your-Own Picture: Dolphins 145
Jellyfish 147
Lobster 148
Octopus 149
Salmon 150
Sea Horse 151
Shark 152
Starfish 153
Whale 154
Word Search: Whale Watch 155
Hidden Pictures: Ocean Animals 156

Farm Animals

Duck 158
Pig 159
Horse 160
Pull-Out Storybook: Horses 161–168
Color-Your-Own Picture: Horses 169

TABLE OF CONTENTS

Cow 171
Chicken 172
Sheep 173
Goat 174

Favorite Pets

Cat 176
Pull-Out Storybook: Cats 177–184
Color-Your-Own Picture: Cat 185
Dog 187
Animal Friends 188
Rabbit 189
Guinea Pig 190
Frog 191
Compare and Contrast 192
Pull-Out Storybook: Frogs 193–200
Color-Your-Own Picture: Frogs 201

Science and Animals

Classification Systems 204
Classifying Animals 205
Classifying Vertebrates 206
Backbones 207
Classy Vertebrates 208
Animals With Backbones 209
Parts of a Fish 210–211
Life Cycle of a Frog 212–213
Parts of a Bird 214–215
Bird Beaks 216–217
Feathered Friends' Feet 218
Strangers in the Night 219
What's a Mammal? 220–221
The Mammal With Wings 222–223
Animals Without Backbones 224–225
Kinds of Insects 226–227
Animal Adaptations 228–229
Animal Defenses 230
Animal Locomotion 231
Food Chains 232

Answer Key 233–256

PRONUNCIATION KEY

As you read, you may find words that you do not know or words that are difficult to pronounce. In this book, the difficult words are respelled the way you say them. A syllable in capital letters will have the most stress. The key below gives examples of how words are respelled.

Letters	Example	Respelling	Letters	Example	Respelling
a	sat	(sat)	m	moose	(moos)
ah	mop	(mahp)	n	nature	(NAY cher)
ahr	car	(cahr)	oh	no	(noh)
air	fair, pear	(fair), (pair)	oi	foil, toy	(foil), (toi)
aw	law, all	(law, (awl)	oo	moon, blue	(moon), (bloo)
ay	pay, late	(pay), (layt)	or	corn, more	(corn), (mor)
b	bat	(bat)	ow	now, house	(now), (hows)
ch	chin, beach	(chihn), (beech)	ng	sing	(sihng)
d	dime	(dighm)	p	pen	(pehn)
eh	net	(neht)	r	ring	(rihng)
ee	see, eat	(see), (eet)	s	say, cent	(say), (sehnt)
er	fern, stir, turn	(fern), (ster), (tern)	sh	ship, brush	(shihp), (bruhsh)
f	fan, phone	(fan), (fohn)	t	tail	(tayl)
g	gate, dog	(gayt), (dahg)	th	three	(three)
h	hat	(hat)	u	book	(buk)
ih	him	(hihm)	uh	sun	(suhn)
igh	fine, buy	(fighn), (bigh)	v	valley	(VA lee)
j	jeep, gem,	(jeep), (jehm)	w	win	(wihn)
k	kit, can	(kiht), (kan)	y	yes	(yehs)
ks	fox	(fahks)	yoo	few, mule	(fyoo), (myool)
kw	quit	(kwiht)	z	zebra, size	(ZEE bruh), (sighz)
l	lamp	(lamp)	zh	treasure	(TREH zher)

ARCTIC AND ANTARCTIC

LAND AND SEA ANIMALS

Orca

Lemming

Seal

Caribou

Caribou (CAIR ah boo) are sometimes called *reindeer*. They are large animals weighing 300 to 600 pounds. Both male and female caribou have very large antlers. In fact, the female caribou is the only female member of the deer family able to grow antlers. Caribou have long hair and woolly fur. They are great long-distance runners and can easily outrun a pack of wolves. Their wide hooves help them walk easily through snow. Caribou can also swim.

In summer, caribou feed on grass, leaves, and other low-growing plants of the tundra—the flat, treeless land of the arctic. In winter, caribou migrate to wooded areas and feed on small, dry plants that grow on rocks and trees called *lichens* (LEYE kuhnz).

Think and Learn

1. How much do caribou weigh? ____________________
2. Caribou are members of the ____________________ family.
3. Where do caribou migrate in winter? ____________________
4. What do caribou eat during summer? ____________________

____

Ermine

Ermine (ER mehn) are members of the weasel family. They are tiny animals, weighing less than a pound. Ermine have huge, dark eyes and long whiskers. They have smooth, silky fur. During the spring and summer, their fur is brown. When autumn approaches, ermine grow a new coat of thick, snow-white fur. This white fur helps ermine blend in with their snowy environment.

Ermine live in northern regions of North America along riverbanks and at the edges of forests. They are good hunters and feed on small animals, such as rabbits and rats. In April, ermine have litters of 3 to 13 fuzzy white babies. By late summer, these babies are fully grown.

Think and Learn

1. During spring, ermine have ____________________ fur.
2. What color fur do ermine have in winter? ____________________
3. Where do ermine live? ____________________

   ____
4. What do ermine eat? ____________________

   ____

Lemming

Lemmings are chubby little animals belonging to the rodent family. They look very much like hamsters and guinea pigs. Lemmings dig in the soil to build their nests, which they line with grass. They eat plants and live in areas where food is often scarce.

An old legend about lemmings says that every few years, lemmings march to the ocean, jump in, and drown. Scientists have learned that some lemmings will move to a new area when the number of lemmings in an area is too high. Lemmings always migrate in a straight direction, crossing anything in their path. If they come to a river, they jump in and swim across it. When they come to the ocean and jump in, they cannot swim across it, so they drown.

Think and Learn

1. What other animals do lemmings look like? ______
2. Where do lemmings build their nests? ______
3. What do lemmings eat? ______
4. When do lemmings migrate? ______

Musk Ox

Musk oxen are huge animals with large heads and short legs. They grow to 5 feet tall at the shoulders and weigh up to 900 pounds. Musk oxen have long, dark brown hair that almost touches the ground. Thick, woolly fur under the hair keeps them warm and dry. They use their hooves to scratch through the snow to find grass, willows, and other plants to eat.

Musk oxen live together on the tundra in herds of 20 to 100. When danger is near, the adult musk oxen gather in a circle, facing outward. The calves stay in the center of the circle for protection. When the adult oxen lower their heads, showing their enormous horns, even a pack of wolves will not come near.

Think and Learn

1. Musk oxen have ______________________________ legs.
2. Musk ox hair almost touches the ______________________________.
3. How do musk oxen find food? ______________________________

____

4. How big are herds of musk oxen? ______________________________

Orca (Killer Whale)

The black and white orca (OR kuh) is a large dolphin that is often called a *killer whale*. It grows up to 30 feet long and weighs 3 to 10 tons. The orca has 40 to 48 large pointed teeth that it uses to catch and hold its prey. It eats over 100 pounds of food every day.

Orcas live and travel in family groups called *pods*. They are affectionate animals and are often seen touching each other. Female orcas give birth to one baby every 3 to 10 years. The baby will stay with its mother for 10 years. Orcas are very intelligent animals. They communicate with each other by making sounds.

Think and Learn

1. Is an orca a dolphin or a whale? __________
2. What color is an orca? __________
3. How much food does an orca eat each day? __________
4. Orcas travel in family groups called __________.
5. Orcas communicate by making __________.

PENGUINS

Pull-Out Storybook

What animal seems dressed for a fancy party? A penguin, of course. The penguin's black-and-white coloring looks like a tuxedo. There are 17 different kinds of penguins. The emperor penguin is the largest. It can weigh up to 90 pounds and grow to be 4 feet tall. The little blue penguin is the smallest. It weighs 2 pounds and is about 1 foot tall.

Penguins have bodies that are built for water. Their short wings serve as flippers. A penguin uses its tail as a rudder to steer. Penguins get their food from the sea. Their favorite foods are krill—small, shrimplike animals—fish, and squid, which they catch and eat underwater.

If there is snow, penguins like to get around by tobogganing. They flop on their bellies and slide, using their wings and feet to paddle forward. Some penguins can leap from the water several feet into the air! Imagine if you could pop out of a pool like a penguin!

King Penguin chicks

Like all other birds, a penguin's feathers wear out. So, each year, the penguin sheds its old feathers and grows new ones. During this time, a penguin cannot go in the cold water because it is no longer waterproof. Therefore, it cannot eat. Penguin chicks shed their downy feathers when they are about a year old. The feathers underneath are waterproof.

Most penguins build nests to keep their eggs safe. Emperor penguins, however, do not build nests. The egg is kept warm on the tops of the parents' feet. The fathers huddle together to keep the eggs warm while the mothers go to the sea to feed. The mothers return after the chicks have hatched, and the fathers go to the sea.

A penguin chick must peck its way out of the eggshell. Both the mother and father penguins will care for the chick. Penguin parents must go to the sea for fish, then come back to feed their hungry chicks. When chicks get older, they gather in groups for warmth and protection. Once a young penguin molts, or sheds its feathers, it grows adult feathers. Then, the penguin is ready to feed and live on its own.

Here are a variety of penguins. The giant **emperor penguin** and the little **Adelie** (AD uh lee) **penguin** both live in Antarctica. The **black-footed penguin** lives off the southern coast of Africa. Like other warm-water penguins, it brays like a donkey. The **rockhopper** is an aggressive little penguin that will bite humans or slap them with a flipper if they get too close. The **Galapagos** (guh LAH puh gohs) **penguin** lives on islands where temperatures reach 100°F. **Chinstraps** are noisy penguins that hiss, growl, and stamp their feet! The **gentoo** is the shyest penguin. The **little blue penguin** lives in Australia and New Zealand. The **yellow-eyed penguin** is the rarest penguin. Fewer than 5,000 are left.

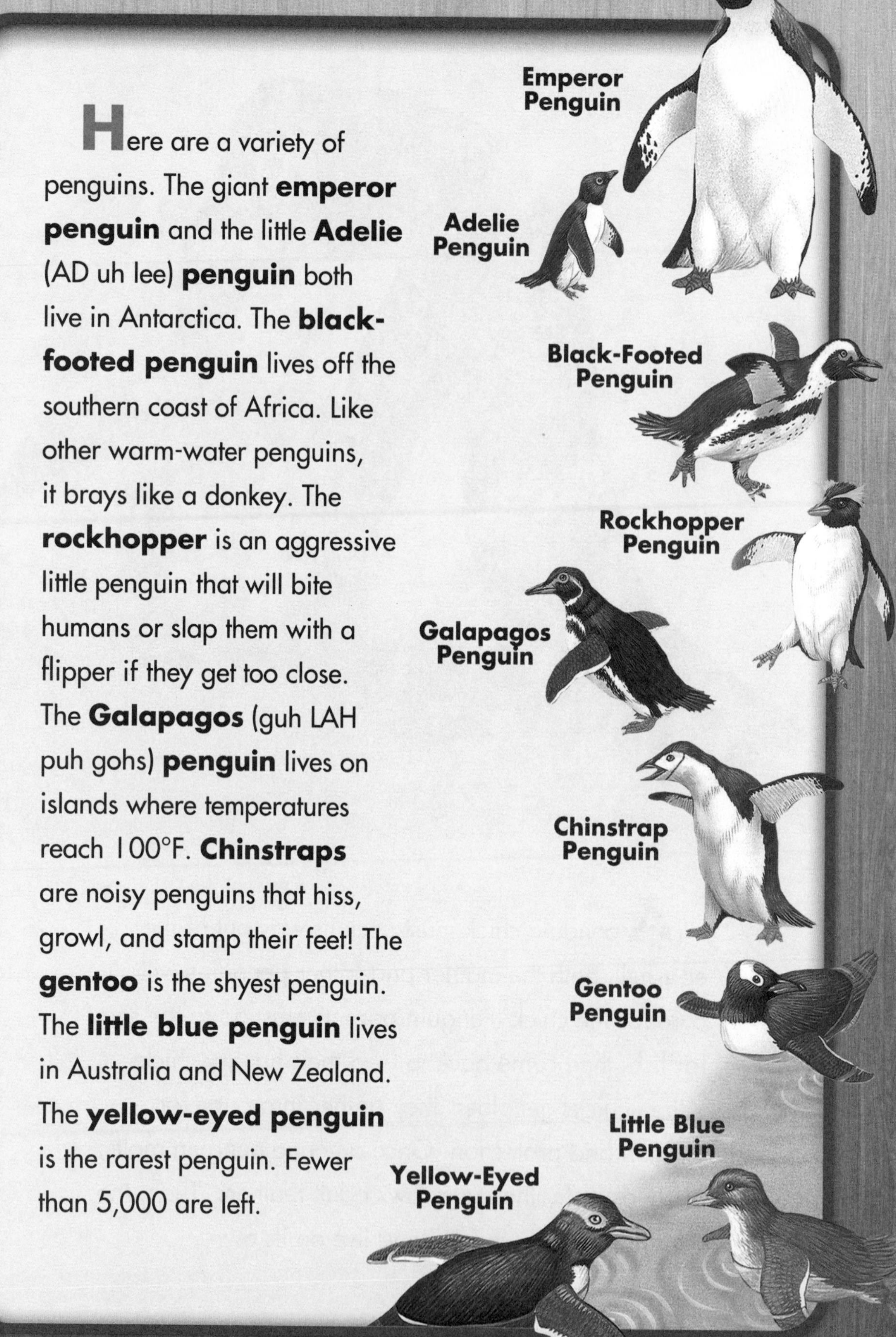

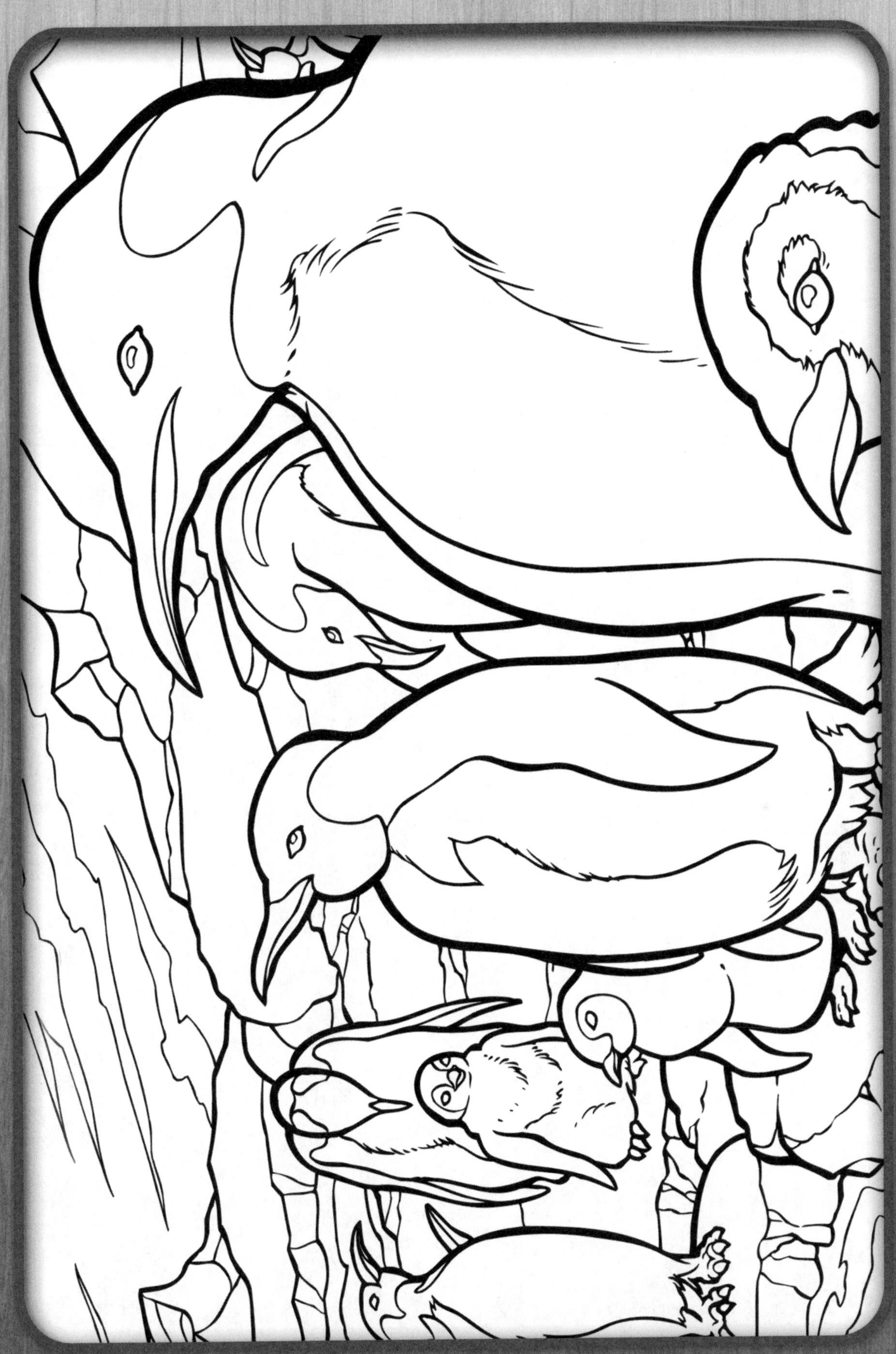

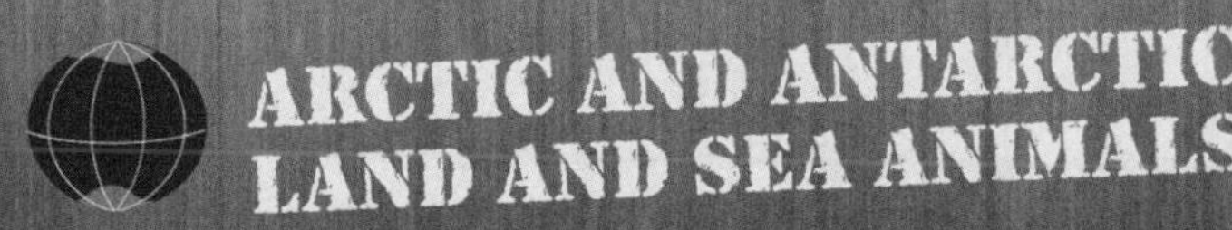

Polar Bear

Polar bears are the world's largest four-legged meat-eating animals—9 feet tall and 1,600 pounds! They have special features to help them live in the arctic. Their thick fur and a layer of fat keep them warm. Their small ears lose less body heat. Pads on the bottom of their feet keep them from slipping on ice. Polar bears are excellent swimmers. Webbing between their clawed toes helps them swim. Polar bears hunt seals, walruses, small whales, and fish. In the summer months, they eat berries and plants.

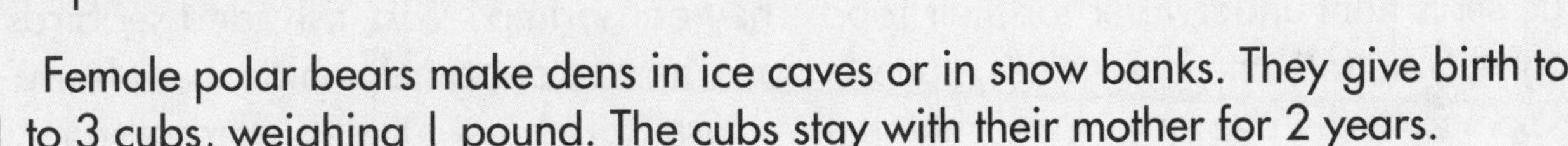

Female polar bears make dens in ice caves or in snow banks. They give birth to 1 to 3 cubs, weighing 1 pound. The cubs stay with their mother for 2 years.

Think and Learn

1. What features keep polar bears warm? ______________________________

____

2. Polar bears have webbed toes to help them ______________________.

3. What do they eat in the summer? ______________________________

4. How long do polar bear cubs stay with their mother? ______________

____

Seal

Seals are animals with special features to live in water. Their flippers move them quickly and gracefully through water. Their bodies are covered with oily fur and a layer of blubber, or fat, to keep them warm. There are two kinds of seals—sea lions and true seals. Sea lions have ears outside their heads, but true seals have no outer ears. While sea lions can move easily on land, true seals must use their chest muscles to move on land. True seals never have to leave the water.

True seals hunt underwater for their food. They eat shrimp, crab, fish, and seabirds. Seals give birth to white baby seals, called *pups*. Their coloring helps hide them from polar bears. As the pup grows, its white fur will turn dark brown like its parents' fur.

Think and Learn

1. Seals are adapted to live in ____________________.
2. ____________________ move seals quickly through water.
3. What keeps seals warm? ____________________
4. Which kind of seal moves easily on land? ____________________
5. What color are seal pups? ____________________

Predator and Prey

Polar bears live along frozen shores and on ice floating in arctic waters. The polar bear is a predator (PRED uh tur) because it hunts other animals for food. The animals hunted by predators are called *prey*. When hunting for seals, polar bears like to wait by a seal's breathing hole in the ice. The seal may not see the polar bear waiting by the breathing hole. The polar bear's white fur helps it blend in with its snowy environment. When the seal comes up to breathe, the polar bear catches it. Seals are dark brown to help them blend in with their environment. When a polar bear looks down into the water, the water reflects the color of the ocean bottom, which is dark brown or black. Sometimes, the polar bear does not see the seal.

1. Color the picture to show how the animals blend into the environment.

2. Label the predator and the prey in the picture.

Snowy Owl

The snowy owl gets its name from the snow-white feathers covering its body. It has thick feathers covering its feet and legs for warmth. Like other owls, snowy owls must turn their heads to look around because their eyes cannot move. Their ears are tiny slits on their faces. Owls raise their face feathers when they are listening.

Snowy owls hunt for rats and arctic hares, but lemmings are their main food source. If lemmings are plentiful, snowy owls will lay more eggs. When lemmings are scarce, snowy owls may not lay any eggs. Snowy owls live on the treeless tundra, so they build their nests on the ground in places where they can watch for predators.

Think and Learn

1. Snowy owls have ________________ covering their feet and legs.
2. Why must owls turn their heads to look around? ________________

   ____
3. What is the main food source for snowy owls? ________________
4. Snowy owls build nests on the ________________.

Walrus

The walrus is a huge animal, weighing between 2 and 3 tons. Its thick skin and layer of blubber protect it from the cold. Both male and female walruses have ivory tusks. They use their tusks to pull themselves across ice and for protection against polar bears.

Walruses are excellent swimmers. They can stay out at sea for days. They feed on the ocean floor by using their "moustache" bristles to feel for clams. Then, they use their snouts to dig the clams out. Walruses live together in herds containing thousands of walruses. One of their favorite things to do is sleep. When one walrus is awakened, it slaps another walrus. This goes on until the whole herd is awake. In time, they will fall back to sleep.

Think and Learn

1. How much does a walrus weigh? ______________________________

2. Why are the tusks of a walrus important? ______________________________

____

3. What do walruses eat? ______________________________

4. Walruses live together in ______________________________.

Wolverine

The wolverine is the largest member of the weasel family. It reaches a height of 1 foot at the shoulder and weighs 30 to 50 pounds. Wolverines are covered with long, shaggy, dark brown hair. Water does not freeze to their fur.

For their size, wolverines are probably the strongest and fiercest animals of the North. Often, wolverines chase away a bear or a mountain lion from its food so they can eat the food. After a wolverine eats a large meal, it will not eat again for a few days. Female wolverines give birth to two or three cubs in a litter. They are born in early summer already covered in woolly fur coats. By winter, the cubs can live on their own.

Think and Learn

1. The wolverine is the largest member of the ______________ family.
2. What is special about wolverine fur? ______________
3. Why are wolverines thought of as fierce animals? ______________

____
4. When are wolverine cubs born? ______________

NORTH AMERICAN ANIMALS

Bald Eagle

The bald eagle is a bird of prey, or a bird that catches and eats other animals. It is a large bird, with a wingspan reaching 8 feet. The bald eagle is well-known for its white head and neck. Most bald eagles live near water because they love to eat fish. Their hooked bills and long, curved claws help them to catch fish.

Of all the eagles, bald eagles build the largest nests. Some nests have been measured at 8 feet across! Eagles lay two ivory-white eggs. The eaglets are born brown. They do not look like adults until they are 3 years old. The bald eagle has been the national bird of the United States since 1782. It is a symbol of freedom and courage.

Think and Learn

1. The bald eagle has a wingspan of ____________________.
2. What color is the bald eagle's head? ____________________
3. What helps bald eagles catch fish? ____________________

____.

4. The bald eagle is the national bird of ____________________

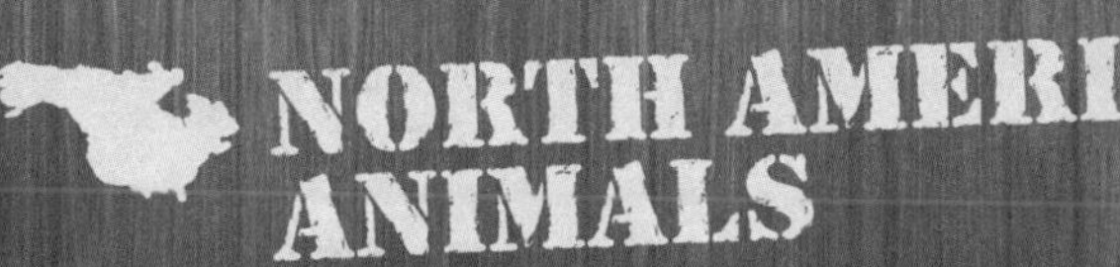

Beaver

The beaver is a member of the rodent family. It grows to a length of 2 feet and usually weighs 35 to 40 pounds. The beaver has dark brown fur that keeps the animal warm and dry. Its strong jaws have two cutting teeth, called *incisors*. The incisors keep growing all through a beaver's life so that these teeth are never worn down. Beavers use their incisors to cut down trees. Beavers eat twigs and bark from trees that grow near water.

Beavers are graceful swimmers. They move easily through the water with their webbed toes. Their tail helps steer them. Beavers mate for life and live in colonies. All the beavers in a colony work together and build lodges as their homes.

Think and Learn

1. What are the beaver's cutting teeth called? ______________________________

2. What do beavers eat? ______________________________

3. How does a beaver use its tail? ______________________________

4. What is a beaver's home called? ______________________________

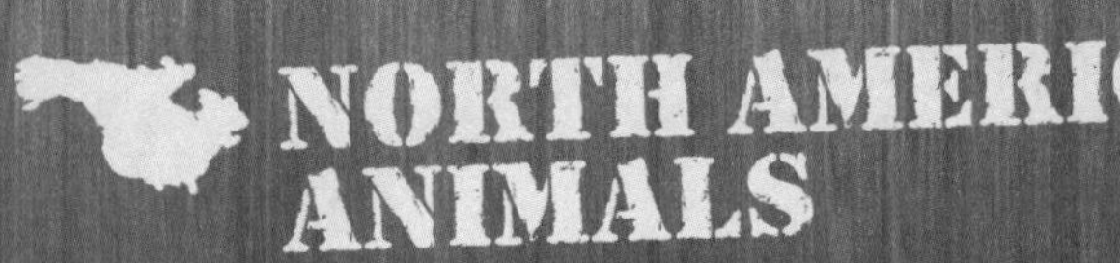

Gray Wolf

The gray wolf is the largest member of the wild dog family. This animal can reach a length of 4 feet and can weigh 100 pounds. Gray wolves live in northern forests. They hunt for deer, elk, and moose in packs of 3 to 24. Wolves, like other members of the dog family, can go for several days without food.

The leader for the wolf pack is the strongest male. Other wolves show respect by lowering their ears and putting their tails between their legs. Wolves mate for life. A female gives birth to a litter of 3 to 13 young, called *pups*. The pups are helpless at first. Other members of the pack help the parents care for the pups.

Think and Learn

1. The gray wolf is a member of the ________________ family.
2. Where do gray wolves live? ________________
3. Gray wolves hunt in ________________.
4. How do wolves show respect to the leader? ________________

____

WOLVES
Pull-Out Storybook

What do you think of when you hear the word *wolf*? A sly animal that tricks girls in red hoods? Wolves have had a bad reputation. But wolves are actually shy animals that avoid people. With each other, they are caring, protective, and loyal.

There are two main species, or kinds, of wolves—the gray wolf and the red wolf. Male wolves are larger than females. The wolves below are timber wolves—a type of gray wolf.

Wolves look like large dogs. In fact, they are members of the dog family. Wolves have longer legs and bigger paws than dogs. Their fur is also thicker and bushier. This helps keep them warm in freezing temperatures.

Wolves have excellent eyesight and a keen sense of hearing. They can hear sounds 10 miles away. Wolves also have an excellent sense of smell.

Gray wolves live in family groups called *packs*. Most packs have between 6 and 20 wolves. Pack members care for and protect each other. They work together to hunt food. They also help raise the wolf pups.

Wolves are curious, intelligent animals. They sometimes remind us of dogs. But as friendly as wolves may look, they are wild animals and do not make good pets.

Wolves communicate in many ways. A wolf pack howls to tell other wolves to stay away. They may howl to signal the start of a hunt. Wolves also howl to call each other back to the pack.

Wolves often communicate with their bodies. A happy wolf has its ears forward, its tongue hanging out of its mouth, and its tail wagging. An angry wolf has its ears forward, its teeth bared, and its tail up. A frightened wolf has its ears back, its mouth closed, and its tail down.

Wolves are carnivores, meaning they eat other animals. Wolves use their excellent sense of smell to help them find deer, beavers, rabbits, and other prey. When the wolves spot their prey, they chase it until the prey tires. Then, the wolves surround it.

Wolves can run at speeds of up to 40 miles per hour. But many times, the pack does not catch its prey. Some animals can outrun the wolves.

Wolves are caring parents. The mother wolf finds or digs a den before her pups are born. Wolf pups are born blind and helpless. The mother cares for the pups inside the den for a few weeks. She feeds them milk from her body. In the meantime, the father wolf brings food for the mother.

Wolves belong to a group of animals that also include foxes, coyotes, jackals, wild dogs, and pet dogs. The **maned wolf** of South America is called the *fox on stilts*. Can you see why? The **husky** looks like the wolf, but is smaller. **African wild dogs** live in packs. They hunt large animals like zebras. The **gray fox** will climb a tree to escape from danger or search for prey. Thousands of years ago, the **dingo** was brought to Australia as a tame dog. Since then, it has become wild. **Coyotes** usually live alone or in pairs. Although the wolf's range has decreased, the areas where coyotes live have increased. The **raccoon dog** has a face like a raccoon. This small foxlike animal lives in eastern Asia.

Grizzly Bear

Grizzly bears once lived in large numbers from Canada to Mexico. Now, most grizzly bears live in national parks. Male grizzly bears stand 8 feet tall and weigh 800 to 1,000 pounds. Grizzly bears have very good senses of smell and hearing. These senses make up for their poor eyesight.

Grizzly bears are omnivores—they eat both plants and animals. Their favorite foods are berries, leaves, fish, and small animals. In autumn, grizzly bears spend a lot of time eating. They are fattening up to get ready for their winter sleep, or hibernation. Grizzly bears hibernate differently from other animals. Their body functions do not slow down, and they are easily awakened.

Think and Learn

1. Where do most grizzly bears live today? ______________________

2. Which senses make up for the grizzly bear's poor eyesight? ______________________

____

3. What do omnivores eat? ______________________

4. How do grizzly bears get ready for hibernation? ______________________

____

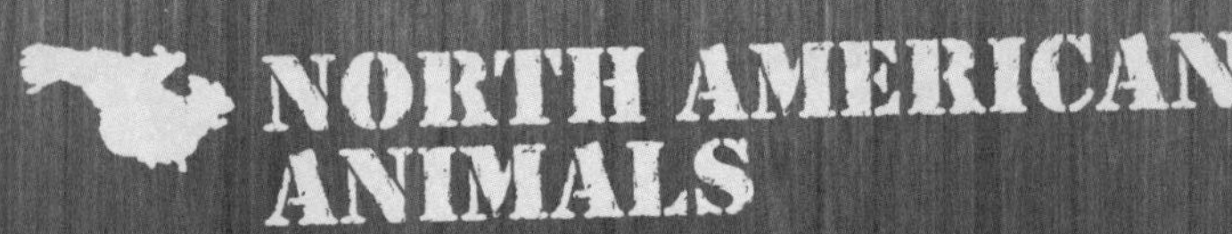

Moose

The largest member of the deer family is the moose. These huge animals are 10 feet long and weigh about 1,800 pounds. Male moose have very large, flattened antlers. Every year, they shed their antlers and grow a new pair in spring. Moose enjoy water and are excellent swimmers. They usually live near marshes, lakes, or in moist forests.

During the summer months, moose eat water plants, roots, leaves, and grass. In winter, moose walk easily through the deep snow. They find tree shoots and twigs to eat. Moose live alone in the summer. When winter arrives, it is common for small bands of moose to stay together in the woods for warmth and protection.

Think and Learn

1. The moose is a member of the ______________________ family.

2. Each year, moose shed their ______________________, then grow a new pair.

3. Where do moose usually live? ______________________

____

4. Why do moose stay together in small bands in winter? ______________________

____

Otter

Otters are members of the weasel family. Their long bodies have special features, or adaptations, that allow them to live most of the time in water. Otters have flat tails and webbed feet that help them swim. Their coarse, outer fur is waterproof. They also close their nostrils and ears when underwater.

Otters make their homes by digging burrows or finding caves near water. They mainly eat fish that they catch while swimming. But they also eat crayfish, frogs, snails, and insects. Otters are fun to watch because they are so playful. They love to slide on their bellies down banks of mud or snow and splash into the water. They communicate with each other by barking, chirping, and growling.

Think and Learn

1. Where do otters spend most of their time? ______________________

2. Otters have ______________________ feet.

3. What do otters eat? ______________________

____

4. How do otters communicate with each other? ______________________

____

Wild Turkey

Wild turkeys are large birds that live mainly on the ground. Males, or toms, may weigh as much as 24 pounds. Females, or hens, weigh only 12 pounds. Tom turkeys look different from hens. They have a flap of skin, called a *snood*, that falls over the beak. They also have a wattle, a flap of skin that grows from the throat. Both toms and hens have short rounded wings and heavy bodies. They fly for only short distances. They also have strong feet with four toes. This makes them very fast runners.

Wild turkeys live in woods near water. They eat seeds and insects, but sometimes eat frogs or lizards. When threatened, they usually run away and hide. Wild turkeys sleep in tree branches at night.

Think and Learn

1. Where do wild turkeys live? ________________

2. What features do toms have that hens do not? ________________

3. What makes turkeys fast runners? ________________

____

4. Where do wild turkeys sleep? ________________

Porcupine

The porcupine (POR kyoo pighn) is a gnawing animal that is best known for its strong, sharp quills. Quills are bunches of hair that have grown together. The quills are white with black tips. They cover a porcupine's tail, sides, and back. Porcupines are rather small, weighing between 15 and 20 pounds. They are also peaceful and never attack other animals.

Porcupines are nocturnal. This means they sleep during the day and are active at night. They spend most of the night in trees looking for food. They might climb 60 to 70 feet up a tree to reach young leaves. In summer, they eat seeds, fruits, and leaves. In winter, they eat twigs, leaves, bark, and pine needles.

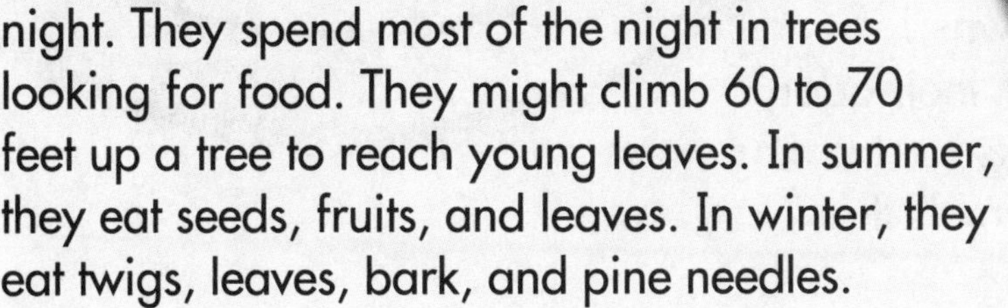

Think and Learn

1. What are quills? ______________________________

2. Why don't porcupines attack other animals? ______________________________

____

3. Porcupines are ______________________________, they sleep during the day.

4. What do porcupines eat during the summer? ______________________________

____

Striped Skunk

The skunk is known for its black and white fur and its horrible odor. The striped skunk is the most common kind of skunk. It gets its name from the white stripes running down its back. Skunks are about the size of a small cat, measuring 15 inches long. They weigh 5 to 6 pounds. Skunks have short legs, an arched back, a long bushy tail, and a patch of white fur on their forehead.

Skunks make their dens in burrows, hollow trees, and under buildings. They are found in forests, grasslands, and in towns. Even though skunks annoy people with their odor, skunks are very helpful animals. Skunks eat harmful insects, rats, mice, and other small animals that damage crops and fields.

Think and Learn

1. What two things are skunks known for? ____________________

____

2. A skunk is about the same size as a small ____________________.

3. Where are skunks found? ____________________

4. How are skunks helpful to people? ____________________

____

White-Tailed Deer

The white-tailed deer is easy to recognize by its snow-white tail. White-tailed deer are found throughout North America, but they are most common in southern Canada and northern United States. Only the males, called *bucks*, grow antlers. These antlers are shed each winter. White-tailed deer eat nuts and berries, as well as the buds and twigs from trees.

White-tailed deer are fast runners and great jumpers. Bucks frequently fight during mating season. They use their antlers and hooves as weapons. Female deer, called *does*, give birth to 1 to 3 fawns in the spring. The fawns are covered with white spots that disappear in six months.

Think and Learn

1. What are white-tailed deer recognized by? ______________________________

2. Only bucks grow ____.

3. What do deer eat? ____

4. How is a fawn's coloring different from an adult deer? ____________________

____

Pronghorn

The pronghorn is North America's fastest animal. It can run about 40 miles per hour and jump very high. The pronghorn is mostly covered with reddish-brown fur and has white fur on the lower parts of its body, including the tail. The pronghorn lifts its fur straight up to cool its body in hot weather. In cold weather, it holds its fur flat against its body for warmth. The pronghorn has long horns that it never sheds.

Pronghorn live in the grasslands of western United States and Canada. They eat shrubs, sagebrush, grass, and twigs. In the summer, they live in small groups. As winter comes, they form large herds of 100 or more.

Think and Learn

1. The pronghorn is North America's ______________________ animal.
2. How does a pronghorn keep cool in hot weather? ______________________

   ____
3. Where do pronghorn live? ______________________

   ____
4. What do pronghorn eat? ______________________

ASIAN ANIMALS

Tiger

Wild Boar

Chevrotain

Chevrotains (SHEHV ruh taynz) are very small animals with cowlike hooves. They are sometimes called *mouse deer* because they look like tiny deer. Chevrotains have two long tusklike teeth and no other upper teeth. They use their long upper teeth to defend themselves from other animals.

Chevrotains live in the tropical forests of India and Southeast Asia. They eat at night, keeping hidden in the underbrush. They feed on fruit, leaves, twigs, and grass. During the day, chevrotains hide behind rocks or in the bushes. They are quiet, timid animals. Chevrotains live alone except during the mating season. A female chevrotain usually gives birth to two babies, called *fawns*.

Think and Learn

1. Chevrotains are also called ____________________.
2. What do chevrotains use to defend themselves? ____________________

   ____
3. Where do chevrotains live? ____________________

   ____
4. When do chevrotains eat? ____________________

Giant Panda

The giant panda is a very large black and white furry animal. Scientists used to classify pandas as part of the raccoon family. Now, they classify pandas as bears. The giant panda is found in bamboo forests in the mountains of west central China.

Pandas reach a height of 5 feet and weigh about 200 pounds. They easily climb trees and spend most of their time eating bamboo plants. They eat every part of the plant. Pandas have a special thumblike toe on their front feet used for holding bamboo stems. Their teeth are large and wide to help them grind up the bamboo.

Think and Learn

1. Scientists now classify the giant panda as a ________________.
2. Where do giant pandas live? ________________
3. Pandas eat all parts of the ________________ plant.
4. How do pandas use the thumblike toe on their front feet? ________________

____

A Vanishing Act

The panda is one of many endangered animals. Endangered animals may soon disappear from Earth. That's what happened to dinosaurs, dodo birds, and passenger pigeons. They disappeared, or became extinct.

Write the letter that comes before each letter in the alphabet to decode the names of some endangered animals.

A B C D E F G H I J K L M N O P Q R S T U V W X Y Z

N P V O U B J O   H P S J M M B

B G S J D B O   F M F Q I B O U

X I P P Q J O H   D S B O F

C M B D L   S I J O P

H J B O U   Q B O E B

T F B   M J P O

H S B Z   X P M G

D I F F U B I

Gibbon

Gibbons (GIHB uhnz) are the smallest members of the ape family. Gibbons are built for swinging through the trees. In fact, it is awkward for them to walk on the ground. Their long arms enable them to "fly" from branch to branch, with leaps over 30 feet.

Gibbons are found in the rainforests of Southeast Asia. They live in the trees, where they get most of their food. They eat seeds, leaves, fruits, young birds, and insects. Gibbons live in family groups made up of a male, a female, and their young. Gibbons mate for life. At night, the gibbon family huddles together for safety.

Think and Learn

1. Gibbons are the smallest member of the ______________________ family.
2. How are gibbons built for swinging through trees? ______________________

   ____
3. Where are gibbons found? ______________________________
4. Gibbons live in ______________________________ groups.

Malayan Tapir

The Malayan tapir (muh LAY uhn TAY per) is related to the horse and the rhinoceros. It canters and gallops like a horse. Its snout is an upper lip that works much like an elephant trunk. It has a pig-shaped body and weighs about 650 pounds. Its coat is brownish-black and cream-colored.

Malayan tapirs are found in Sumatra and Malaysia in tropical rainforests near rivers and lakes. At night, they look for leaves, grass, and water plants to eat. Malayan tapirs love to dive and swim in the water. They lie in mud holes where they get relief from ticks and insects.

Think and Learn

1. To what animals are the Malayan tapirs related? ______________________________

____

2. Describe the tapir's snout. ______________________________________

____

3. When do Malayan tapirs find food? ______________________________

4. What do tapirs do in water? ____________________________________

Orangutan

Orangutan (oh RANG uh tan) is a Malay word that means *forest man.* Do you think an orangutan looks like a person? It is a large animal that grows to be 5 feet tall. Its arms, hands, and feet help the orangutan to live in the trees. An orangutan is easily identified by its long, shaggy, reddish-brown hair.

Orangutans are found in Borneo and Sumatra. They eat fruits, nuts, seeds, and leaves, as well as lizards, tree frogs, eggs, young birds, and insects. Orangutans build sleeping platforms in the trees. They sometimes use large leaves as blankets when it rains. Orangutans do not live in family groups like other apes.

Think and Learn

1. What does the word *orangutan* mean? ______________________
2. Where do orangutans live? ______________________
3. What color is orangutan hair? ______________________
4. What do orangutans build for sleeping? ______________________
5. How do orangutans sometimes use leaves? ______________________

Sloth Bear

The sloth bear is a huge, shaggy bear. It has a mane of fur around its neck. Sloth bears have very long snouts. They live in the rocky canyons and hills of India and Sri Lanka. They hunt for termites and bee nests at night. A sloth bear can climb any tree to find food. It uses its long claws to rip open a termite or bee nest. The sloth bear is so noisy when it eats that people can hear it 600 feet away!

Sloth bears sleep in caves during the day. They are also very noisy sleepers. They snore as loud as they eat! Sloth bears live in family units. Both parents care for the cubs. The cubs stay with their parents for 3 years.

Think and Learn

1. Sloth bears have very long ________________.
2. Where do sloth bears live? ________________
3. What do sloth bears eat? ________________
4. What do sloth bears do during the day? ________________

Snow Leopard

The snow leopard (snoh LEHP erd) is a large cat that lives in the mountains of central Asia. It is 5 feet long and weighs about 90 pounds. The snow leopard is known for its beautiful fur. Its dense undercoat is covered with long gray and cream-colored hair and speckled with black spots. The snow leopard's large paws are padded for warmth.

The fierce snow leopard does not roar like a lion but purrs like a house cat. Like most cats, snow leopards hunt animals for food. The snow leopard is endangered. It has been overhunted for its fur. It has also lost its natural prey due to the clearing of land for farming.

Think and Learn

1. Where do snow leopards live? ______________________________

2. The snow leopard's paws are padded for ______________________________.

3. What sound do snow leopards make? ______________________________

4. Why are snow leopards endangered? ______________________________

____

Tiger

The tiger is the largest member of the cat family. It is known by its orange and black stripes. Tigers are found only in Asia. They live in different environments—from cold regions to rainforests. Tigers live alone. Every tiger claims its own territory. Tigers, like all cats, stalk their prey and swiftly attack. Tigers hunt at night. They hunt deer, antelope, and wild pigs.

Female tigers, called *tigresses*, give birth every 2 years to a litter of 3 or 4 cubs. The tigress is a loving mother. She teaches her young how to hunt and care for themselves. The cubs stay with their mother for 2 years.

Think and Learn

1. The tiger is the largest member of the ______________________ family.
2. Tigers are found only in ______________________.
3. What animals do tigers hunt? ______________________

____

4. What do tigresses teach their cubs? ______________________

____

Water Buffalo

The water buffalo is a gigantic animal that is 10 feet long and 6 feet tall. It has thick, grayish-black skin. Water buffalo have large horns. The horns grow out of each side of the head and curve upward. Water buffalo love water. They are often found resting in water up to their noses. Water buffalo also roll in mud until they are covered with it. This helps protect them from insects.

Water buffalo are wild cattle. Some have been tamed and help with rice farming. Rice is grown in flooded fields. Water buffalo can easily pull a plow through water that is knee deep. Although they look like gentle animals, water buffalo can become very fierce. However, they are friendly to people they know.

Think and Learn

1. Large ________________ grow out of a water buffalo's head.

2. What do water buffalo like to rest in? ________________

3. Why do water buffalo roll in mud? ________________

____

4. How do water buffalo help with rice farming? ________________

____

Wild Boar

The wild boar is a wild hog found in forests throughout Asia. It can reach a length of 4 to 5 feet and weighs an average of 300 pounds. Its long, piglike snout is used for lifting, pushing, and digging. The wild boar has two long tusks that grow out of its lower jaw. These tusks are 1 foot long. Wild boars use their tusks to protect themselves.

Wild boars like to eat almost anything. They use their snout to search for leaves, fruit, roots, worms, and insects. Wild boars can see and hear well. However, they rely mainly on their sense of smell. Male and female boars travel in separate herds. The female boars raise their young alone.

Think and Learn

1. Where are wild boars found? ________________

2. How do wild boars use their snouts? ________________

3. Wild boars use their ________________ for protection.

4. Which sense do wild boars rely on most? ________________

CENTRAL AND SOUTH AMERICAN

ANIMALS

Chinchilla

Chinchillas (chihn CHIHL uhz) look like large mice, but they are actually related to squirrels. They have thick, soft fur. Their blue-gray color is beautiful. In the 1500s, Spanish explorers brought chinchillas back to Europe. The demand for chinchilla fur nearly caused this animal to be killed off. Today, a small chinchilla population lives in the Andes Mountains.

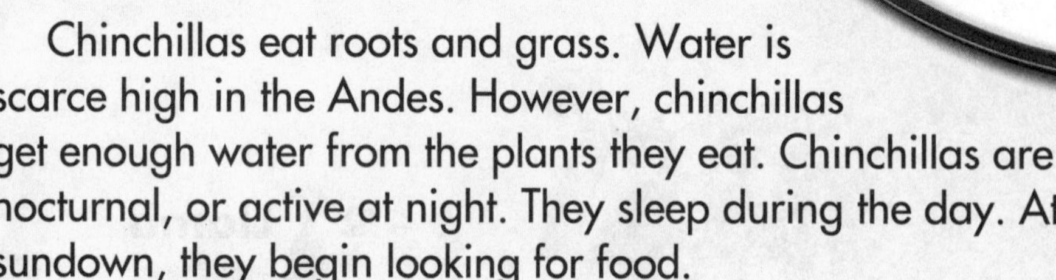

Chinchillas eat roots and grass. Water is scarce high in the Andes. However, chinchillas get enough water from the plants they eat. Chinchillas are nocturnal, or active at night. They sleep during the day. At sundown, they begin looking for food.

Think and Learn

1. Chinchillas are related to ____________________.
2. Describe chinchilla fur. ____________________

   ____
3. Where do chinchillas live? ____________________
4. How do chinchillas get water? ____________________

   ____

Giant Anteater

The giant anteater is an animal that eats ants and termites. Giant anteaters have three large claws on each paw. They use their claws to rip open ant nests. Giant anteaters have a sticky tongue that is 2 feet long. They push their tongue into an anthill to get the ants. Giant anteaters cannot see well. Instead, they find ants with their sharp sense of smell.

Giant anteaters are found only in Central and South America. They never dig burrows or make homes. Instead, they wander alone looking for food until they tire. Then, they lie down in a hidden place, cover their heads with their long bushy tails, and fall asleep.

Think and Learn

1. What do giant anteaters eat? ____________________________

2. How do giant anteaters use their claws? ________________________

____

3. Giant anteaters have ______________________________ tongues.

4. Where do giant anteaters sleep? ____________________________

____

Giant Armadillo

The giant armadillo (ahr muh DIHL oh) is the largest of all armadillos. It can reach a length of 5 feet and weigh as much as 130 pounds. Giant armadillos are found only near rivers in the eastern part of South America. Early Spanish explorers named the armadillo. The name means *little armored one*. Armadillos are covered with hard bony plates called *scutes*.

Giant armadillos use their long curved claws for digging burrows and for finding food. They eat termites, worms, snakes, and insects. Armadillos are quiet animals that prefer to live alone. When threatened, they either run away or crouch low. Their scutes protect their soft undersides.

Think and Learn

1. Where are giant armadillos found? ______________________________

____

2. What does the word *armadillo* mean? ______________________________

3. What are scutes? ______________________________

4. What do armadillos use their claws for? ______________________________

____

Jaguar

The jaguar (JAG wahr) is a member of the cat family. It is 6 feet long and weighs about 300 pounds. This beautiful animal has yellowish-tan fur with black dots encircled by black rings. Some jaguars are almost entirely black. The jaguar is found throughout Central and South America in many different habitats. It can live in shrub country, rainforests, mountains, and woods.

Jaguars like to hunt almost any kind of animal, including fish, turtles, deer, and wild pigs. They often lie on tree branches and wait until they can pounce down on their prey. Not only are jaguars skilled climbers, they are also great swimmers. They will often hunt in the water, especially when the rivers have flooded.

Think and Learn

1. The jaguar is a member of the ______________________ family.
2. In what habitats do jaguars live? ______________________

____
3. Where do jaguars often wait for prey? ______________________
4. Jaguars are skilled ______________ and great ______________ .

Llama

Llamas (LAH muhz) belong to the camel family. They are 4 to 5 feet tall and weigh over 200 pounds. Llamas come in many colors—white, tan, brown, and black. Llamas live in the semi-desert region near the Andes Mountains. They eat shrubs and other plants. Like the camel, a llama can live for weeks without water. The llama gets the water it needs from the plants it eats.

Llamas have been tamed for centuries. Their wool is used for making clothing, ropes, and blankets. Llamas are useful pack animals. They travel easily through mountains carrying heavy loads. However, if a llama thinks it has worked long enough for one day, it sits down and refuses to move.

Think and Learn

1. Llamas belong to the ____________________ family.
2. What do llamas eat? ____________________
3. Llamas can live for weeks without ____________________.
4. Why are llamas useful pack animals? ____________________

____

____

Macaw

Macaws (muh KAWZ) are the largest members of the parrot family. They come in many bright colors. All macaws have powerful hooked bills. They use their bills to help them climb and to break open nuts and seeds. Macaws have four toes on each foot. Their feet are well-suited for perching, climbing, and holding objects. Macaws are only found in rainforests. They live in holes that they make in tree trunks.

Macaws are in danger of extinction, or dying out. They are losing their homes as the rainforest is destroyed. Laws protect these birds, but people still capture them to sell as pets. Macaws are not good pets because they like to scream and bite.

Think and Learn

1. Macaws are members of the ______________________ family.
2. All macaws have powerful, hooked ______________________.
3. What do macaws use their feet for? ______________________

____
4. Why are macaws in danger of extinction? ______________________

____

Spider Monkey

Spider monkeys are small monkeys well-suited for living in trees. In fact, they rarely come down to the ground. These monkeys move quickly through trees by swinging and jumping from branch to branch. Spider monkeys have tails that are longer than their bodies. These tails can easily grab and pick up things.

Spider monkeys are found in rainforests from southern Mexico to the northern part of South America. They eat nuts, fruit, and sometimes eggs. Spider monkeys live in groups, or bands, of 10 to 40 monkeys. Every band of monkeys lives in its own area, or territory. One band of monkeys will not go into the territory of another band.

Think and Learn

1. How do spider monkeys move quickly through trees? ______________________
____
2. Their ______________________ can grab and pick up things.
3. What do spider monkeys eat? ______________________
4. Spider monkeys live in groups called ______________________.

Spider Monkey Dot-to-Dot

Spider monkeys live in rainforests. They usually run away and hide if another animal scares them. Connect the dots to find the hidden monkey. Then, color the picture.

Toucan

Toucans (TOO kanz) are birds with large, colorful bills. Although a toucan bill looks heavy, it is really very light. The bill is hollow. It is made from a hornlike material. Toucans live in the rainforests of Central and South America. Toucans eat fruit, large insects, lizards, and young birds. A toucan sits on a branch and reaches for fruit with its long bill. The curved end of the bill helps the toucan pick the fruit and hold on to it.

Toucans make their nests in the holes of trees. Both the male and female take turns sitting on the eggs. Newly hatched toucans are blind and have no feathers. After 6 to 7 weeks, the young toucans are ready to live on their own.

Think and Learn

1. Toucans have large, colorful ______________________________.
2. Where do toucans live? ______________________________

   ____
3. What do they eat? ______________________________

   ____
4. Where do toucans make nests? ______________________________

Two-Toed Sloth

A sloth (slawth) is an animal that lives in trees. Sloths rarely go down to the ground. In fact, they cannot walk at all. The two-toed sloth has two long, curved claws on its front legs. Sloths use their claws to hold onto tree trunks and branches. They often hang upside down. Sloths move very slowly along tree branches, paw over paw, while hanging upside down.

Two-toed sloths are found from the southern part of Central America to central Brazil and Peru. They eat leaves, twigs, and buds. Sloths are nocturnal, or active at night. It is hard to see sloths sleeping in the trees during the day. Green algae often grow on the sloths' fur, so the sloths blend in with the leaves.

Think and Learn

1. Sloths cannot ______________________________ at all.

2. What do sloths use to hold onto branches? ______________________________

3. When are sloths active? ______________________________

4. How do sloths blend in with tree leaves? ______________________________

____

Woolly Monkey

Woolly monkeys are named for their beautiful thick, woolly coats. They are found in forests along the Amazon River in Columbia, Ecuador, Peru, and Brazil. They eat fruit, flowers, and leaves. Unlike other tree-living monkeys, woolly monkeys are often found on the ground. While on the ground, they stand straight up, using their tails for support.

Woolly monkeys live in groups, or bands, of 10 to 30 monkeys. They move more slowly than other monkeys. When frightened, they swing through tree branches and hide. Woolly monkeys are friendly. They are often seen in the company of other kinds of monkeys.

Think and Learn

1. Woolly monkeys are named for their ____________________.
2. How do woolly monkeys stand while on the ground? ____________________

   ____
3. Woolly monkeys live in groups called ____________________.
4. Woolly monkeys move more ____________________ than other monkeys.

AUSTRALIAN ANIMALS

Wallaby

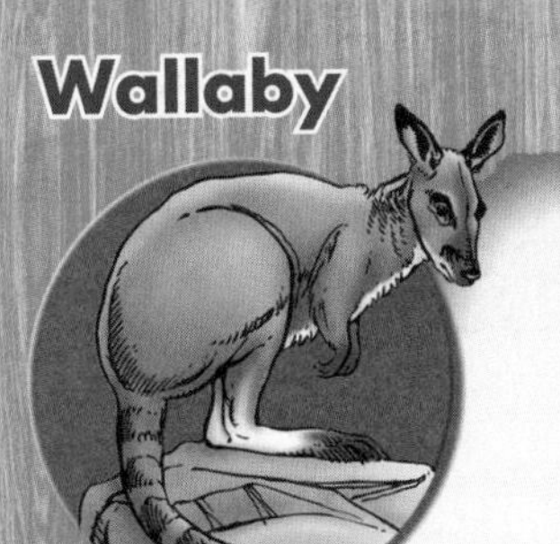

Giant Gray Kangaroo

Koala

Dingo

Tasmanian Devil

Echidna

Kookaburra

Dugong

Wombat

Platypus

Dingo

The dingo (DIHNG goh) is the only wild member of the dog family found in Australia. Dingoes are about the same size as medium-sized dogs. Their ears stand up, and they have bushy tails. Dingoes cannot bark, but can yelp and howl. Dingoes are excellent hunters. They hunt alone or in family groups for small animals to eat. Scientists think Aborigines, or native Australians, brought dingoes to Australia thousands of years ago.

Dingoes give birth only once a year to 3 to 6 puppies. Both parents care for the puppies and keep them hidden. The Aborigines search for the puppies to train them for hunting. Adult dingoes cannot be trained.

Think and Learn

1. The dingo is a member of the ______________________ family.
2. Dingoes cannot ______________________, but they can yelp and howl.
3. What do dingoes hunt for? ______________________
4. Why do Aborigines look for dingo puppies? ______________________

____

Dugong

The dugong (DOO gahng) is related to the manatee. Dugongs are mammals—animals that feed their young with their mothers' milk. Even though dugongs breathe air, they spend their entire life in water. They surface only to breathe about every 1 to 10 minutes. They have an unusual snout. It is rounded, with a large whiskered upper lip. Only male dugongs grow tusks.

Dugongs are found in the Indian Ocean, the Red Sea, and off the northern coast of Australia. Dugongs eat only sea grass. They are often called *sea cows* because they graze on sea grass just as cows graze on field grass.

Think and Learn

1. What are dugongs related to? ______________________________

2. Only male dugongs grow ______________________________.

3. Where are dugongs found? ______________________________

____

4. Dugongs are often called ______________________________.

Echidna

The echidna (ih KIHD nuh) is sometimes called a *spiny anteater*. It is found throughout Australia in open forests. The echidna's body is covered with coarse hair and pointed spines. Echidnas sleep in hollow logs during the day. At night, they use their sharp claws to scratch up insects. They eat the insects by licking them up with their long sticky tongues. Echidnas do not have teeth.

Echidnas are mammals that lay eggs. Mammals are animals whose young feed on the mother's milk. Female echidnas lay one egg each year. The mother keeps the egg in her pouch, where it hatches. The baby stays in the pouch for several weeks, drinking the mother's milk and growing.

Think and Learn

1. What is another name for an echidna? ______________________

2. When do echidnas sleep? ______________________

3. How do echidnas eat insects? ______________________

____

4. Echidnas are ______________________ that lay eggs.

Giant Gray Kangaroo

The giant gray kangaroo is the largest of all kangaroos. It grows to 7 feet tall. Kangaroos have huge feet and long, powerful tails. When kangaroos stand, they lean on their tails for balance. Kangaroos are found in the open forest and bush country of Australia. They eat fruit, leaves, and roots. Kangaroos travel in groups called *mobs.*

Kangaroos have excellent hearing, vision, and sense of smell. They are gentle, timid animals. Their senses and speed help them escape from danger. Kangaroos are marsupials. This means that they carry their babies, called *joeys,* in pouches. At birth, a joey is the size of a bee. It lives in its mother's pouch for 1 year.

Think and Learn

1. What does a kangaroo use its tail for? ____________________
2. Where do kangaroos live? ____________________

   ____
3. Kangaroos travel in groups called ____________________.
4. A baby kangaroo is called a ____________________.

Australian Animal Scramble

Unscramble the words below to find the names of Australian animals. The words below will help you.

1. O G N I D

____

2. L A B W Y A L

____

3. G O U D G N

____

4. D I H A C E N

____

5. S Y P A L T P U

____

6. M A S T A N N A I V L I E D

____________ ________

7. R A O K A O R B U K

____

8. G N A K A O O R

____

9. A L K O A

____

10. B W O T A M

____

Koala

Although many people call the koala (koh AW luh) a *koala bear*, it is not a bear. The koala is a marsupial—a mammal with a pouch for carrying its young. The koala has beautiful gray, woolly fur. If threatened, koalas defend themselves with their sharp claws.

Koalas eat the leaves of eucalyptus trees. Koalas are found in the eucalyptus forests on the east coast of Australia. The only time a koala climbs down from a tree is to move to another tree. They get the water they need from the leaves they eat. Koalas are nocturnal and sleep 18 hours during the day. Female koalas have one baby at a time. The baby crawls into the mother's pouch, where it stays for 6 months. Then, the mother carries the baby on her back for 4 or 5 months.

Think and Learn

1. What is a marsupial? ______________________________

____

2. What do koalas eat? ______________________________

3. When do koalas climb down a tree? ______________________________

4. How long does a baby koala stay in its mother's pouch? ______________________________

____

Kookaburra

The kookaburra (KOOK uh ber uh) is a bird that lives in forests in the southern parts of Australia. It is best known for its loud, screaming laughter. The kookaburra screams its laughing sounds at dawn and at dusk. Kookaburras make their homes in holes in trees. They eat a wide variety of foods, such as caterpillars, fish, small mammals, frogs, and worms. Insects, however, are their favorite food.

Kookaburras usually lay 1 to 4 eggs in spring. Male kookaburras protect the nest. Young kookaburras stay in their parents' territory for up to 4 years. The young kookaburras even help to feed their parents' new babies.

Think and Learn

1. The kookaburra is known for its loud screaming ____________________.

2. Where do kookaburras make their homes? ____________________

   ____

3. A kookaburra's favorite food is ____________________.

4. How do young kookaburras help their parents? ____________________

   ____

Platypus

The platypus (PLAT ih pus) is a mammal that has a bill like a duck and a flat, beaverlike tail. It is found near rivers and streams in eastern Australia and Tasmania. The platypus is awkward on land but swims gracefully. It has claws under its webbed toes. It uses its claws for digging burrows and getting food. The platypus eats large amounts of snails, worms, shrimp, and small fish.

The male platypus is poisonous. It has a poison gland attached to a hollow claw on each hind leg. A scratch from this claw can kill an animal or make a human very sick. The female platypus lays her eggs in a burrow lined with leaves. When the babies hatch, she holds them with her tail. The babies drink milk from her body.

Think and Learn

1. The platypus has a ______________________________ like a duck.
2. What does a platypus use its claws for? ______________________________

____

3. The male platypus is ______________________________.
4. How does a mother platypus hold her babies? ______________________________

____

Tasmanian Devil

The Tasmanian devil is a marsupial—a mammal with a pouch to raise its young. It is found only on the island of Tasmania, off the southern coast of Australia. The Tasmanian devil looks somewhat like a small bear. It has a large head, stocky body, and strong jaws and teeth. It is named for its bad temper and loud, throaty growl.

The Tasmanian devil is nocturnal. It rests during the day in a hollow log or between rocks. At night, it hunts for food. It is a scavenger—it eats the remains of dead animals. It also eats sheep, chickens, reptiles, and other small animals. The female Tasmanian devil keeps her young in her pouch for 15 weeks. When the furry babies come out, they still need their mother's milk for several months.

Think and Learn

1. The Tasmanian devil looks like a small ______________________.
2. What is the Tasmanian devil named for? ______________________

____
3. What does the Tasmanian devil do at night? ______________________
4. A ______________________ eats the remains of dead animals.

Wallaby

Wallabies (WAHL uh beez) belong to the kangaroo family. Like kangaroos, they stand on their hind legs and use their tail for balance. Wallabies are found in Australia, New Guinea, and Tasmania. They live in grasslands or in woods. They graze on plants in the early morning and late afternoon. During the heat of the day, they rest in the shade. When the weather is very hot, wallabies lick their forearms and paws to cool themselves. Wallabies do not drink much water. They get enough water from the plants they eat.

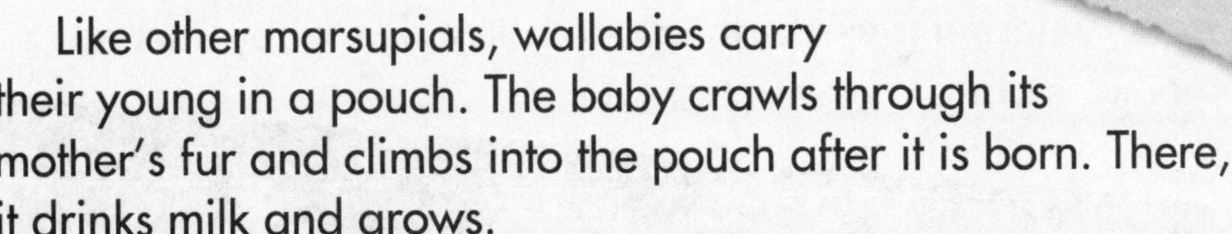

Like other marsupials, wallabies carry their young in a pouch. The baby crawls through its mother's fur and climbs into the pouch after it is born. There, it drinks milk and grows.

Think and Learn

1. Wallabies belong to the ______________________ family.

2. During the heat of the day, wallabies rest in the ______________________.

3. How do wallabies cool themselves in hot weather? ______________________

____

4. Wallabies get water from the ______________________ they eat.

Wombat

A wombat (WAHM bat) is a marsupial that looks like a small bear. However, it acts more like a rabbit or a mouse. Wombats have two upper and two lower front teeth that never stop growing. They use their strong legs and claws for digging and burrowing. Adult wombats weigh up to 75 pounds.

Wombats live in dry climates in southern Australia and Tasmania. They can go without water for a long time. Wombats stay in underground burrows all day. At night, they come out to eat roots and leaves. A wombat builds a nest of leaves and bark, where it gives birth to one baby. The baby spends the first part of its life in its mother's pouch. A wombat can live up to 25 years.

Think and Learn

1. What do wombats use their claws for? ______________________

____

2. Wombats live in ______________________ climates.
3. When do wombats eat? ______________________
4. How long can a wombat live? ______________________

AFRICAN
ANIMALS

Vulture

Ostrich

Lion

Zebra

Chimpanzee

Gorilla

African Elephant

Giraffe

Black Rhinoceros

Hippopotamus

African Elephant

The African elephant is the world's largest land animal. A male, or bull, can grow to 11 feet tall and 24 feet long. It can weigh as much as 14,000 pounds. Females, called *cows*, are smaller. Elephants have trunks that they use like hands. They can easily pick up small fruits or lift tree branches with their trunks. Elephants spend most of the day eating leaves, grass, small branches, bark, coconuts, and berries. They also drink large amounts of water every day.

African elephants are found in the warm grasslands and forests of Africa. They live with other animals, such as lions, hyenas, giraffes, and zebras. Lions and hyenas will attack baby elephants and sick elephants. Adult elephants are safe from most predators.

Think and Learn

1. The female elephant is called a __________________________.

2. Elephants use their __________________________ like hands.

3. What do elephants eat? __________________________

____

4. Adult elephants are safe from most __________________________.

ELEPHANTS

Pull-Out Storybook

Elephants are the largest animals on land. They are the only animals with long, flexible trunks. There are two kinds of elephants. The African elephant lives in Africa. The Asiatic, or Indian, elephant lives in India. It is easy to tell the two elephants apart. African elephants are bigger. Their larger ears cover their shoulders. Asiatic elephants have much smaller ears.

Almost everything about an elephant's body is huge. An elephant's trunk can be 5 feet long. Elephant tusks are actually upper front teeth that never stop growing. The tusks can grow to 8 feet long. An elephant's heart is five times bigger than a human heart. Its large, stumplike legs are strong enough to support the elephant's weight—about the weight of 100 people.

Elephants use their trunks in many ways. They use them to sniff the air and ground to find food. They use them to reach into treetops and pull down branches and leaves. They even use them like straws to drink water. Did you know that an elephant's trunk holds more than 2 gallons of water? Elephants also use their trunks to take a "shower." They fill up their trunks with water and spray themselves.

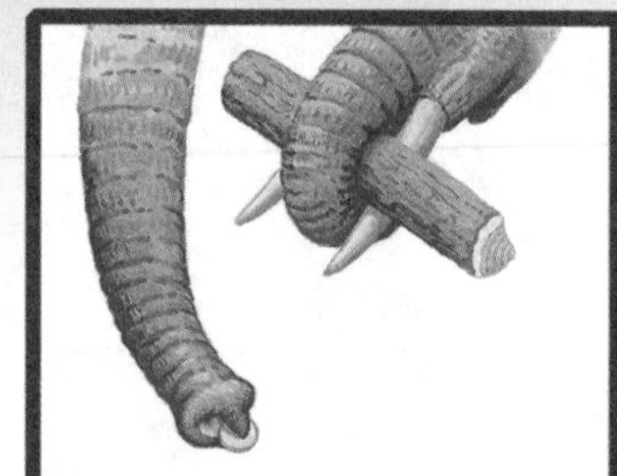

Elephants give birth to one baby at a time. When the baby is born, the other females in the herd sniff it and touch it gently. Later, they help look after the baby as it grows. A baby elephant stands about 3 feet at birth and weighs about 200 pounds. The baby grows quickly, gaining 30 pounds a month. Baby elephants stay with their mothers until they are 12 to 14 years old.

Baby elephants love to play. They chase and push one another. They grab each other's tail with their trunks. They also climb on top of each other and have play-fights. As the young elephants play, an older sister or aunt usually watches them. Playing helps young elephants learn the rules of the herd. It also teaches them how to get along with other elephants.

Elephants communicate, or talk, to each other by making different kinds of sounds. They also communicate by touching each other. Elephants show fondness by rubbing their trunks together. They might also stand with their heads touching. Mother elephants touch their babies gently with their trunks to comfort them or to get their attention. When elephants meet, they twist their trunks together and sniff each other.

For thousands of years, people have trained elephants to help them do work. In India and other parts of Asia, elephants are still used in the logging industry to move fallen trees. Working elephants are generally found in places where the ground is too rough for trucks and machines. In some Asian countries, elephants also take part in religious ceremonies. These elephants are colorfully painted or dressed. Then, they are led in parades.

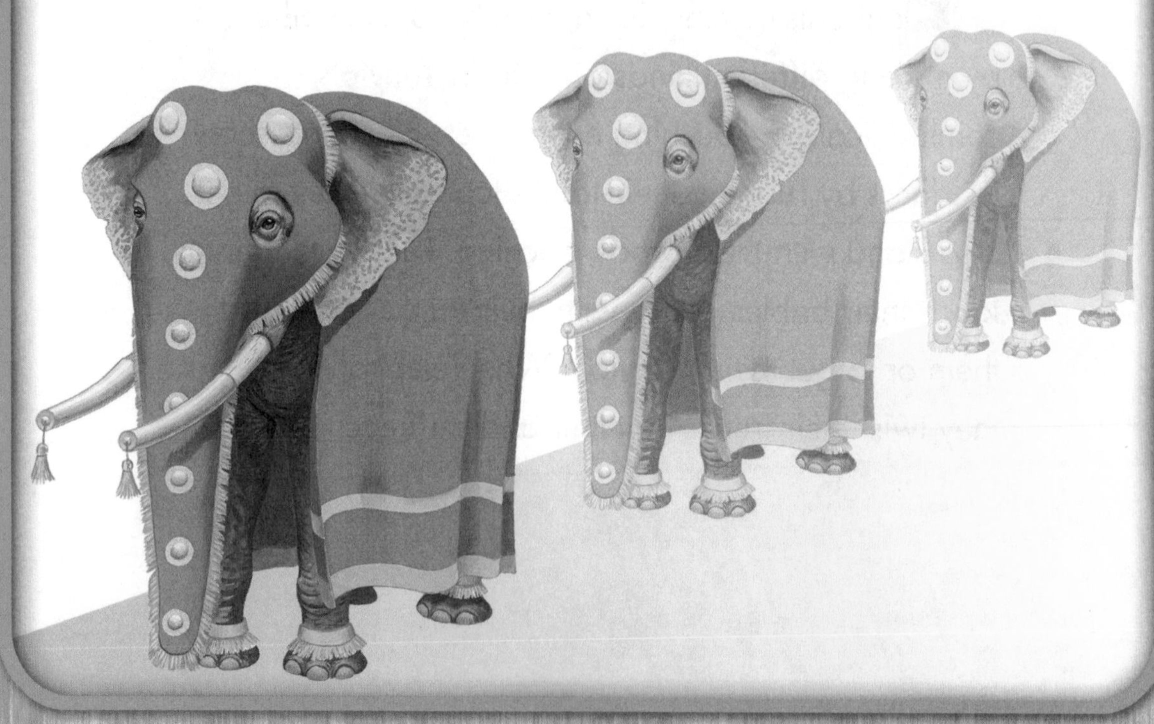

Giraffe

Giraffes are the tallest of all animals. They stand over 18 feet tall and weigh over 4,000 pounds. Even though their necks are so long, they have the same number of neck bones as other animals. Giraffes have sharp eyesight. They can see in all directions without moving their heads. Every giraffe has a different pattern of patches, just as every human has different fingerprints.

Giraffes live in herds on the dry grasslands in Africa. They mainly eat leaves from acacia (uh KAY shuh) trees, which are the most common trees in the area. Giraffes can go weeks without water. When they drink, giraffes spread apart their front legs and lower their long necks to reach the water.

Think and Learn

1. Giraffes are the ______________________ of all animals.
2. Compare the number of neck bones in giraffes to other animals. ______________________

   ____
3. What do giraffes eat? ______________________
4. How do giraffes bend down to get a drink? ______________________

   ____

Chimpanzee

Chimpanzees (chihm pan ZEEZ) belong to the ape family. They are found in rainforests in Africa. Like apes, they can walk on two feet. However, they prefer to move about on all four legs like monkeys do. Chimpanzees have hands that look like human hands, but their thumbs are shorter. Chimpanzees eat fruit, leaves, and insects.

Chimpanzees are one of the few animals that make and use tools. To get termites, chimpanzees trim sticks and put them inside termite hills. Then, they eat the termites that cling to the stick. Chimpanzees also build platforms in trees for sleeping. To communicate with each other, chimpanzees use different sounds.

Think and Learn

1. Is a chimpanzee a monkey or an ape? ______________________

2. Where are chimpanzees found? ______________________

____

3. What do chimpanzees eat? ______________________

4. What can chimpanzees do that most other animals cannot do? __________

____

Gorilla

The gorilla is the largest member of the ape family. Adult males grow to 6 feet tall and weigh 400 pounds. Females are smaller. Gorillas have broad chests, wide shoulders, long arms, and short legs. Their entire body, except for the face, is covered with dark fur. Gorillas are peaceful animals that live in family groups. An adult male always leads the group. Females and their babies make up the rest of the group.

Gorillas are found in different parts of central Africa. Some live in mountain forests. Others live in forests on low ground. Gorillas spend most of the day eating leaves and fruit. At night, gorillas build sleeping platforms on the ground or in trees.

Think and Learn

1. Gorillas belong to the ______________________________ family.
2. What makes up a gorilla family group? ______________________________

   ____
3. Where are gorillas found? ______________________________
4. Where do gorillas sleep? ______________________________

   ____

Apes and Monkeys

Apes and monkeys are the animals most closely related to humans. Apes and monkeys are different. Monkeys have tails. Apes do not. Apes have larger brains than monkeys. Larger brains allow for more difficult actions.

Even though they are different, apes and monkeys are alike in some ways. Both monkeys and apes can stand up on two legs. This keeps their hands free to do some kind of task. They both have hands and feet that look like human hands. Their hands and feet have "thumbs" that move in opposite directions to their fingers. This action lets apes and monkeys use their hands and feet to pick up things and hold them.

Think and Learn

1. Label the monkey and the ape in the picture.

2. In what ways are monkeys and apes different? ______________________

____

3. How are monkeys and apes similar? ______________________

____

____

Hippopotamus

The hippopotamus (hihp uh PAHT uh muhs) is second only to elephants in size. Hippos are about 12 feet long and weigh up to 8,000 pounds. Hippos have very thick, bluish-gray skin. They have small eyes and ears on their large heads. Their enormous mouths can open 3 to 4 feet wide.

Hippos live by streams and marshes in many parts of Africa. During the day, they rest and sleep in the water. They keep their entire body under water, except for their eyes, ears, and nose. Hippos are very graceful swimmers. At night, they leave the water to eat grass. They spend up to 6 hours a night eating. Hippos live in herds with 15 to 30 members.

Think and Learn

1. Hippos have very thick ________________________________.
2. Where do hippos live? ________________________________

   ____
3. What do hippos do during the day? ________________________

   ____
4. Hippos are very graceful ________________________________.

Lion

The lion is one of the largest and fiercest members of the cat family. Lions range in size from 270 to 500 pounds. Only male lions have a mane—the thick fur around the head. The mane protects lions when they fight to defend their territory, or area in which they live.

Lions sleep during the day and hunt at night. They hunt for antelope, zebras, young elephants, and other smaller animals. Lions are social animals. They live in groups called *prides*. A pride is usually made up of 1 to 6 males and 4 to 12 females with their cubs. Each pride has its own territory. The members of a pride hunt only in their territory.

Think and Learn

1. Why do male lions have manes? ______________________

____

2. When do lions hunt? ______________________.

3. Lions live in groups called ______________________.

4. Each pride hunts in its own ______________________.

Ostrich

The ostrich (AHS trihch) is the world's largest bird. It stands 8 feet tall. Ostriches cannot fly. Their wings are too small. However, ostriches run very fast. They can run as fast as 45 miles per hour. Ostriches have very good eyesight. Their large eyes and long necks help them to see for several miles.

Ostriches live on dry, grassy plains and sandy deserts in Africa. They can go for a long time without water. Ostriches eat leaves, seeds, flowers, insects, and small animals. Ostriches live and travel in flocks. A flock is usually made up of one male and several females. The male ostrich digs a hole as a nest. Each female lays as many as 10 eggs in the nest.

Think and Learn

1. How tall is an adult ostrich? ______________________

2. How fast can an ostrich run? ______________________

3. Where do ostriches live? ______________________

____

4. Ostriches live and travel in ______________________.

Black Rhinoceros

The black rhinoceros (righ NAHS er uhs) has tough, wrinkled skin and a two-horned snout. A rhinoceros grows to 12 feet long and weighs about 2 tons. It is a relative of the horse. Surprisingly, it can run as fast as a horse for short distances. Rhinoceros horns grow from the same material as hair and claws. Rhinos use the longer front horn to dig and to defend themselves. They use the smaller back horn to dig up bushes and small trees to eat.

The black rhino stays hidden during the day. It comes out at night to search for food and water. Rhinos have very poor eyesight. They rely mostly on their sense of smell. A new odor or sound can cause a rhinoceros to charge.

Think and Learn

1. The black rhinoceros is related to the ____________________.
2. How does a rhinoceros use its front horn? ____________________

   ____
3. What do rhinoceroses eat? ____________________
4. What sense do rhinoceroses rely on most? ____________________

Vulture

Vultures (VUL cherz) are large birds of prey, or birds that eat animals. Their wingspan can reach 6 to 9 feet. Vultures have bare, wrinkled skin on their heads and necks. Their bills are slightly hooked. Vultures live in mountains, grasslands, and deserts. They generally do not live in forests or in areas that receive a lot of rain.

Vultures are scavengers. Scavengers feed on the remains of dead animals. Vultures use their sharp eyesight and keen sense of smell to find dead animals. When one vulture finds food, other vultures are quick to follow. Vultures are strong fliers. They come from miles away when food is found.

Think and Learn

1. Vultures are large birds of ______________________.
2. Where do vultures live? ______________________

____
3. What do vultures eat? ______________________
4. How do vultures find food? ______________________

____

Zebra

The zebra is a striped animal related to the horse. The zebra's stripes help the animal blend in with its surroundings. A zebra standing in tall grass is very hard to see. Each zebra has its own stripe pattern, like each human has his or her own fingerprints.

Zebras are found in the deserts and grasslands of eastern and southern Africa. They mainly eat grass, and they spend most of their time eating. Zebras live in herds made up of a male, several females, and their babies. Zebras protect themselves by staying together in a herd. If they are in danger, they try to run away. Zebras can run as fast as 45 miles per hour.

Think and Learn

1. A zebra's ______________ help it blend in with its surroundings.
2. Where are zebras found? ______________________________________
____.
3. Zebras live in ______________________________________
4. What do zebras do when they are in danger? ______________

INSECTS

Fly

Butterfly

Cricket

Beetle

Grasshopper

Bee

Moth

Mosquito

Ant

Ant

Ants are social insects that live and work together in large groups. Ants have two bent antennae on top of their heads. The antennae are used to taste, touch, and smell. An ant is helpless if its antennae are damaged. Ants have very strong jaws that are used for digging and for getting food.

Ants are found all over the world, except for the North and South poles. Ants build different kinds of homes. Some ants live in trees. Some build nests in wood or under leaves. Others burrow under rocks. It is common for ants to dig homes in the dirt. Some dig underground tunnels and rooms in the dirt. Others build large anthills that look like tall mounds of dirt.

Think and Learn

1. Why are ants described as social insects? ______________________

____

2. Ants have two bent ______________________ on top of their heads.

3. Ants use their jaws for ______________________ and for getting food.

4. Where do ants not live? ______________________

Ant Colonies

Ants live in groups called *colonies*. There are three different groups of ants in a colony—the queen ants, the workers, and the males. Each ant in the colony has a special job. The queen ants are the largest females. Their only job is to lay eggs. The worker ants are usually females that do not lay eggs. The workers have many jobs. Some workers are nursery ants who care for the eggs. Other worker ants find food and bring it back to the colony. The largest workers are soldier ants who guard the nest. Male ants live in the nest only at certain times. Their job is to mate with the queen ants. After mating, the male ants soon die.

1. Label the ant in the colony that is a nursery ant. Label the soldier ant.

2. What are the three different groups of ants living in an ant colony? ____________

____

____

Bee

Bees are the only insects that make a food that people eat. Bees have a special stomach, called a *honey stomach*, where they store nectar, the sugar from flowers. Their long, hollow tongues work like straws to suck up nectar. Female bees have a stinger that they use for defense.

Bees live all over the world, except for the North and South poles. Bees build their homes in hollow trees or in beehives. Some bees live in social groups like ants. The queen bee lays eggs. The worker bees build the hive, care for the eggs, find nectar and pollen, and defend the hive. The drones are male bees that mate with the queen.

Think and Learn

1. What is a honey stomach? ______________________

____

2. Female bees have a ______________ they use for defense.

3. Where do bees build their homes? ______________________

____

4. What are drones? ______________________

Honeybees

Some farmers build wooden hives for honeybees. Then, the bees move in and make honeycombs. Honeycombs look like a wall with many six-sided rooms. Worker bees build the honeycomb out of beeswax, which they make in their stomach. The rooms in the honeycomb are used for storing eggs, young bees, and honey.

Worker bees make honey from the nectar they collect from flowers. As bees collect nectar from flowers, they spread pollen from one flower to another. Pollen grains are the male sex cells of a flowering plant. A flower needs pollen to form fruit and seeds. Farmers often keep bees to help spread the pollen on their fruit trees. Then, the fruit trees will have a lot of fruit. Farmers also collect the honey.

Think and Learn

1. What are honeycombs made of? ____________________

2. Why do farmers keep bees? ____________________

____

____

____

____

Beetle

Beetles are the largest group of insects and come in every color of the rainbow. All beetles have two pairs of wings. The outer wings are hard. They protect the inner, or flight, wings. The flight wings are thin and clear. They stay folded under the outer wings until needed for flight. Beetles have very strong jaws to grab and chew food.

Beetles are found all over the world. Beetles make their homes in many different places, from in water to under the ground. Beetles can be harmful or helpful to people, depending on what they eat. Some beetles damage the plants in gardens and farmers' fields. Other beetles eat harmful insects.

Think and Learn

1. Beetles are the ______________________________ group of insects.

2. Which wings do beetles use for flight? ______________________________

____

3. Beetles have strong ______________________ to grab and chew food.

4. How are beetles helpful to people? ______________________________

____

Butterfly

Butterflies are beautiful insects. The body of a butterfly is long and slender. They have knobs at the ends of their antennae, which are used for smelling. Their wings are covered with tiny scales that give the wings their color. All butterflies hatch as caterpillars, which look like worms. The caterpillars change to adult butterflies in a cocoon, or paperlike case.

Butterflies are found everywhere. They live on mountains and in deserts. As caterpillars, they eat leaves and fruit, often damaging crops. As butterflies, they cannot bite or chew. For food, they drink nectar, the sugary liquid, from flowers. Butterflies fly only during the day. When resting, they fold their wings straight up.

Think and Learn

1. What do butterflies use their antennae for? ______________________

2. Tiny ______________________ give butterfly wings their color.

3. What do caterpillars eat? ______________________

4. When do butterflies fly? ______________________

Cricket

Crickets are jumping insects. Most crickets are either black or brown in color and are about 1 inch long. Crickets have two pairs of wings. Both pairs of wings lie flat over the cricket's back. Only male crickets make the chirping sound that crickets are known for. They make the sound by rubbing their wings together. They make this sound to attract female crickets. Crickets hear sounds with a special body part on their front legs.

Crickets are found in many parts of the world. They hide during the day and are active at night. This is when they chirp and search for food. Crickets eat grain and the remains of other insects.

Think and Learn

1. Crickets are ______________________________ insects.

2. How do male crickets chirp? ______________________________

____

3. How do crickets hear? ______________________________

____

4. When do crickets search for food? ______________________________

Fly

Flies are very common insects. People see and hear them everywhere. There are many different kinds of flies, such as house flies, fruit flies, gnats, and deer flies. Flies have only one pair of wings. The buzzing sound you hear when a fly flies by is the sound of its wings beating together. Flies use their antennae to touch and smell things. Flies have tiny, hairy pads on the bottoms of their feet. These help flies cling to walls and walk upside down on ceilings.

Although flies look harmless, they can carry and spread germs. Some flies, however, are helpful. They spread pollen from flower to flower like bees do.

Think and Learn

1. What are some kinds of flies? ______________________________

____

2. Flies have ______________________________ pair of wings.

3. Flies use their ______________________ to touch and smell things.

4. Flies can carry and spread ______________________________.

Grasshopper

Grasshoppers are built for jumping. Grasshoppers have long, thin legs with powerful muscles. Most grasshoppers have large fragile wings that are protected by a second pair of wings. Like crickets, male grasshoppers make sounds by rubbing their wings together. Although grasshoppers can fly, they fly for only short distances. They move mainly by leaping and jumping.

There are two kinds of grasshoppers—long-horned grasshoppers and short-horned grasshoppers. Long-horned grasshoppers have long antennae. They eat plants and, sometimes, the remains of animals. Short-horned grasshoppers are locusts. They have short antennae and eat only plants. Some locusts damage crops.

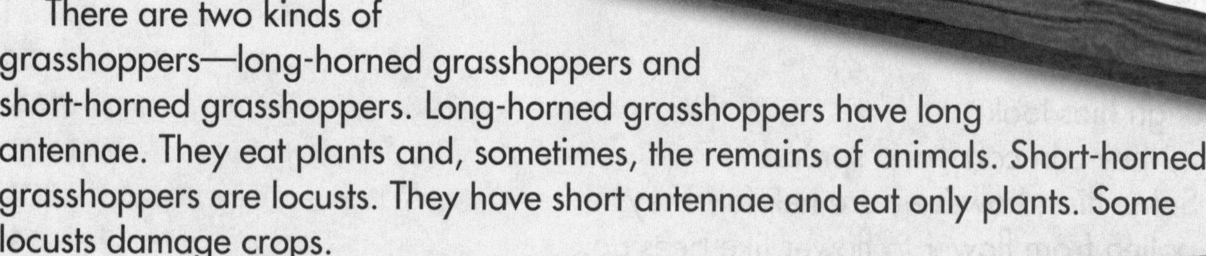

Think and Learn

1. Grasshoppers are built for ______________________.

2. How far do grasshoppers fly? ______________________

____

3. Long-horned grasshoppers have ______________ antennae.

4. Locusts are ______________ -horned grasshoppers.

Mosquito

The mosquito is a kind of fly. Like all flies, mosquitoes have only one pair of wings. Mosquito wings can beat 1,000 times each second. The mosquito's head is almost entirely covered by its two large eyes. The antennae, used for hearing and smelling, are located between the eyes. Female mosquitoes have thin antennae. Male mosquitoes have feathery antennae.

Mosquitoes are found in all parts of the world. Some mosquitoes in tropical parts of the world spread diseases. Mosquitoes are most annoying because their bites hurt and itch. Only female mosquitoes bite. They bite to get the blood they need for their eggs to grow.

Think and Learn

1. The mosquito is a kind of ______________________________.
2. Mosquito wings can beat ____________________ times each second.
3. What do mosquitoes use their antennae for? ____________________

   ____
4. Why do female mosquitoes bite? ____________________

   ____

Moth

Moths are closely related to butterflies. Butterflies and moths are so much alike that it is sometimes hard to tell them apart. Unlike butterflies, moths have chubby bodies and usually fly only at night. Moth antennae look feathery. The antennae give moths their senses of touch and smell. Moths cannot bite or chew. They have a mouth that looks and works like a drinking straw. Moths eat sap and nectar.

Moths are found everywhere. They have many enemies, such as frogs, birds, snakes, and spiders. Some moths protect themselves by flying away. Others blend into their surroundings. Some moths taste so awful that other animals leave them alone.

Think and Learn

1. Moths are closely related to ____________________.
2. When do moths fly? ____________________
3. Moth antennae look ____________________.
4. What are some enemies of moths? ____________________

____

REPTILES

Tuatara

Turtle

Sea Turtle

Tuatara

The tuatara (too uh TAW ruh) looks like a lizard but is actually the last remaining animal in its group. Tuataras lived during the time of the first dinosaurs, about 220 million years ago. They have not changed since that time. Tuataras have a third eye on top of their head. They also have two rows of upper teeth. A row of horny plates runs along their back. These plates rise straight up when tuataras are frightened.

Tuataras are found only on some islands near New Zealand. They live in burrows made by seabirds. They can dig their own burrows, but seem to prefer ones already made. Tuataras lay hard-shelled eggs that take 15 months to hatch.

Think and Learn

1. Tuataras lived during the time of the first ______________.
2. How many eyes do tuataras have? ______________
3. Where are tuataras found? ______________
____
4. How long do tuatara eggs take to hatch? ______________

Crocodile

Crocodiles (KRAHK uh dighlz) are the largest reptiles. They can reach 25 feet in length. Of all the animals belonging to the crocodile group, crocodiles are the most dangerous. Crocodiles have long narrow snouts. When their mouths are closed, their lower teeth show.

Crocodiles are found in the tropical parts of the world. They catch fish and small land animals for food. Like alligators, crocodiles, are most active at night. During the day, they rest in the sun. Often a crocodile lies with its mouth open to help cool its body. When its mouth is open, the crocodile lets birds go in it and peck out leftover pieces of food.

Think and Learn

1. Crocodiles are the ______________________ reptiles.
2. Describe the shape of a crocodile's snout. ______________________

____
3. What do crocodiles eat? ______________________
4. How does a crocodile cool its body? ______________________

____

Alligator

Alligators (AL ih gay terz) belong to the crocodile group of reptiles. Although they are members of this group, alligators and crocodiles are two different animals. Alligators have wide, rounded snouts. When their mouths are closed, their lower teeth are inside. Alligators are smaller than crocodiles. They grow up to 12 feet long.

Alligators are found in southeastern United States and in parts of China. They eat frogs, fish, snakes, turtles, and small mammals. Like crocodiles, alligators are good swimmers. Alligators move through the water by moving their tails from side to side. Female alligators lay as many as 50 eggs and guard the eggs until they hatch. Mother alligators care for their young for up to a year.

Think and Learn

1. Alligators belong to the ______________________ group of reptiles.

2. Describe the shape of an alligator's snout. ______________________

____

3. How do alligators move through water? ______________________

____

4. Mother alligators care for their young for up to a ______________________.

Compare and Contrast

Read about crocodiles and alligators. Then, use the Venn diagram and the facts you have learned to compare and contrast these two animals.

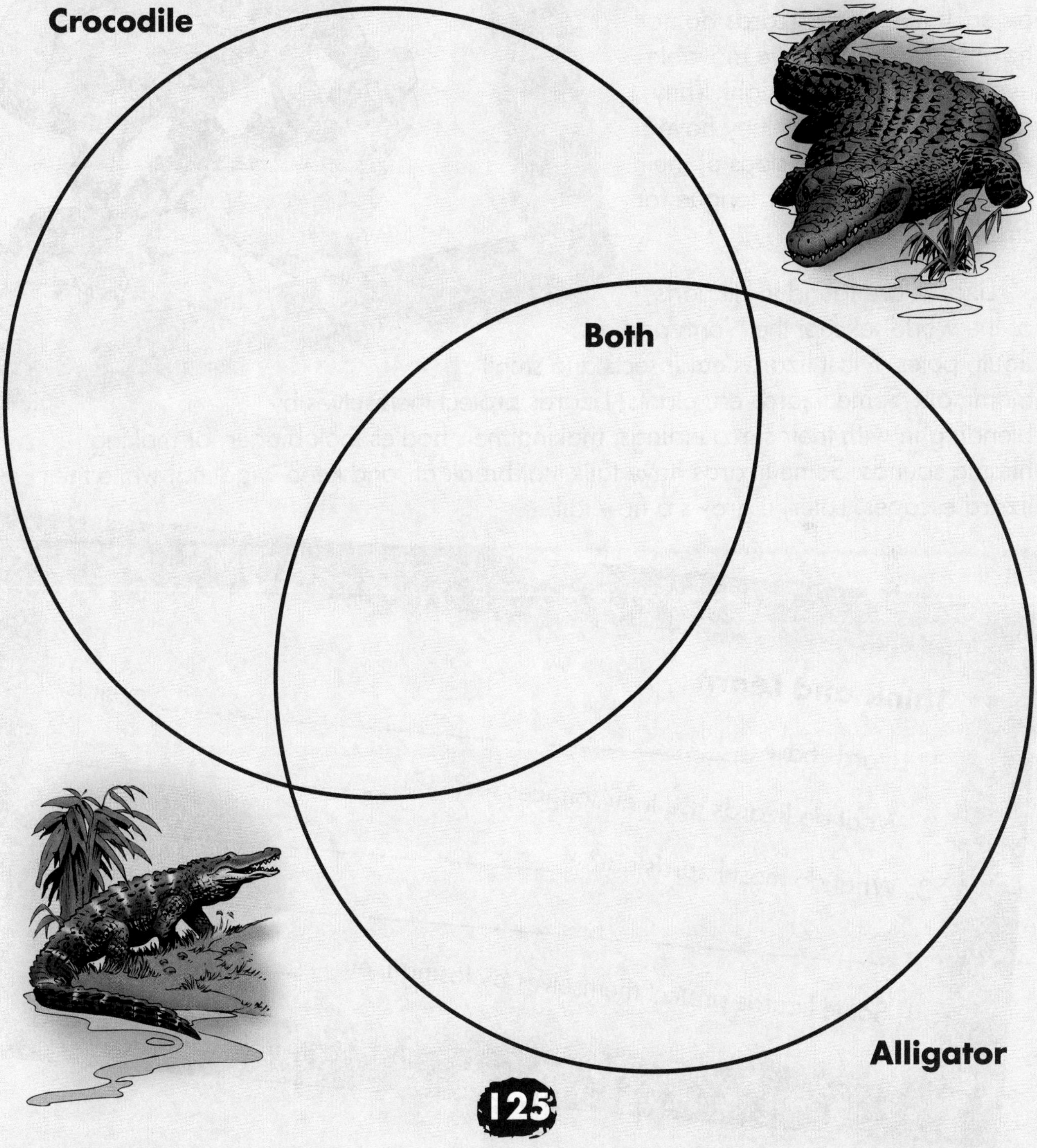

Crocodile

Both

Alligator

Lizard

Lizards and snakes make up the largest group of reptiles. Most lizards have four legs with five clawed toes on each leg. Some lizards do not have legs. Lizards have movable eyelids and good eyesight. They do not have ears, but they have ear openings on the sides of their head. Lizards use their tongue for smelling.

Lizards are found in all parts of the world, except the North and South poles. Most lizards eat insects and small mammals. Some lizards eat plants. Lizards protect themselves by blending in with their surroundings, making their bodies look bigger, or making hissing sounds. Some lizards have tails that break off and keep wiggling, while the lizard escapes. Later, it grows a new tail.

Think and Learn

1. Lizards have ______________________ eyelids.
2. What do lizards use their tongues for? ______________________
3. What do most lizards eat? ______________________

______________________.
4. Some lizards protect themselves by losing their ______________________

Chameleon

Chameleons (kuh MEEL yuhnz) are lizards that can change their body color to match their surroundings. They can blend in so well that they actually look invisible! Chameleon bodies are flat on the sides. Their eyes are large and bulging. Each eye works separately from the other. They can look in different directions at the same time.

Chameleons are slow-moving lizards. They do not chase down their food. Instead, a chameleon sits quietly and waits for food to come to it. When a chameleon sees an insect, it shoots out its sticky tongue and catches the insect. Chameleons are found only in Africa and Madagascar.

Think and Learn

1. What changes on chameleons? ______________________

2. How can chameleons look in different directions at the same time? ____________

____

3. Chameleons catch insects with their sticky ______________________.

4. Where are chameleons found? ______________________

Snake

Snakes are reptiles that have long bodies and no legs. Snakes move by sliding on their belly. Snakes cannot shut their eyes, because they do not have eyelids. Their eyes are covered with clear scales. Snakes do not have ear slits. Instead, they hear sounds by feeling the movement of air around them. Snakes have a long, forked tongue that helps them smell.

Snakes eat other animals. The size of animal they can eat depends on the size of their mouth. A snake swallows its food whole. Snakes do not eat often. Most snakes eat only a few times a year. Snakes, like all other reptiles, lay eggs or give birth to live young. They do not take care of their young.

Think and Learn

1. How do snakes move? ________________________

2. What covers a snake's eyes? ________________________

3. Snakes use their long, forked ________________ to help them smell.

4. How often do most snakes eat? ________________________

____

Garter Snake

Garter snakes are harmless snakes found in Central and North America. Female garter snakes grow 20 to 30 inches long. Males are slightly smaller. Garter snakes living in different areas look different from each other. They come in many different colors. However, most garter snakes have three stripes running along their body.

Garter snakes are most active in the spring and autumn. That is when most people see them in their yards or in parks. Garter snakes catch and eat small animals, such as frogs, salamanders, and fish. Garter snakes do not lay eggs. Instead, they give birth to live young.

Think and Learn

1. Garter snakes are ______________________________ snakes.
2. What feature do most garter snakes have? ______________________________

____
3. When are garter snakes most active? ______________________________
4. Garter snakes do not lay ______________________________.

Rattlesnake

Rattlesnakes are poisonous snakes with rattles on their tails. The rattles are pieces of bone that are loosely connected. Each time a rattlesnake grows enough to shed its skin, a new section of the rattle forms. Many people believe that a rattlesnake will shake its rattle before striking. That is not always true.

Rattlesnakes are most commonly found in the desert areas of the United States and in the mountains of Mexico. Rattlesnakes eat small animals. They catch animals by pouncing on them and biting them. The poison in their fangs, or long front teeth, kills the animal. All rattlesnakes give birth to live babies. Young rattlesnakes can take care of themselves right away.

Think and Learn

1. Where are rattlesnakes found? ______________________________ ______________________________.
2. Their rattles are pieces of loosely connected ______________________________.
3. What do rattlesnakes eat? ______________________________
4. Rattlesnakes have ______________________________ in their fangs.

Turtle

Turtles are reptiles with shells. Turtle shells are made of either horny plates or tough, leathery skin. The shell protects the turtle's body. Many turtles can pull their legs and head inside their shell. Turtles do not have teeth. They cut their food with their hard, sharp beak. They also breathe air with lungs. All turtles lay eggs and bury them in soil. The warmth from the sun helps the eggs hatch.

Turtles are found all over the world. Some turtles spend most of their time in water. Other turtles spend some time both in the water and on land. There are also turtles that live only on land. Turtles eat both plants and animals.

Think and Learn

1. Turtles are reptiles with ______________________.
2. How do turtles cut their food? ______________________

   ____
3. All turtles lay ______________________.
4. What do turtles eat? ______________________

Sea Turtle

Sea turtles are turtles that live in the ocean. Sea turtles are very large. They range in size from 2 to 8 feet and weigh from 100 to 1,800 pounds. Instead of claws, sea turtles have flippers to help them swim easily through water. Sea turtles have flat shells instead of rounded shells like land turtles. Flat shells also help them move more easily through water.

Sea turtles are found in warm oceans throughout the world. They eat fish, shrimp, crabs, jellyfish, and plants. Sea turtles dig holes and lay their eggs on sandy beaches. The eggs lay buried in the sand for a couple of months before they hatch. When the eggs hatch, the babies dig out of the sand and head for the ocean.

Think and Learn

1. Flippers and ______________ shells help sea turtles move in the water.
2. Where are sea turtles found? ____________________________
3. Sea turtles eat fish, shrimp, crabs, jellyfish, and ________________.
4. Sea turtles lay their eggs on sandy ______________________.

ANIMALS THAT LIVE IN THE WATER

Starfish

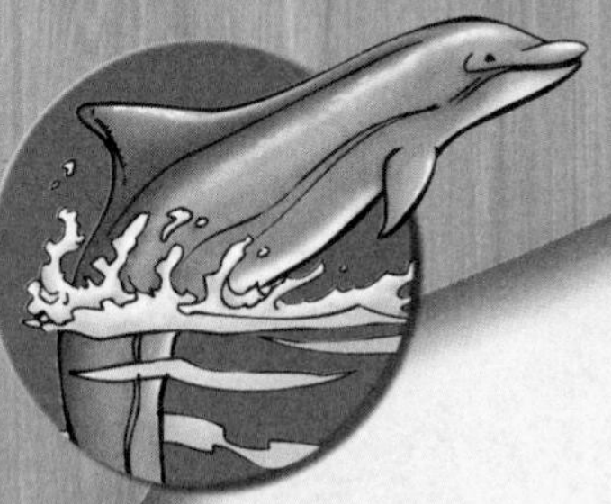

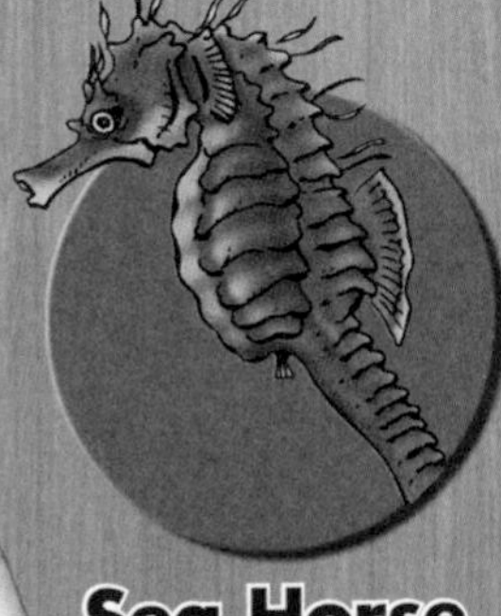

Octopus

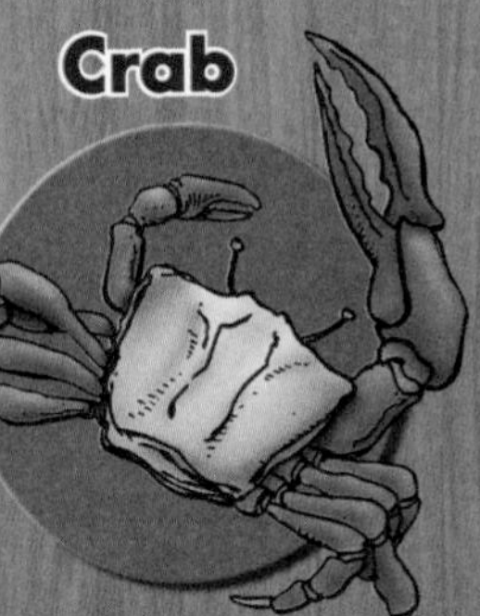

Salmon

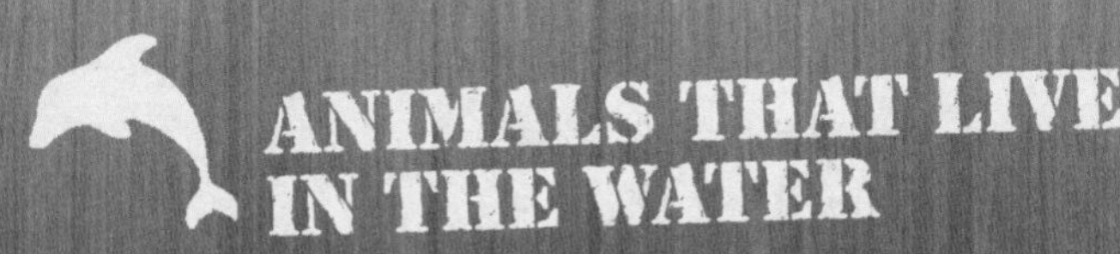

Crab

A crab is a sea animal covered by a hard shell. Crabs have five pairs of jointed legs. The first pair of legs has large claws. Crabs use their claws to attract mates, defend themselves, and get food. On crabs that swim, the last pair of legs is shaped like flippers. On land, crabs often walk sideways on their last four pairs of legs. Crabs come in all sizes, from less than 1 inch long to 12 feet long.

Crabs are found in oceans all over the world. Some crabs live on land, but must lay their eggs in the sea. Their young grow in the sea until they are adults. Then, they move to the land. Crabs eat both plants and animals.

Think and Learn

1. Crabs have ____________ pairs of jointed legs.
2. How do crabs use their claws? ____________

   ____
3. Crabs walk ____________ on their last four pairs of legs.
4. What do crabs eat? ____________

Dolphin

Dolphins (DAHL fihnz) are small-toothed whales that live in the ocean. They are mammals, not fish. A mammal is an animal whose young feed on its mother's milk. Dolphins also breathe with lungs, not gills like fish. They must come to the surface of the water to breathe. Dolphins have bodies well-suited for living in water. They have long, narrow bodies, flippers, and fins on their backs.

Dolphins are social animals. They live together in groups. They also talk to each other using many different sounds. Dolphins are very smart animals. Many have been trained by humans to do different jobs and to entertain people. Dolphins mainly eat fish and squid.

Think and Learn

1. Dolphins are ______________________________, not fish.

2. Dolphins breathe with ______________________________.

3. How are dolphin bodies suited for living in water? ____________________

____

4. What do dolphins eat? ______________________________

Dolphin Dot-to-Dot

Connect the dots. Color the picture.

DOLPHINS

Pull-Out Storybook

A dolphin is a type of toothed whale. There are more than 30 different kinds of dolphins. Most kinds live in the ocean, but some live in freshwater rivers and lakes in South America and Asia. Although dolphins live in water, they are mammals, not fish. Dolphins flap their tails up and down when they swim. Most fish move their tails from side to side. Dolphins also must come to the surface of the water to breathe air.

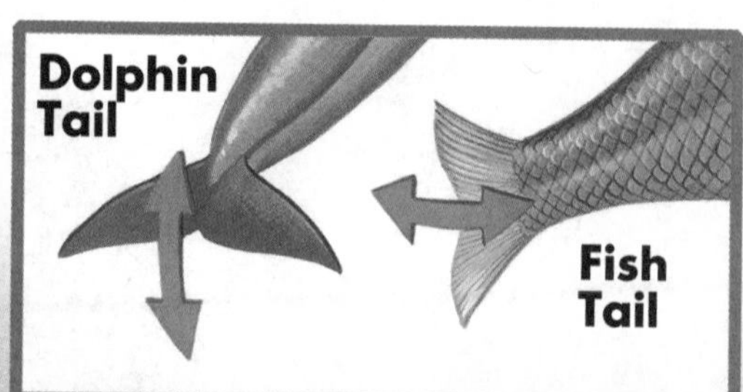

Bottlenose Dolphins

A dolphin uses its two flippers to steer and the dorsal fin on its back for balance. Instead of having a fur coat to keep it warm, a dolphin has a layer of fat called *blubber* under its skin. The blubber allows the dolphin to live in cold ocean water.

Like its whale cousins, a dolphin breathes through a blowhole at the top of its head. A dolphin usually comes to the surface two to three times a minute to breathe. It closes its blowhole underwater, just as you might plug your nose.

If dolphins could talk, their most common words might be "Let's play!" They race, leap, surf, spin, flop, splash, somersault, and even do back flips in the air. They play tag, catch, and tug-of-war. Play is a sign of intelligence. Dolphins enjoy playing games, learning new ones from each other, and even teaching humans how to play.

These spinner dolphins are amazing acrobats. They get their name from the spins they do in the air.

Dolphins are social animals that live in groups called *pods* or *schools*. Living in groups helps dolphins hunt for food and protect themselves from enemies, like sharks. And of course, it's more fun to play with a buddy. Dolphins talk to each other by making many different sounds. They also slap their tails on the water.

Dolphins will help another dolphin that is sick or hurt. They sometimes lift the dolphin in need to the surface so it can breathe.

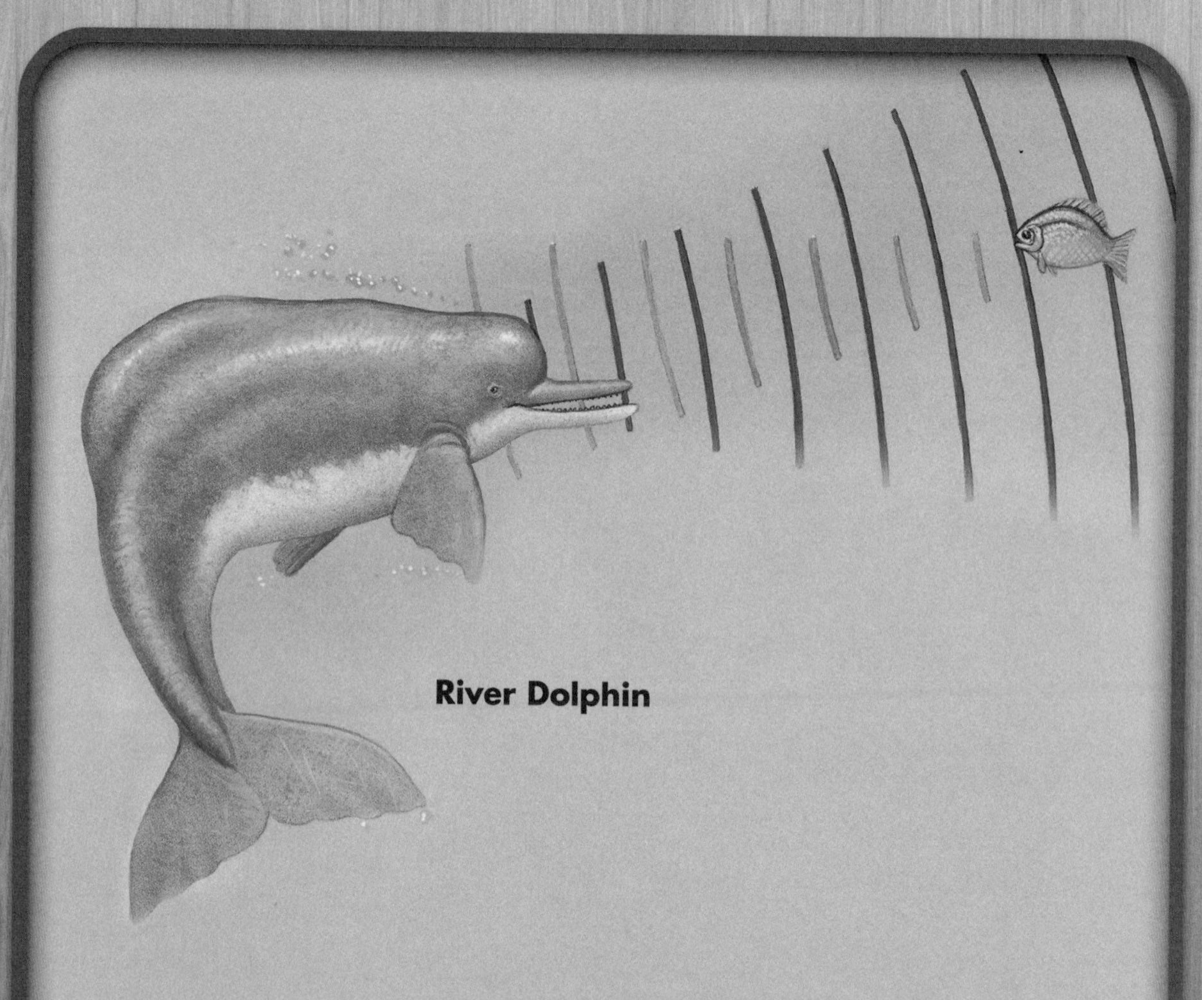

River Dolphin

Dolphins probably have the best hearing of all animals. They use their sense of hearing to find their way, hunt for food, and be aware of danger. Dolphins send out a series of clicking sounds. The sounds travel fast through the water. When the sounds strike an object, such as a fish or a rock, they bounce back as an echo. Dolphins can tell from the echoes the size, shape, speed, and location of the object.

Mother dolphins are very good parents. A baby dolphin grows inside its mother for about 1 year. The mother dolphin, often with the help of another female dolphin, guides her newborn calf up to the surface for air. A baby dolphin can swim quite well within 30 minutes of birth.

A mother dolphin is very protective of her baby. When the calf is about 6 months old, it begins to eat fish scraps left by adults. Later, its mother teaches it to hunt. Dolphin calves stay with their mothers for up to 3 years.

Dolphins face many dangers throughout the world. Some are accidentally caught in nets set by fishermen searching for tuna and other fish. Other dolphins are hunted as food. In the past 30 years, efforts have increased to protect dolphins and their habitats.

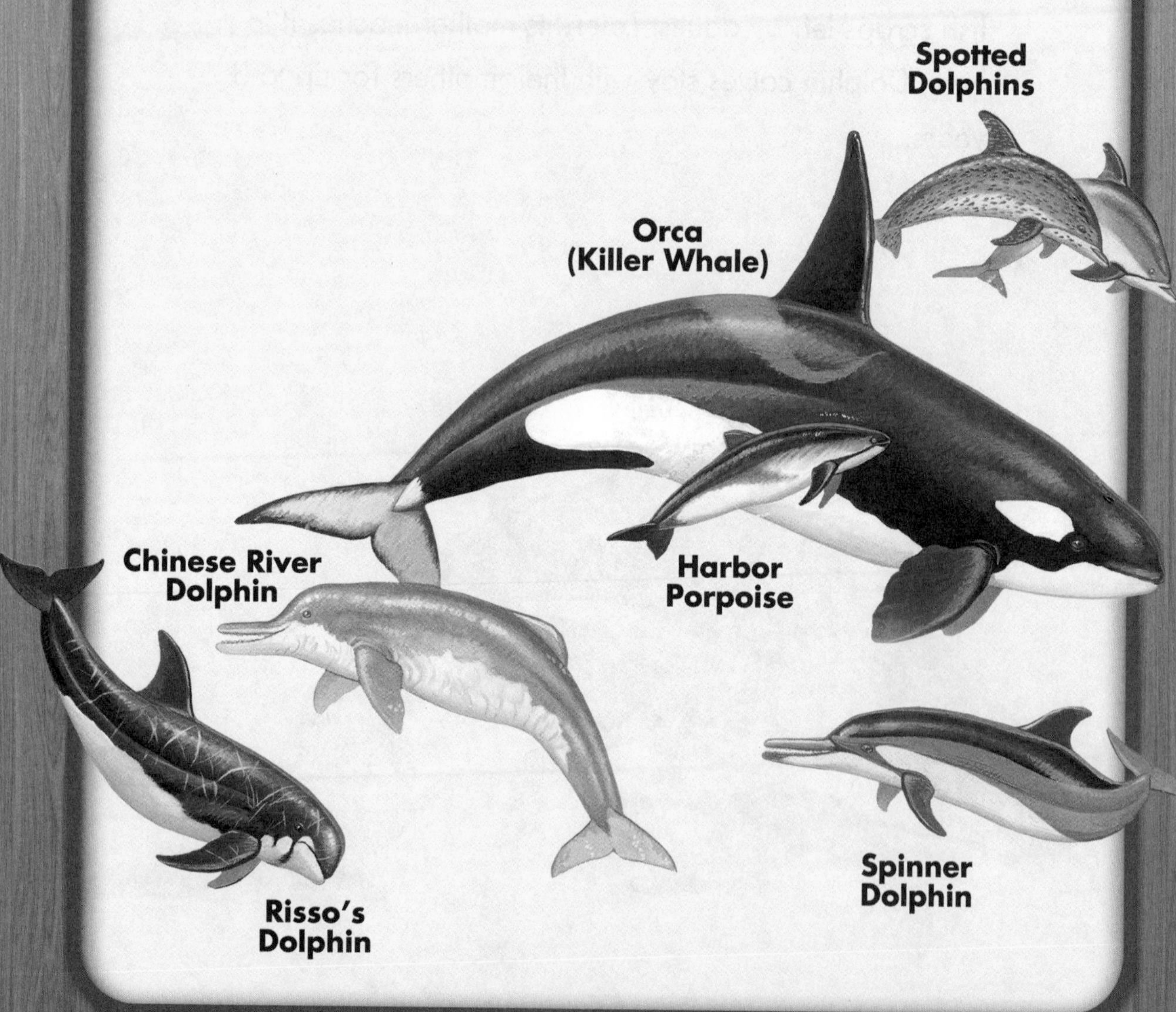

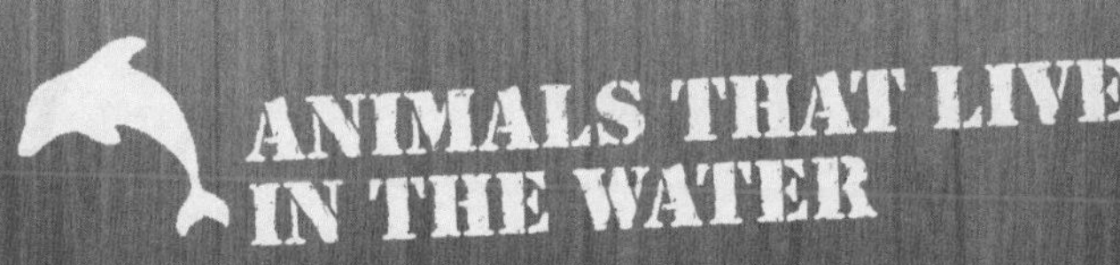

Jellyfish

Jellyfish are soft-bodied animals that live in oceans. Jellyfish get their name from the stiff, jellylike material that makes up their body. Jellyfish have no bones. Their body is shaped like an open umbrella. Their mouth hangs down from the center of their body. Long tentacles hang down around the outside of their body. These tentacles are poisonous.

Jellyfish swim by opening and closing their body. This action pushes the jellyfish through the water. To get food, jellyfish first swim upward. Then, as they float down to the bottom, they catch fish and other small animals by stinging them with their poisonous tentacles.

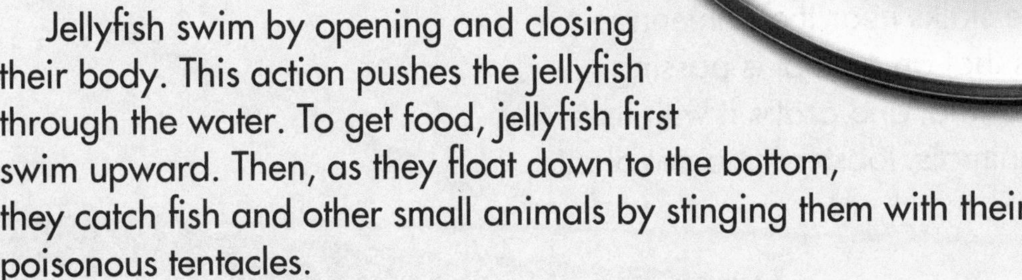

Think and Learn

1. What are jellyfish named for? ______________________________

____

2. What are jellyfish shaped liked? ______________________________

3. Jellyfish have ______________________________ tentacles.

4. How do jellyfish swim? ______________________________

____

Lobster

Lobsters (LAHB sterz) are sea animals that are related to crabs. Like crabs, lobsters have hard shells and five pairs of jointed legs. The first pair of legs has claws. Lobsters use their claws to grab food and tear it apart. Lobsters have long bodies divided into three parts—the head, the thorax or middle, and the abdomen or tail.

Lobsters live on the ocean floor near the shore. They usually hide in holes or under rocks and wave their antennae outside. Lobsters have eyes on the ends of the stalks near their antennae. When a lobster senses that an animal is passing by, it pounces on the animal and grabs it with its claws. Besides small animals, lobsters also eat plants.

Think and Learn

1. Lobsters are related to ______________________________.
2. How do lobsters use their claws? ______________________________

   ____
3. Lobster bodies are divided into ______________ parts.
4. Where do lobsters live? ______________________________

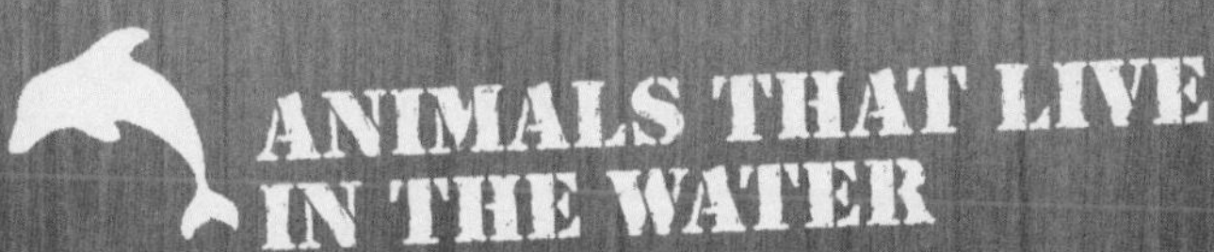

Octopus

An octopus (AHK tuh puhs) is a sea animal with a soft body and eight arms. These arms are called *tentacles*. The bottom sides of the tentacles are lined with suckers. Suckers are round and help octopuses stick to rocks. An octopus uses its arms and suckers to catch food and to move along the ocean floor.

Octopuses are found in oceans all over the world. They eat crabs, lobsters, clams, and snails. Many other sea animals eat octopuses. An octopus defends itself by squirting a dark cloud to hide itself. It can also change colors to either scare an enemy or help the octopus blend in with its surroundings. An octopus can shoot out a jet of water from its body and move quickly away.

Think and Learn

1. An octopus has ______________________________ tentacles.
2. How does an octopus use its tentacles? ______________________________

____
3. What do octopuses eat? ______________________________

____
4. Octopuses can change ____________________ to scare away enemies.

Salmon

Salmon are large fish that are born in freshwater streams. After birth, the young fish swim to the saltwater ocean. Some kinds of salmon go to the ocean right away. Other kinds stay in the streams for several years. Salmon live most of their lives in the ocean. When salmon are ready to lay eggs, they swim back to the freshwater stream where they were born. The return trip is not easy. Salmon must swim against strong river currents and jump up waterfalls.

Salmon are found in the Pacific and Atlantic oceans. They eat shrimp, squid, and small fish. When they return to freshwater rivers and streams to lay eggs, they do not eat. They live off the fat that is stored in their bodies.

Think and Learn

1. Where are salmon born? ______________________________

2. Where do salmon live most of their lives? ______________________________

3. Why is the return trip to lay eggs not easy? ______________________________

____

4. What do salmon living in the ocean eat? ______________________________

____

Sea Horse

A sea horse is a small fish with a head that looks like a horse's head. Its body is only about 5 inches long. Sea horses have long tails. They use their tails to hold onto plants. Their spiny coat protects them like armor. Sea horses are not strong swimmers. They swim in an upright, or standing up, position. They move through the water by moving their dorsal, or back, fin back and forth.

Sea horses are found in shallow ocean water in warm climates. They feed by sucking in small animals through their long snout. Female sea horses lay eggs in a pouch on the male sea horse's body. The male sea horse carries the eggs until they hatch.

Think and Learn

1. A sea horse is a small ____________________.
2. How do sea horses use their tails? ____________________
3. Sea horses swim in an ____________________ position.
4. Where do female sea horses lay eggs? ____________________

____

Shark

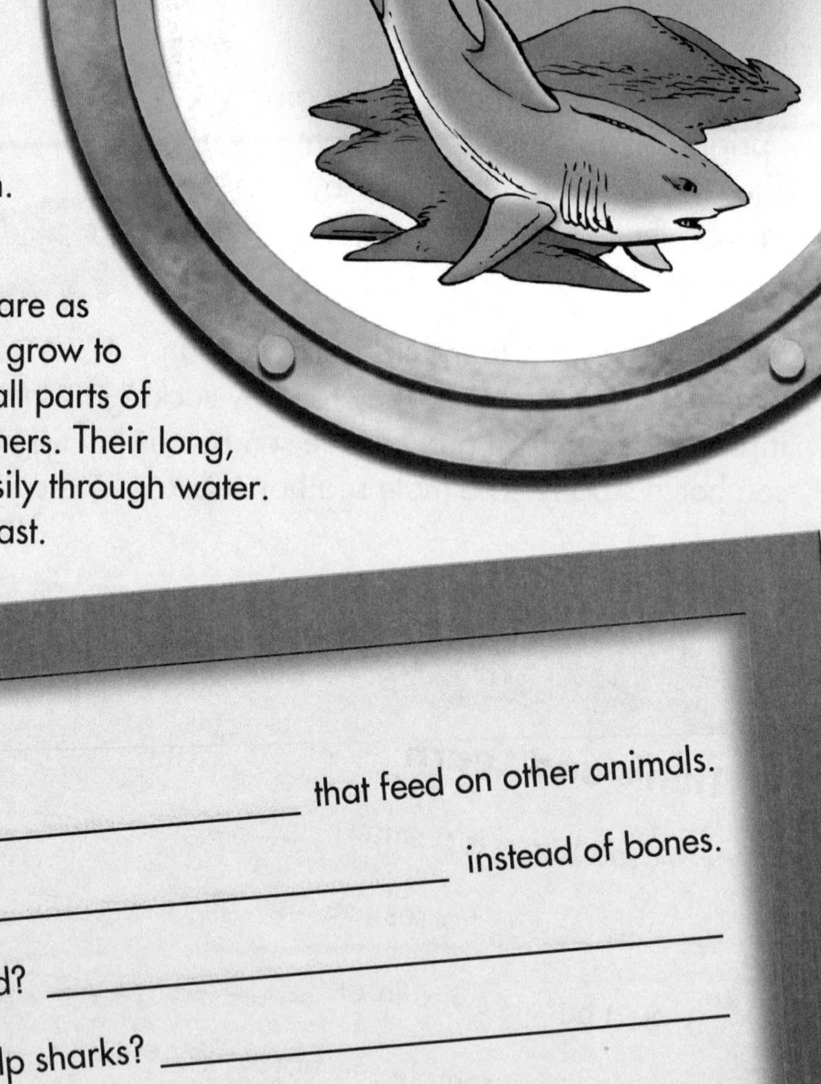

Sharks are fish that feed on other animals. Unlike most fish, sharks do not have bones. Instead, their bodies are supported with cartilage (KART I ij). Cartilage is a tough, bendable material. You have cartilage at the tip of your nose. Most sharks have mouths on the bottom side of their head. Some kinds of sharks have grinding teeth. Others have tearing teeth.

Sharks come in all sizes. Some are as small as 6 inches long. Others can grow to 40 feet long. Sharks are found in all parts of oceans. They are very good swimmers. Their long, narrow bodies help them move easily through water. Their curved tails help them swim fast.

Think and Learn

1. Sharks are ______________________ that feed on other animals.
2. Sharks have ______________________ instead of bones.
3. Where are sharks found? ______________________
4. How do curved tails help sharks? ______________________

____

Starfish

Starfish are sea animals with spines on their skin. Starfish are sometimes called *sea stars* because they are shaped like stars. Many starfish have five arms pointing out from their body. However, some starfish have as many as 40 arms. Starfish have rows of tiny, tube-shaped feet along their arms. These tube feet help starfish move and get food.

Starfish are found in oceans all over the world. They eat animals with shells, such as clams and oysters. A starfish opens up a shell by attaching its tube feet to both halves of the shell. Then, it pulls apart the shell and pushes its stomach through the opening in the shell.

Think and Learn

1. Starfish have ______________________________ on their skin.
2. Starfish have a body shaped liked a ______________________________.
3. How do starfish use their tube feet? ______________________________

   ____
4. What do starfish eat? ______________________________

   ____

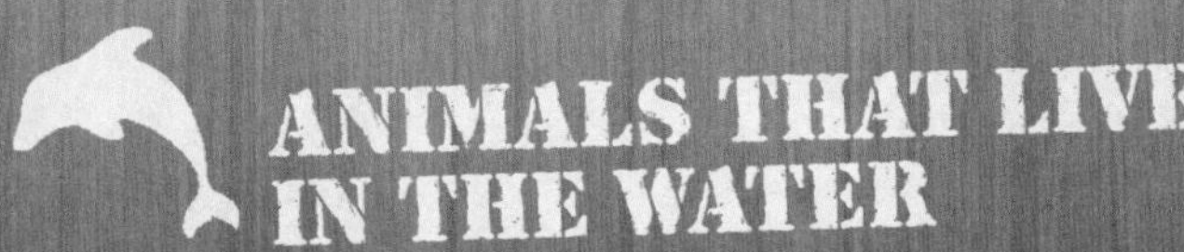

Whale

Whales are large mammals that live in the ocean. Mammals are animals whose young feed on their mother's milk. Although whales look like fish, they are very different. Whales have lungs and must come to the water's surface to breathe. Whales also have tails that move up and down, not back and forth.

Some whales have teeth. These whales usually eat fish and other animals. Other whales do not have teeth. These whales feed on tiny plants and animals that float in the water. Whales are social animals that live in groups. Whales talk to each other by making many different sounds. Whales have a keen sense of hearing and can hear sounds from far away.

Think and Learn

1. Whales are ______________________________ that live in the ocean.

2. How are whales different from fish? ______________________________

____

3. What do whales without teeth eat? ______________________________

____

4. Whales have a keen sense of ______________________________.

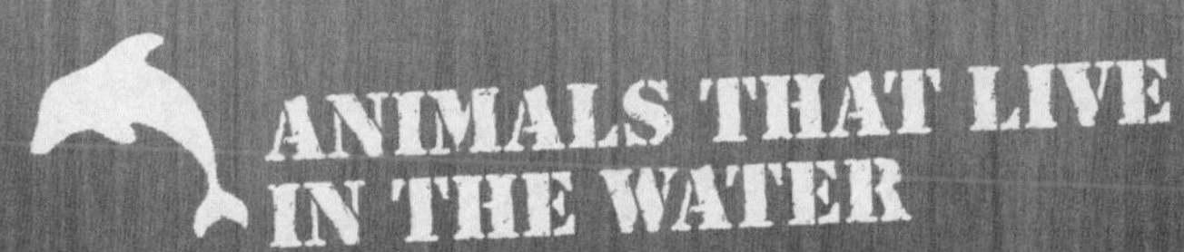

Word Search: Whale Watch

Let's go on a whale watch! Maybe you will see the largest animal on Earth, the blue whale. Find the whales and whale words in the puzzle. They are written **across** and **down**.

B L U E S B R S T F O G A P M P E B

A H U M P B A C K I R N N Y I S E L

L C P L E A R S E N C D B A N N K U

E U O M R B E L U G A L E U K G R B

E P D O M F B B O W H E A D E A S B

N A R W H A L T K Z B L O W H O L E

M A R E L R A K I L L E R T M E W R

blue	**baleen**	**bowhead**	**blowhole**
killer	**blubber**	**sperm**	**orca**
minke	**beluga**	**narwhal**	
fin	**pod**	**humpback**	

Hidden Pictures: Ocean Animals

Find the ocean animals hidden in the picture. Color the picture.

FARM ANIMALS

Duck

Chicken

Cow

Horse

Pig

Sheep

Goat

Duck

Ducks are birds that spend part of the time in water. Their webbed feet act as paddles to move them easily through the water. Most ducks get their food from water or from the areas around water. Some ducks eat fish. Others eat water plants and small water animals. Ducks keep dry by oiling their top feathers with oil from a special gland near their tail. They have a layer of soft fluffy feathers, called *down*, under the top feathers. Down keeps the duck warm.

Farmers raise ducks for their feathers, eggs, and meat. Duck feathers are used to stuff pillows and make winter coats. Ducks raised on farms do not get their food from water. The farmer feeds them a kind of food made just for ducks.

Think and Learn

1. What helps ducks move through water? ______________________

2. Most ducks get their food from ______________________.

3. What is down? ______________________

______________________.

4. Farmers raise ducks for feathers, eggs, and ______________________.

Pig

Pigs are farm animals with short legs and a long, round body. Their body is covered with short bristles. Pigs cannot sweat to cool their body in hot weather. Instead, they lie in the mud during hot weather to cool off. Pigs have a sharp sense of smell but poor eyesight. The end of their flat snout is very sensitive to touch. Pigs use their snout for finding and digging up food.

Farmers all over the world raise pigs. Pigs are raised for their meat, which is called *pork*. Many other products, such as leather, glue, soap, fertilizer, and medicines, are made from other parts of the pig. Farmers feed pigs corn and other grains. Pigs also eat "pig food" made with meat scraps, milk, peanuts, soybeans, and other foods.

Think and Learn

1. How do pigs cool themselves? ______________________________

2. Pigs use their ______________________ for finding and digging up food.

3. Pigs are raised for their meat, which is called ____________________.

4. What are some other products made from parts of the pig? ______________

____

Horse

The horse is a very useful animal. Long ago, people used horses to go places and move things. Now, many people use horses for fun. Some people, however, still use horses to herd cattle and sheep. Horses are built for running. They have long legs and strong feet. Their wide nostrils bring a lot of air into the lungs. They also have sharp senses of sight, hearing, and smell.

Horses eat grass and grains. Their back teeth are wide and flat to grind grass into small pieces. These teeth never stop growing. Their front teeth are narrower and sharp. They help the horse bite off grass from the ground.

Think and Learn

1. What do people use horses for today? ______________________

____

2. Horses are built for ______________________.

3. What do horses eat? ______________________

4. How do horses use their back teeth? ______________________

____

Incredible!

Incredible!

Incredible!

Incredible!

BRAVO!

BRAVO!

BRAVO!

WOW!

WOW!

WOW!

GOOD!

GOOD!

GOOD!

HORSES

Pull-Out Storybook

There are more than 150 breeds of horses. These breeds are divided into three main groups, according to size. Light horses, such as quarter horses, are lean and athletic. Most weigh less than 1,300 pounds. Heavy horses, such as shires, are the biggest and strongest horses. Some weigh more than 2,000 pounds. Ponies, such as Shetland ponies, are the smallest horses. A pony stands less than 58 inches tall and usually weighs less than 800 pounds.

Horses are built for speed. In just a short distance, their strong legs can take them from standing still to a speed of 40 miles per hour. A horse also has a deep chest that holds a large heart and strong lungs. These body parts help the horse run fast for miles. The horse's long neck helps it to stay balanced while running.

When a horse gallops, each hoof touches the ground at a different time. At one point, all four hooves are lifted into the air for a split second before the horse lands with a thud.

Horses usually give birth to one baby at a time. A baby horse is called a *foal*. When it is born, a foal weighs about 100 pounds and is about 43 inches long. A few minutes after birth, a foal tries to stand up. At first, its long thin legs are wobbly. But soon, the foal is standing by itself. After only a few hours, the foal can walk and run next to its mother.

Foals are weaned, or separated, from their mother at about 6 months old. During this time, the young horses often are kept together to help them get used to being away from their mother.

Foals are very lively and playful. They love to jump, kick, and run. They enjoy playing games or galloping across a field with other young horses.

Horses talk by making sounds and using body movements. Horses whinny or snort when they are excited. The position of a horse's ears tells how the horse is feeling. Ears laid back show fear or anger. Ears pricked up show friendliness. Horses often circle and sniff each other when they first meet.

Horses have been helping people for thousands of years. At one time, horses were the fastest way of traveling on land. People have ridden horses to hunt for food, charge into battle, and round up livestock. Horses have also been used to haul heavy loads, pull carts and carriages, and plow land. Today, people use horses for fun and sport.

Horses belong to the animal family called *Equidae.* Other members of this family include zebras, donkeys, and mules. Though these animals are different in size and color, they share many common features. For one thing, each member of the horse family has one hoof at the end of each leg. They also have long, powerful legs, pointed ears, and manes that run down their necks. In fact, the body structures of horses and their relatives are so much alike that only an expert can tell their bones apart.

Cow

Cows are large farm animals with split hooves. They have long tails that help swat insects away. Cows eat grass, hay, corn, and soybeans. They break down their food in a stomach that has four parts. When breaking down food, cows move it from the stomach back into their mouth to chew it again. The food that moves back into their mouth is called a *cud*. Cows chew the cud and swallow it again. Then, the food moves through the other parts of the stomach.

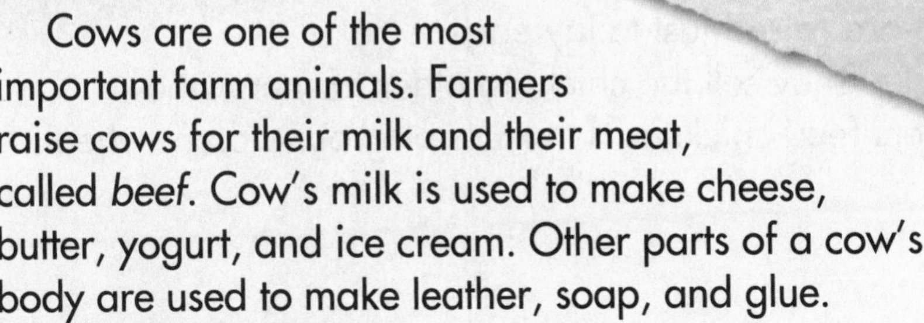

Cows are one of the most important farm animals. Farmers raise cows for their milk and their meat, called *beef*. Cow's milk is used to make cheese, butter, yogurt, and ice cream. Other parts of a cow's body are used to make leather, soap, and glue.

Think and Learn

1. What do cows eat? ____________________

2. Cows have a stomach that has ____________________ parts.

3. Meat from cows is called ____________________.

4. What foods are made from cow's milk? ____________________

____

Chicken

Chickens are ground birds. They have a plump body and rounded wings. Chickens can fly but for only short distances. They fly to get away from danger. Chickens have pointed beaks and strong claws that they use to scratch in the dirt and get food. Different kinds of chickens have feathers of different colors.

Chickens are raised on farms all over the world. Farmers raise chickens for their eggs and their meat, called *poultry*. Some chickens are raised only for their meat. Other chickens are raised just to lay eggs. Some farmers raise only baby chicks. They sell the chicks to other farmers who raise them for meat or eggs. Farmers feed chickens a mixture of ground corn, wheat, and soybeans.

Think and Learn

1. Chickens fly for ______________________ distances.

2. How do chickens use their strong claws? ______________________

____

3. What are chickens raised for? ______________________

4. What do farmers feed chickens? ______________________

____

Sheep

Sheep are related to cows and goats. Like cows, sheep have a stomach that is divided into four parts. Sheep also have split hooves. Sheep do not need a lot of water to live. They like to eat grass and shrubs. When sheep eat, they bite off grass very close to the ground. If sheep are kept in the same pasture for a long time, they can kill all the grass.

Sheep are raised all over the world. However, the most sheep are raised in Australia and New Zealand. Sheep are very important animals because they give wool, milk, and meat, called *lamb* or *mutton*. Wool is used to make clothing, blankets, and rugs. Sheep's milk is used to make cheese.

Think and Learn

1. What other farm animals are sheep related to? ____________________

____

2. Sheep do not need a lot of ____________________ to live.

3. Where are the most sheep raised? ____________________

____

4. What are sheep raised for? ____________________

Goat

Goats are related to sheep and cows. Like sheep and cows, goats have split hooves and a four-part stomach. Goats have long, shaggy hair. Most goats, both male and female, have a beard. Goats are known for eating almost anything. Because they have small mouths and flexible lips, goats can easily pick off only the healthful parts of a plant. They find food even in places where few plants can grow.

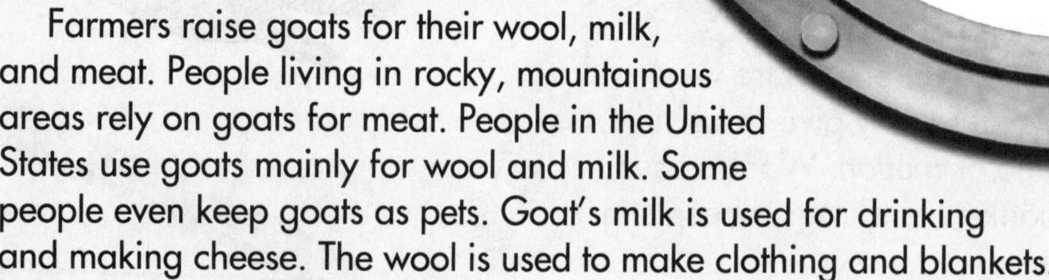

Farmers raise goats for their wool, milk, and meat. People living in rocky, mountainous areas rely on goats for meat. People in the United States use goats mainly for wool and milk. Some people even keep goats as pets. Goat's milk is used for drinking and making cheese. The wool is used to make clothing and blankets.

Think and Learn

1. How are goats like sheep and cows? ______________________________

____

2. Goats can pick off only the ____________________ parts of a plant.

3. Goats are raised for ______________________________.

4. Goat's milk is used for drinking and making ____________________.

FAVORITE PETS

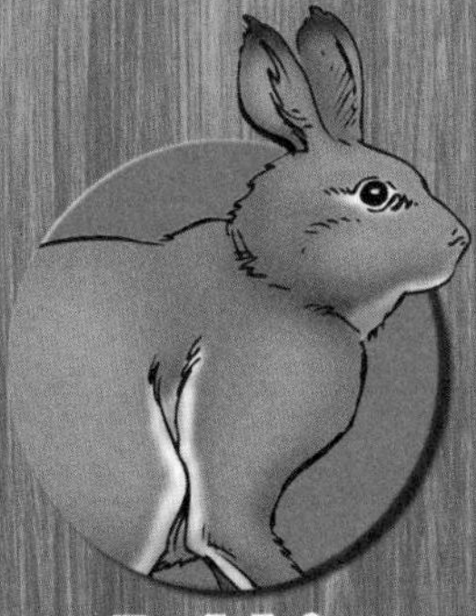
Rabbit

Cat

Guinea Pig

Toad

Frog

Dog

Cat

Cats have been favorite pets for thousands of years. At first, people had cats to get rid of pests, such as mice and snakes. Cats are skilled hunters. They have keen senses, sharp claws, and the ability to jump and climb. Today, most people have cats to keep them company. Cats are smart but rather independent animals. They make good pets for people who are not home often.

Cats need to be fed every day. They must always have fresh water for drinking. Cats are clean animals and groom themselves often. However, cats should be brushed regularly to remove dead hair, especially if the cat has long hair. Cats must also be taken to the veterinarian for medical check-ups.

Think and Learn

1. Why did people first keep cats as pets? ____________________

____________________.

2. Cats have keen senses and sharp ____________________

3. Cats are clean animals and ____________________ themselves.

4. Cats must go to the ____________________ for check-ups.

CATS
Pull-Out Storybook

There are many different breeds of cats. Cats are divided into two main groups, depending on the length of their hair. Long-haired cats have long, silky coats. These cats probably came from cold areas, where thick coats protected them from harsh winters. Short-haired cats have short, sleek coats. These breeds are easier to care for because their coats need less grooming.

Cats are natural athletes. With their flexible body, they can run, leap, and climb. When they fall, they flip and twist their body to land on their feet. Cats have good balance and can walk easily along thin ledges.

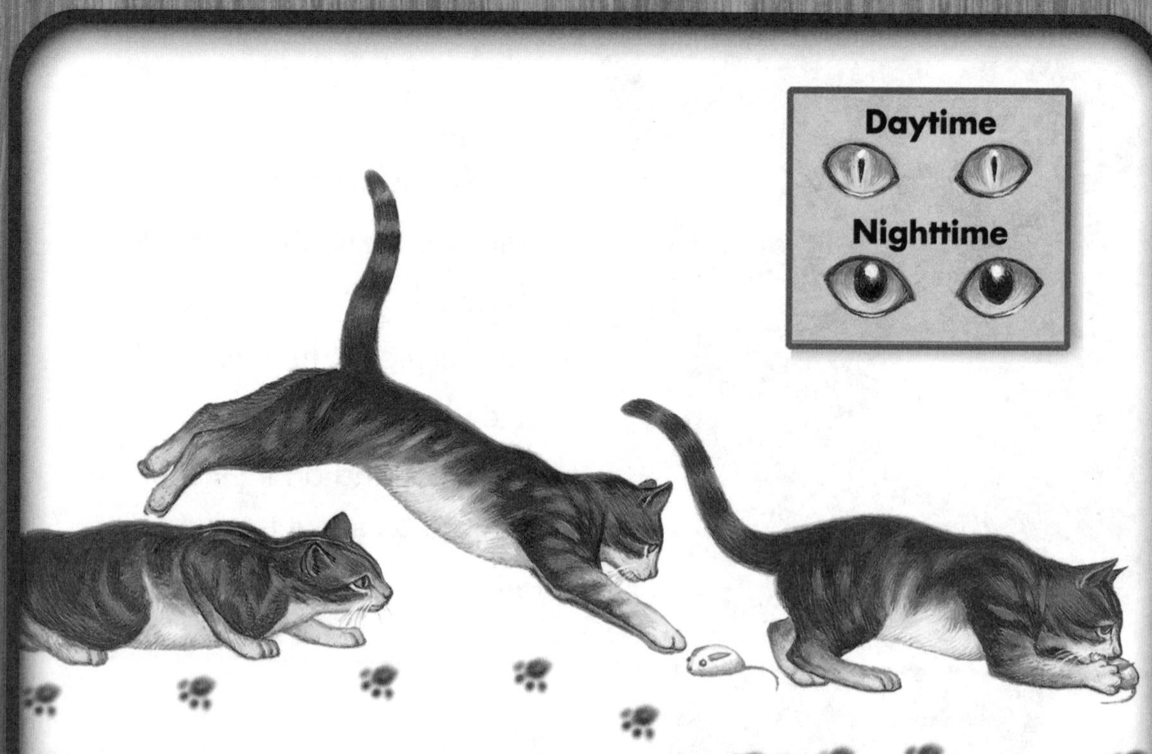

Cats are excellent hunters. Cats have a keen sense of hearing that helps them hear even the slightest movement of another animal. Cats also have sharp eyesight. During the day, a cat's pupils are narrow. The pupil is the dark part in the middle of the eye that opens and closes to let in light. At night, a cat's pupils widen to let more light enter. Cats have a mirror-like layer of skin at the back of each eye. This helps them see even small objects in very dim light.

Cats usually have 3 to 5 kittens at a time. The kittens depend entirely on their mother to feed, clean, and protect them. At first, the mother cat spends almost all of her time caring for her babies, leaving them only to eat or to use the litter box. As the kittens grow older and more independent, the mother leaves them for longer periods of time. Once the kittens are 6 to 10 weeks of age, they can be separated from their mother. By this time, the mother has taught her kittens how to live on their own.

Kittens love to play! When kittens play, they exercise their body to help it grow strong. Kittens learn to hunt when they stalk and pounce on objects. When they play-fight, they learn to defend themselves. All these play activities teach kittens how to live on their own.

Cats use their voice, face, and body to communicate. Cats can make more than 60 different sounds, ranging from soft purrs to loud screams. Each sound has a different meaning. Purrs usually mean a cat is happy. Hisses and screams show that a cat is feeling angry or afraid.

A cat also shows how it's feeling by the look on its face and the position of its body. A friendly cat rubs its face and body against a person. An angry cat curls up its lips and arches its back.

Cats belong to a family of animals called *Felidae*. There are more than 30 different kinds of cats. They include lions, tigers, ocelots, and pumas as well as house cats. Most wild cats live alone. The lion is the only wild cat that lives in a group. The tiger is the largest member of the cat family. Ocelots are skillful climbers. The black leopard has a coat so dark that its black spots are invisible. The jaguar is very strong. It can drag an animal much heavier than itself.

Dog

Dogs are popular pets throughout the world. Dogs have been bred through the years for certain jobs, such as guarding, hunting, and herding. Some dogs have been bred just to be pets. Dogs come in all sizes, colors, and personalities. When choosing a dog for a pet, the dog's qualities must fit in with the family's lifestyle.

Taking care of a dog is a big responsibility. Dogs need to be fed every day. They need clean, fresh water all the time and a warm, dry place to sleep. Dogs also need regular exercise, especially if they are big dogs. Dogs must be brushed and bathed regularly. Dogs also need medical check-ups every year. They must have vaccines and medicines to stay healthy.

Think and Learn

1. What jobs have dogs been bred for? ______________________________

   ____

2. Dogs should be fed ______________________________.
3. Dogs need regular ______________________________.
4. Every year, dogs need medical ______________________________.

Animal Friends

Plants, animals, and people must share our world. How can you be kind to our animal friends? Under each picture, write one way that you can be kind to that animal.

Rabbit

Rabbits are rodents with long ears and fluffy tails. Rodents are animals with front teeth that grow all the time. Pet rabbits must always have something to chew on. If not, their front teeth will grow too long for them to chew food normally.

Pet rabbits need a hutch, or a cage, to live in. They can be kept outside in a shady place during the summer. In winter, they must be kept in a heated garage or a cool basement. Rabbits eat pellets made just for them. They need fresh hay to eat every day. They also like fresh vegetables, clover, and grass. A water bottle filled with clean water should always be kept in the cage. Most rabbits do not like to be held for a long time. Never pick up a rabbit by its ears.

Think and Learn

1. A rodent has front ________________ that grow all the time.
2. What do pet rabbits live in? ________________
3. What do rabbits eat? ________________

   ____
4. Never pick up a rabbit by its ________________.

Guinea Pig

A guinea pig is a small animal with a large head, short legs, and small ears. They grow to 14 inches long and weigh about 1 pound. Guinea pigs are not really pigs. They are rodents. Rodents have front teeth that never stop growing. For this reason, guinea pigs must always have a piece of wood to gnaw on.

Guinea pigs make good classroom pets. They are easy to care for, and they don't often bite. Guinea pigs need a cage through which air can easily move. They should have food and fresh water in their cage at all times. Guinea pigs eat grain, fresh vegetables, and hay. Guinea pigs are most active at night. They are quiet during the day and sleep in a burrow they make in their cage.

Think and Learn

1. Guinea pigs are not pigs; they are ______________________.
2. What is the length of a guinea pig? ______________________
3. Why do guinea pigs make good classroom pets? ______________________

____.

4. Guinea pigs are most active ______________________

Frog

Frogs are animals that spend part of their life in water. Some frogs live mostly in water. Other frogs live mostly on land. Almost all frogs lay their eggs in or near water. Tadpoles hatch from the eggs. Tadpoles swim and grow in water. As they grow, they change from a fishlike animal to an adult frog.

Pet frogs need a lot of care. Frogs are kept in aquariums. The kind of pet frog determines the environment in the aquarium. Some kinds of frogs live in half water and half land environments. Others live in all water environments. Still others live in all land environments. Frogs must be fed regularly. Many frogs eat live insects, such as crickets. Others eat frozen worms.

Think and Learn

1. Frogs spend part of their life in ____________________.
2. ____________________ hatch from frog eggs.
3. Where are pet frogs kept? ____________________
4. What do pet frogs eat? ____________________

____

Compare and Contrast

Read about frogs and toads in the "Frogs" storybook. Then, use the Venn diagram and the facts you have learned to compare and contrast these two animals.

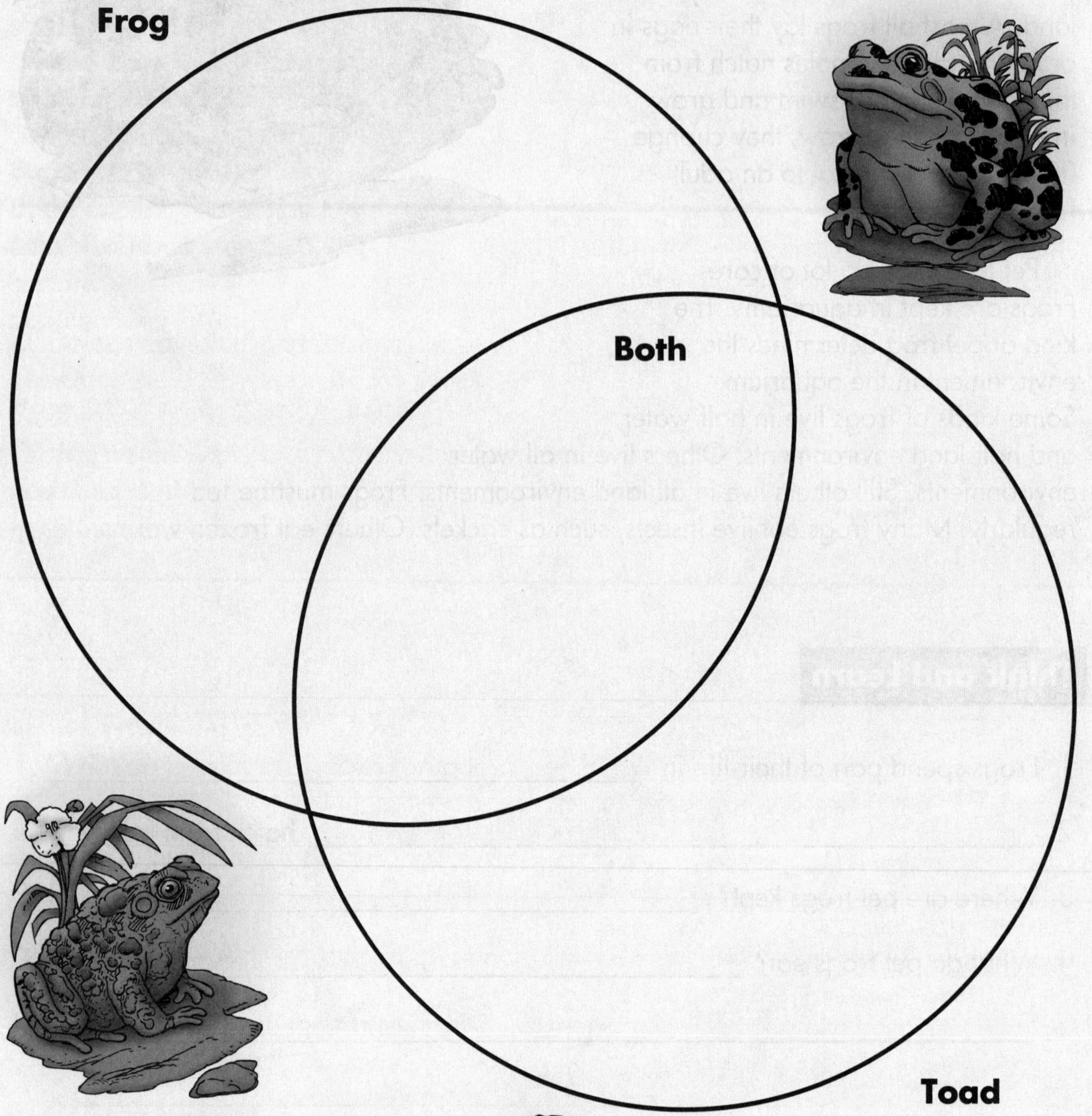

Frog

Both

Toad

FROGS
Pull-Out Storybook

Frogs are amphibians. Amphibians are animals that spend the first part of their life in water and the second part on land. Frogs and their cousins, the toads, make up the largest group of amphibians. Frogs and toads look alike but do have some differences. Generally, frogs have slender bodies and smooth, moist skin. Toads have plump bodies and bumpy, drier skin. Most frogs have long powerful hind legs that help them leap long distances. Toads, on the other hand, have short legs. They tend to waddle or hop.

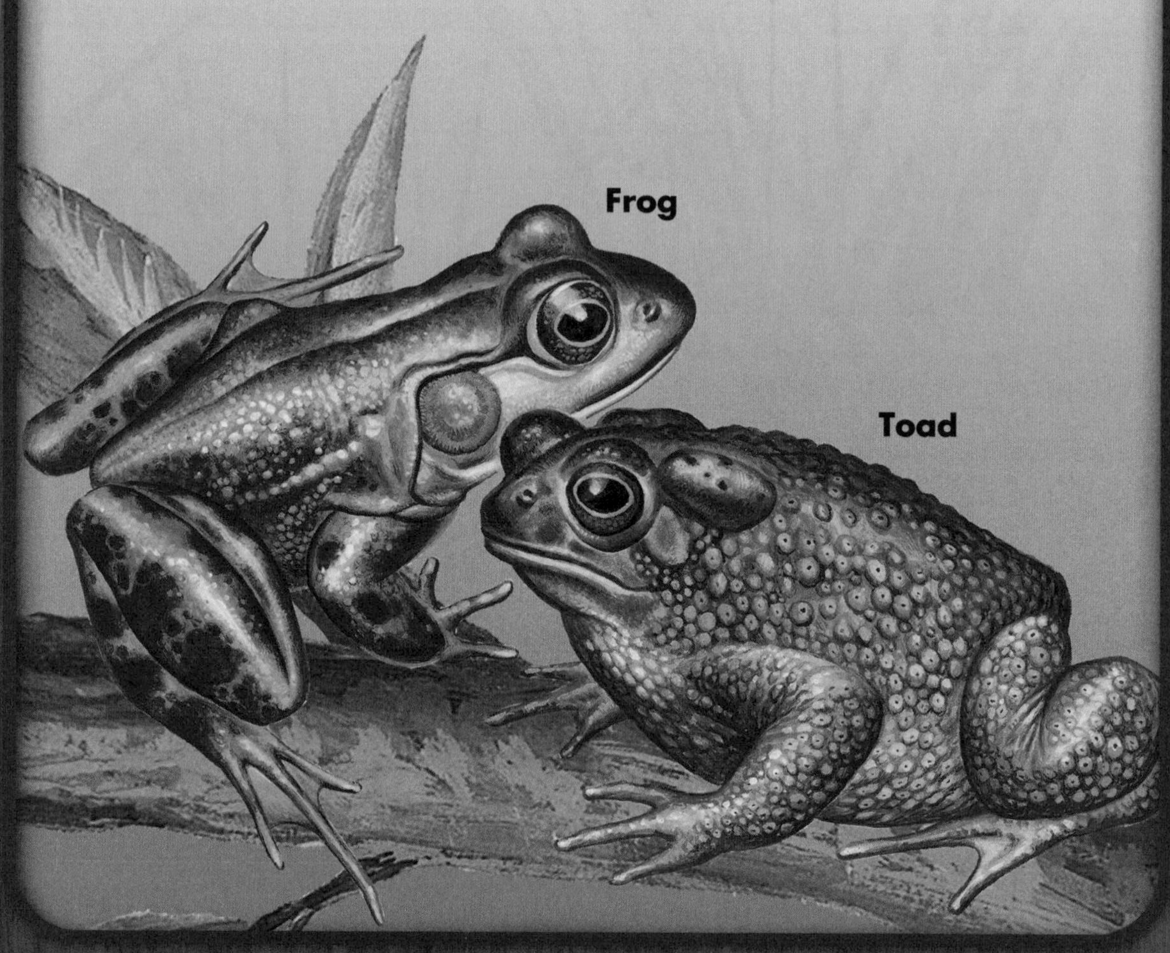

Like all amphibians, frogs are cold-blooded. This means that their body temperature changes to match the temperature of their surroundings.

The smooth, moist skin of frogs does more than protect the body. Although frogs breathe with lungs, they also take in air through their skin. Frogs take in water through their skin, too. Instead of drinking with their mouths, they simply sit in water and soak it up like a sponge.

Frogs are expert swimmers. Their webbed feet act like flippers to push the water backward. As it swims, a frog kicks its hind legs back to push itself forward. Then, it draws its legs up to its body to get ready for the next kick.

Frogs that burrow and dig have pointy feet. Frogs that climb trees have sticky feet. Frogs that swim have webbed feet.

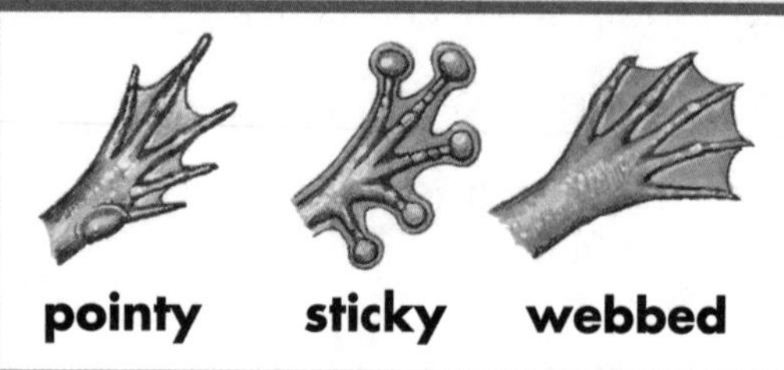

A frog's feet give clues about the way it lives.

Most frogs eat insects. Large frogs even eat mice, rats, and lizards. Frogs hunt mainly by sight. Their large, bulging eyes can see the tiniest movements of their prey. When ready to attack, a frog flicks out its weapon—a long tongue with a sticky tip. The frog traps its prey on the end of its tongue, then whips the prey into its mouth. If the prey is too far for their tongue to reach, frogs jump up and grab the prey in their mouth.

Each kind of frog makes its own special sound. The sounds range from peeps and grunts to pops and whistles. When speaking, a frog pumps air back and forth over its vocal cords. The vocal cords are bands of skin that lie between the mouth and lungs. Many male frogs also have an air sac called a *vocal sac*. The sac swells as the frog calls out, making the sound even louder. Some frogs have one vocal sac under the chin. Others have a vocal sac on each side of the head.

Life Cycle of a Frog

Frogs lay their eggs in water. They may lay hundreds, or even thousands, of eggs at a time. But only a few of these eggs develop into adult frogs.

The babies that hatch from the eggs are called *tadpoles*. With their round head, legless body, and long tail, they look more like fish than frogs. Unlike adult frogs, tadpoles breathe with gills. As tadpoles grow, their lungs start to form, their legs appear, and their gills and tail begin shrinking. Eventually, they lose their gills and tail altogether.

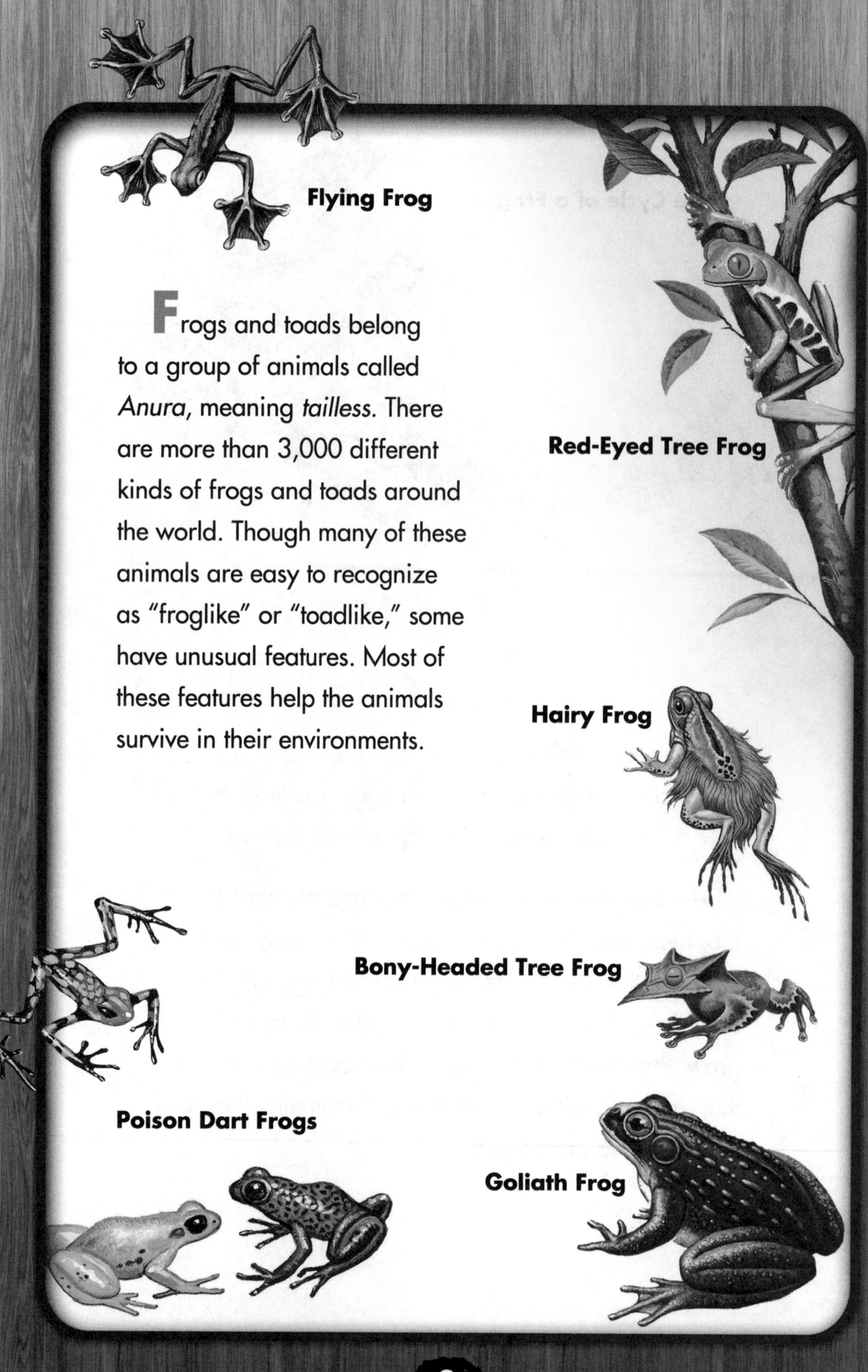

Frogs and toads belong to a group of animals called *Anura,* meaning *tailless.* There are more than 3,000 different kinds of frogs and toads around the world. Though many of these animals are easy to recognize as "froglike" or "toadlike," some have unusual features. Most of these features help the animals survive in their environments.

SCIENCE
AND ANIMALS

Life Cycles

Food Chains

Vertebrates

Reptiles

Birds

Amphibians

Mammals

Invertebrates

Fish

Animal Adaptations

Classification Systems

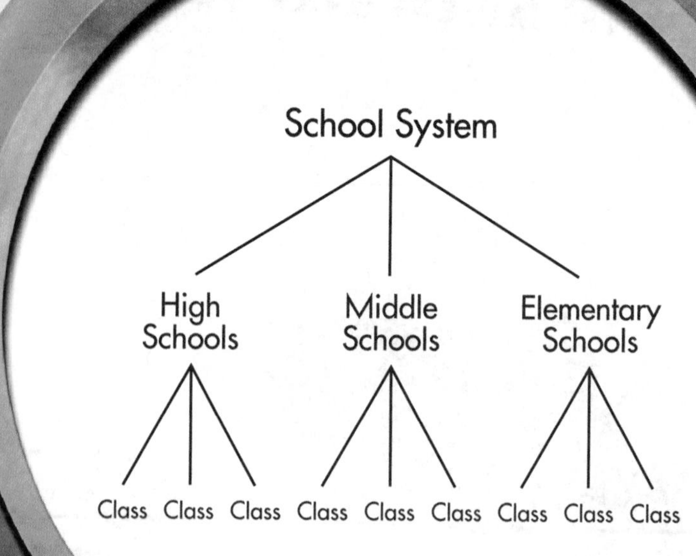

Scientists divide all living things into major groups. Then, they divide these major groups into smaller groups. And, they divide the smaller groups into still smaller groups. This is called a *classification system*.

Your school uses a classification system, too. The whole school system includes all the schools in your area. High schools, middle schools, and elementary schools make up the school system. You go to school in a certain elementary school. You are in a certain class within your school.

Think and Learn

1. Scientists use a classification system to divide ____ into major groups and smaller groups.

2. What are the different kinds of schools that make up your school system? ____

3. What are elementary schools divided into? ________________________________

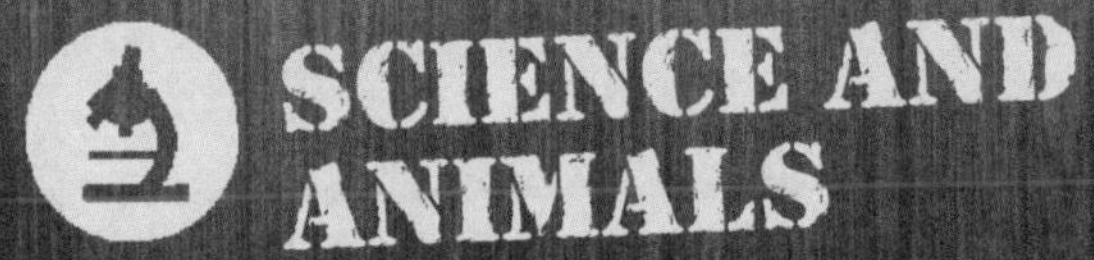

Classifying Animals

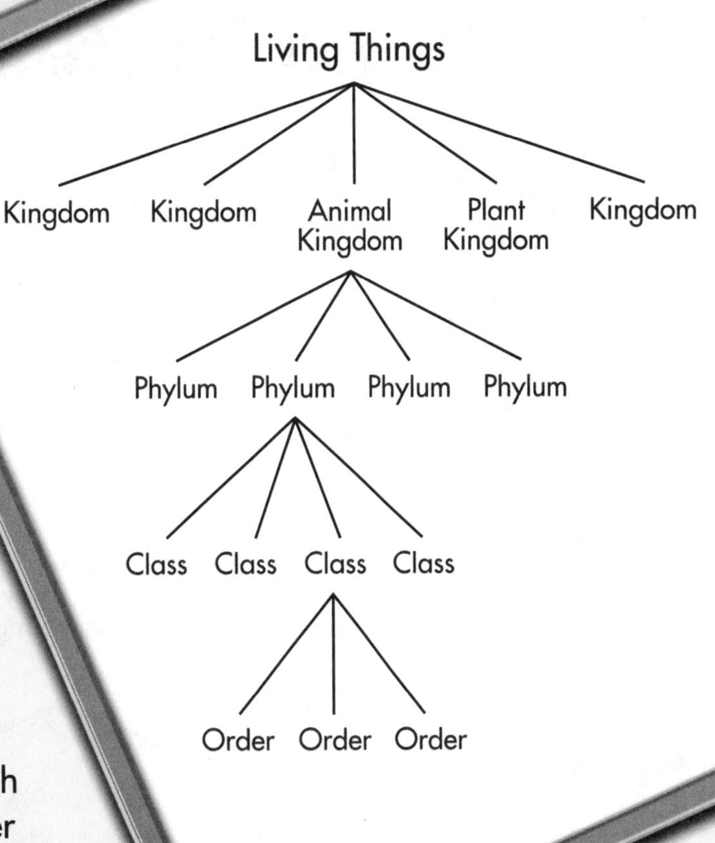

Just as your school system includes the several different kinds of schools, all of Earth's living things make up several major groups. Scientists call these major groups *kingdoms*. Two of the kingdoms of living things are the Plant Kingdom and the Animal Kingdom. The Animal Kingdom contains all the animals in the world.

Scientists divide each kingdom into large groups called *phyla* (FIH luh). Each phylum (FIH luhm) is divided into smaller groups called *classes*. Each class contains smaller groups called *orders*. In this way, scientists classify all living things on Earth.

Think and Learn

1. What do scientists call the major groups of living things? ____________________

____

2. What are two kingdoms of living things? ____________________

____

3. Kingdoms are divided into large groups called ____________________.

4. Scientists divide phyla into ____________________.

Classifying Vertebrates

Animals that have backbones are called *vertebrates* (VER tuh bruhts). Scientists classify vertebrates into five main groups called *classes*. The five main classes of vertebrates are shown below. Write the correct class name under the picture. Then, color each of the vertebrates.

Birds have feathers and wings. Baby birds hatch from eggs.

____

Mammals have hair on their bodies. They feed milk to their young.

____

Amphibians live some of their life in water and some on land. Adults breathe with lungs.

____

Reptiles live on land. They have dry scaly skin and breathe with lungs.

____

Fish live in water and breathe through gills. Scales cover their body.

____

reptile	**fish**	**amphibian**
bird	**mammal**	

Backbones

Each skeleton below shows a different class of vertebrates. Color the backbone in each skeleton. Then, write the class below each animal.

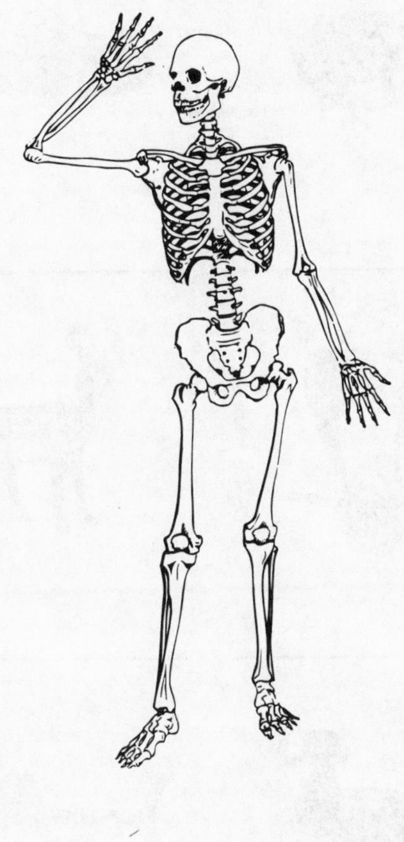

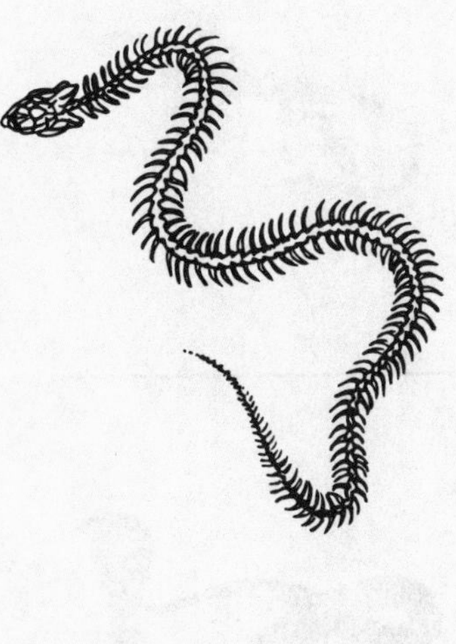

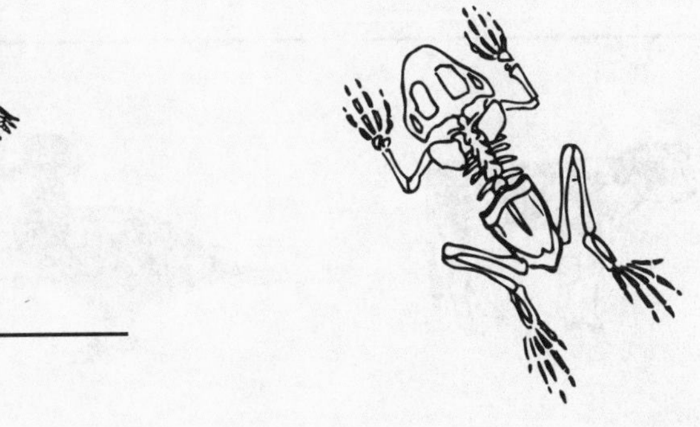

reptile **fish** **amphibian**
bird **mammal**

Classy Vertebrates

Scientists group the vertebrates into five main classes. Write the name of the vertebrate class for each picture.

reptile **fish** **amphibian**
bird **mammal**

Animals With Backbones

Vertebrates are animals that have backbones. There are five main classes of vertebrates. Read the characteristics listed in the second column. Then, write the name of the class in the first column. Write an example of each class in the third column.

class	characteristics	example
	• live in water • breathe with gills	
	• live partly in water and partly on land • breathe with lungs as adults	
	• have dry, scaly skin • breathe with lungs	
	• have feathers and wings • breathe with lungs	
	• body covered with hair • feed young with milk	

reptiles
birds
toad
fish

mammals
turtle
trout
bear

amphibians
hawk

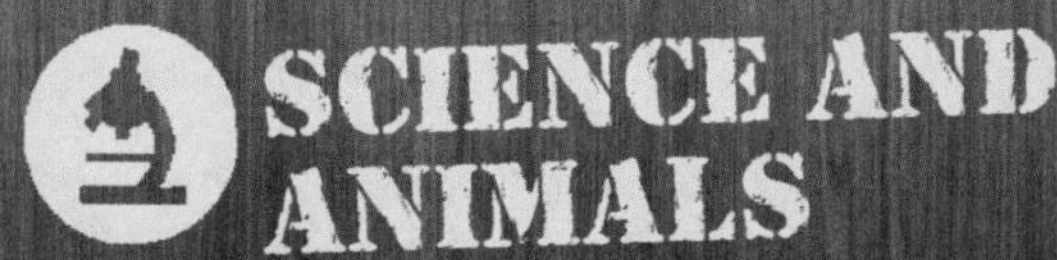

Parts of a Fish

Fish make up one class of vertebrates. There are many different kinds of fish. They vary greatly in size and shape. However, most fish have certain features in common.

Fish eat plants and other animals with a mouth. They see where they're going with their eyes. Fish breathe under water through structures called *gills* on the sides of their heads.

The bodies of fish are covered with tiny scales. Scales make fish smooth on the outside and help them swim easily through the water. Fish move through the water by using their fins. They have several body fins. The tail fin helps them move fast and in the direction they want to go.

Think and Learn

1. ______________________ allow fish to see underwater.

2. Fish use ______________________ to breathe underwater.

3. What do fish use their fins for? ______________________

____

4. Do all fish look alike? ______________________

Parts of a Fish

Label the parts of the fish.

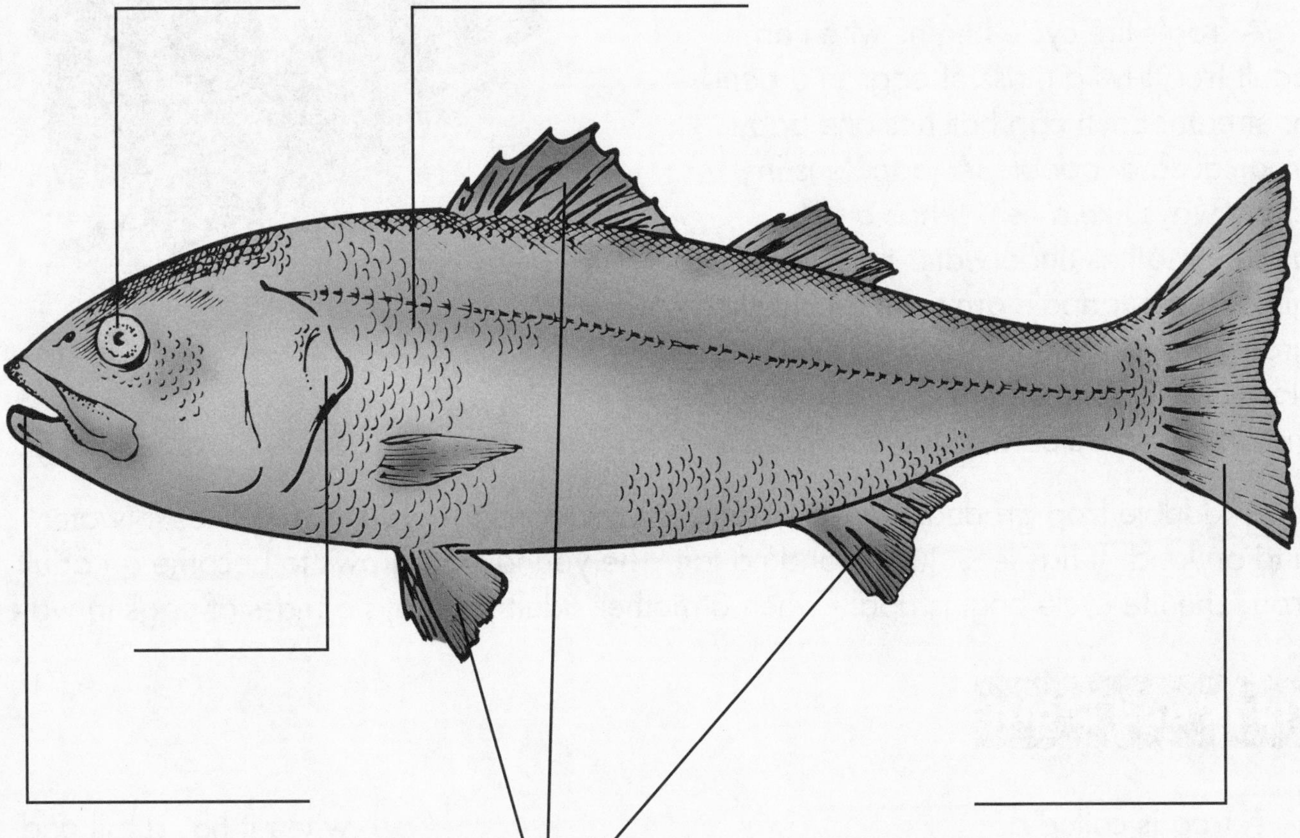

mouth	gill	body fins
eye	scales	tail fin

Life Cycle of a Frog

Frogs are amphibians. They begin their lives as though they were fish but are more like land animals as adults. Frogs pass through stages during their lives. The series of stages in the life of an animal is called its *life cycle.*

A frog's life cycle begins when an adult frog lays a mass of eggs in a pond or stream. Each egg hatches one baby frog called a *tadpole.* A tadpole is in many ways like a fish. It has a tail, and it breathes underwater through gills. As the tadpole grows, it gradually grows legs and begins to lose its tail. Its gills slowly develop into lungs for breathing air. At this stage, the animal is called a *tadpole frog.*

A tadpole frog gradually develops into a young frog. A young frog lives in water and on land. It has legs, lungs, and no tail. The young frog grows to become an adult frog. The life cycle begins again when a mother adult frog lays a mass of eggs in water.

Think and Learn

1. A frog is called a ______________________________ when it has a tail and breathes through gills.

2. When a tadpole becomes a frog, it grows legs and develops lungs.

   What does it lose? ______________________________

3. The series of stages in the life of an animal is called its ______________________________

   ______________________________.

Life Cycle of a Frog

Label the steps in the life cycle of the frog.

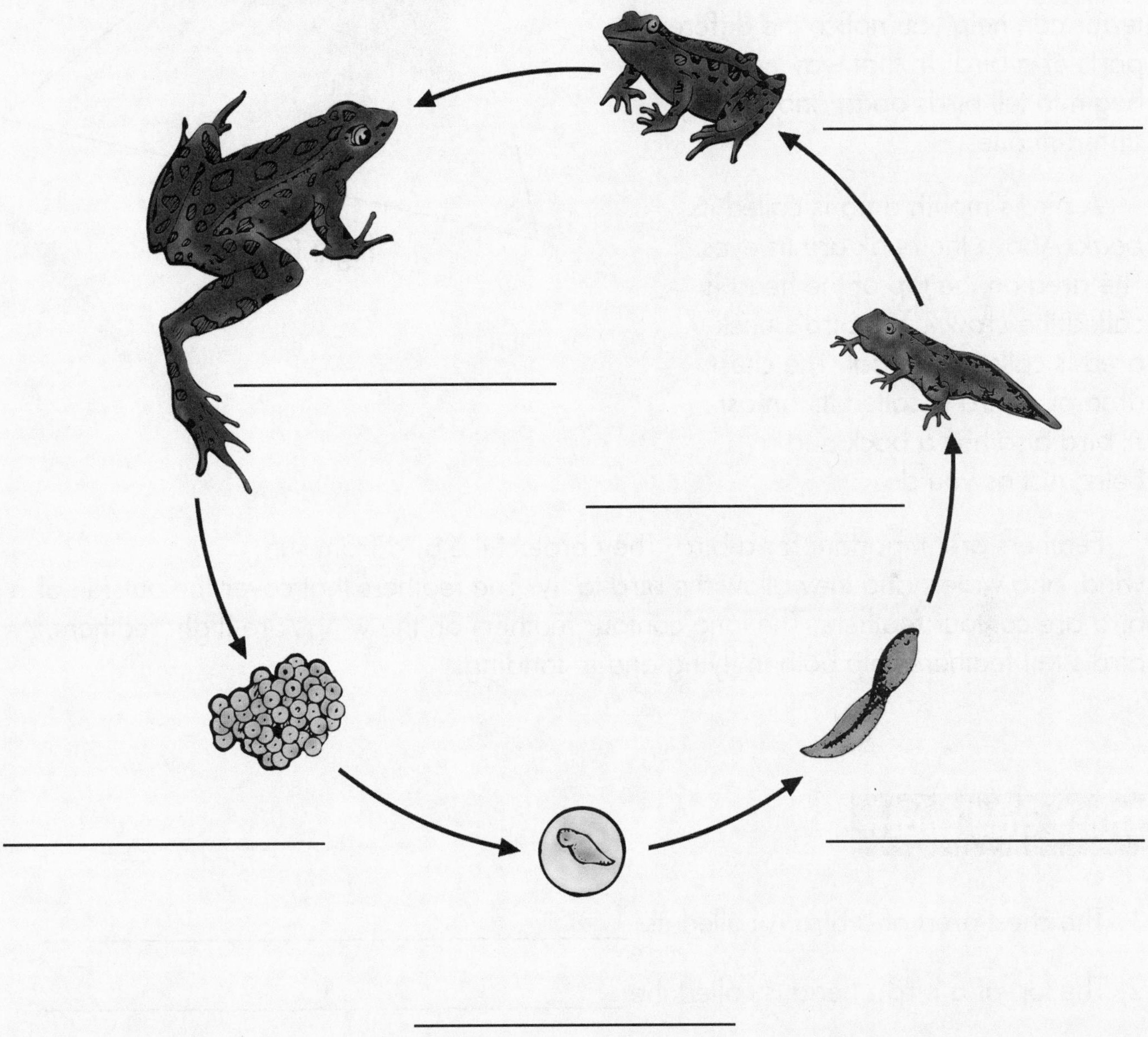

____

____

____

____

____

____

tadpole	**egg**	**tadpole frog**
adult frog	**young frog**	**egg mass**

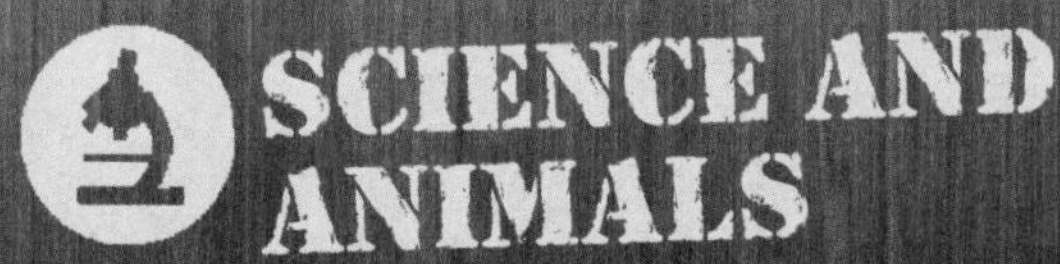

Parts of a Bird

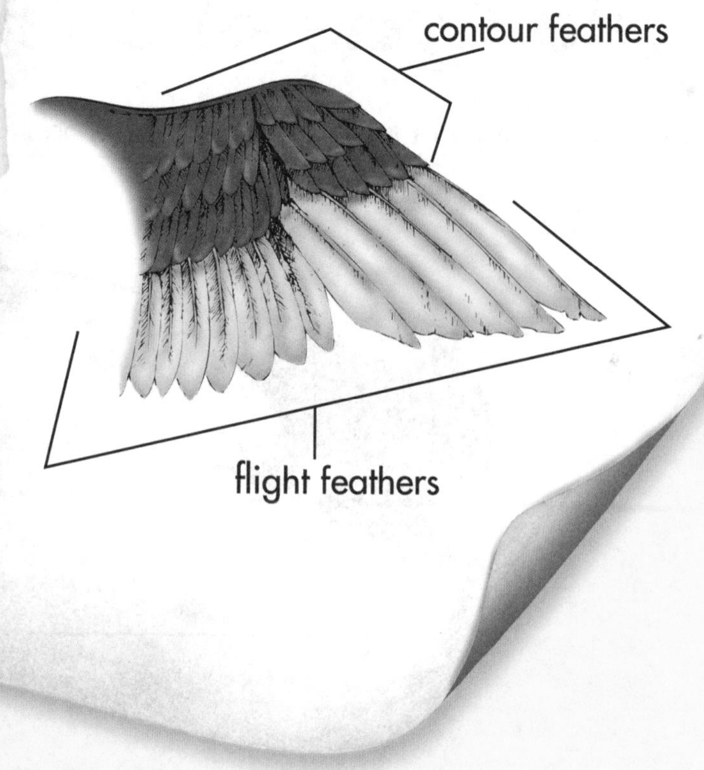

Scientists and bird watchers use special terms to describe a bird. These terms can help you notice the different parts of a bird. In that way, you can begin to tell birds apart and identify different ones.

A bird's mouth area is called its *beak*. Above the beak are its eyes. The area on the top of the head is called the *crown*. The bird's neck area is called its *throat*. The chest area of a bird is called its *breast*. A bird also has a back and a belly, just as you do.

Feathers are important for a bird. They protect the bird from sun, wind, and water, and they allow the bird to fly. The feathers that cover the outside of a bird are contour feathers. The long contour feathers on the wings are flight feathers. A bird's tail feathers help both in flying and in landing.

Think and Learn

1. The chest area of a bird is called its ____________________.

2. The top of a bird's head is called the ____________________.

3. What are the long contour feathers at the end of the wing called? ____________________

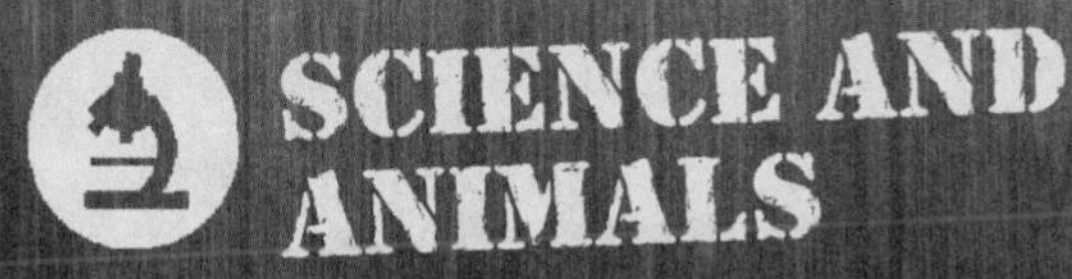

Parts of a Bird

Label the parts of a bird.

crown
eye
beak
belly
throat
breast
back
contour feathers
flight feathers
tail feathers

Bird Beaks

Bird beaks vary greatly in both shape and size. By looking closely at a bird's beak, you can often tell what kind of food that bird eats. Some birds feed on small animals, while other birds eat seeds. Their beaks are different, because they are used differently. Hawks, for example, have a beak made for tearing the meat of small animals, such as mice. The tiny hummingbird has a beak made for sucking liquid from flowers.

Cardinals have a strong beak good for cracking seeds. Fast-flying swallows have small beaks made for catching insects. Robins have pointed beaks for stabbing worms. Woodpeckers have strong beaks just right for pounding holes in wood as they look for insects.

Many water birds also have different kinds of beaks. A pelican has a large beak made for scooping up fishes. An anhinga has a sharp beak good for stabbing fish that swim by.

Write how each bird uses its beak.

Hawk ______________________

____

____

Cardinal ______________________

____

____

Bird Beaks

Write how each bird uses its beak.

Hummingbird ______________

____

____

Pelican ______________

____

____

Swallow ______________

____

____

Robin ______________

____

____

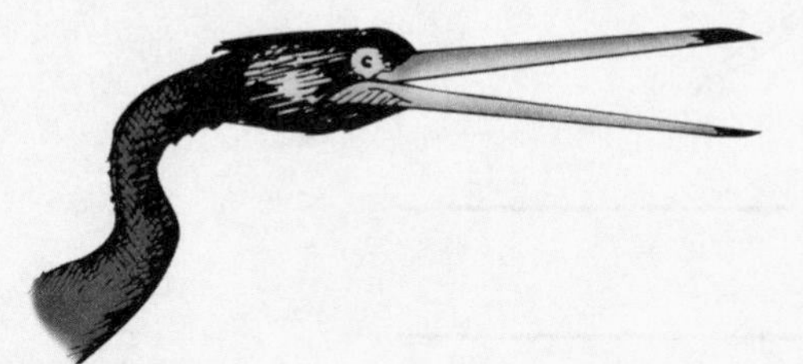

Anhinga ______________

____

____

Woodpecker ______________

____

____

Feathered Friends' Feet

Just as a bird's beak can tell you what it eats, a bird's feet can tell you many things about its habits or home. Think about what you already know about the birds listed below. How do each of these birds use their feet in a special way?

Sparrow ______________________

____

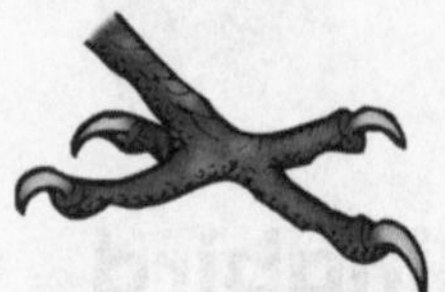

Woodpecker ______________________

____

Duck ______________________

____

Hawk ______________________

____

Heron ______________________

____

for perching on branches
for wading in mud
for climbing
for catching small animals
for swimming

Strangers in the Night

It's much easier to identify a bird when you can see its color, size, and shape. At night, however, it is difficult to see. Identify these birds just by their shapes, or silhouettes.

heron
robin
crow
gull

duck
hawk
owl
hummingbird

cardinal
blue jay

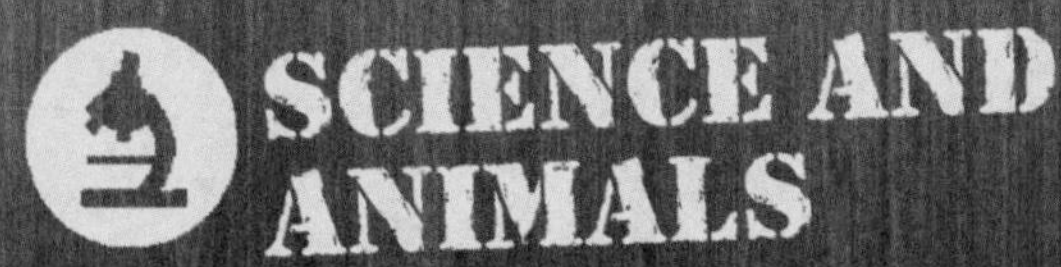

What's a Mammal?

When you think of an animal, you probably think about a mammal. Mammals live in every part of the world. They range from tiny mice to the largest animals on Earth, the whales. Mammals include dogs, cats, cows, bears, kangaroos, raccoons, rabbits, elephants, dolphins, and many others. Human beings are also mammals.

Mammals are the only animals with hair. Any animal with hair is a mammal. Even whales have a few hairs on their body. Most mammals are covered with hair. The hair keeps the body warm and dry. When mammals give birth, the mother feeds her young with milk from her body. No other animals feed their young with milk.

Mammals have large, well-developed brains compared with other animals. These large brains make mammals very intelligent animals.

Think and Learn

1. Mammals have large, well-developed ______________________.

2. The largest mammal on Earth is the ______________________.

3. How does hair protect a mammal? ______________________

____

4. Baby mammals get ______________________ from their mother's body.

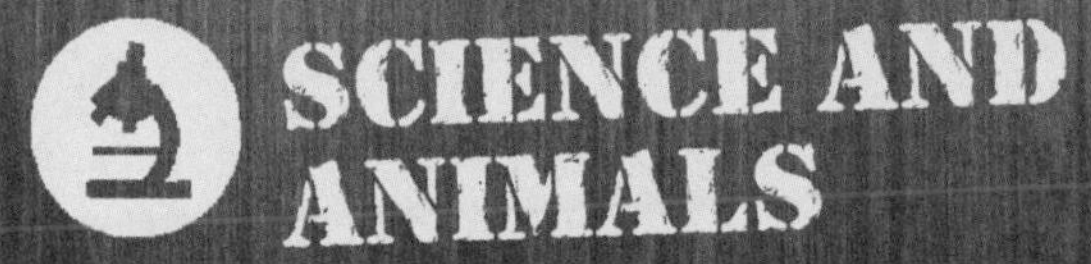

What's a Mammal?

Think and Learn

1. Look at the picture above. How do you know the mother is a mammal? ____________

____

____

2. In the picture above, what are the babies doing that only young mammals do?

____

____

____

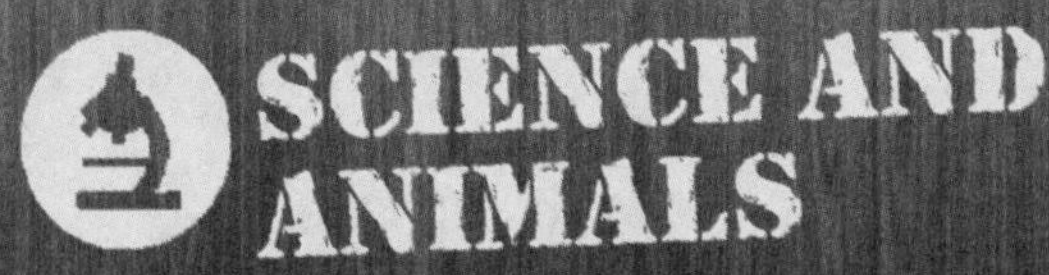

The Mammal With Wings

Bats are the only mammals that can fly. Some squirrels can glide, but bats really fly like birds. They can fly because they have wings.

A bat wing is made of a thin layer of skin called a *wing membrane*. This skin stretches between the long fingers on a bat's hands. The thumb is the only finger not attached to the wing membrane. On most bats, the wing membrane also stretches between the hands and the legs. It even stretches across the tail between the legs. When bats flap their wings, they can fly.

Bats fly mainly at night, when they hunt flying insects. They can find insects in the dark by using their large sensitive ears. During the day, most bats sleep by hanging upside down.

Think and Learn

1. Bats are the only mammals that can ______________________.
2. A ______________________ stretches between a bat's fingers.
3. When do bats hunt for food? ______________________
4. Bats sense where insects are flying with their ______________________.

The Mammal With Wings

Label the parts of a bat.

foot | **ear** | **wing membrane**
thumb | **fingers** | **tail**

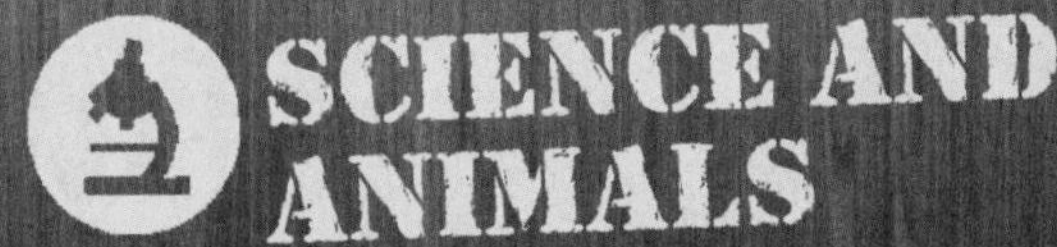

Animals Without Backbones

Animals that have a backbone are called *vertebrates*. Animals without a backbone are called *invertebrates*. There are many more invertebrates than vertebrates. More than 9 out of 10 animals on Earth are invertebrates.

The many different kinds of invertebrates vary greatly in shape and structure. They have only one thing in common. None have a backbone. Some, such as insects and lobsters, have a hard covering on the outside called an *exoskeleton*. Clams and snails have shells around their soft bodies. Other invertebrates, such as sponges and jellyfish, have no hard covering or shell.

What are some invertebrates you have seen? Sponges, jellyfish, earthworms, clams, snails, octopuses, starfishes, spiders, lobsters, and insects are all invertebrates.

Think and Learn

1. Animals without a backbone are called ______________________________.

2. Insects have an ______________________________ on the outside of their body.

3. What are two invertebrates that have no outer covering or shell? ______________

____

Animals Without Backbones

Write whether each animal is a vertebrate or an invertebrate.

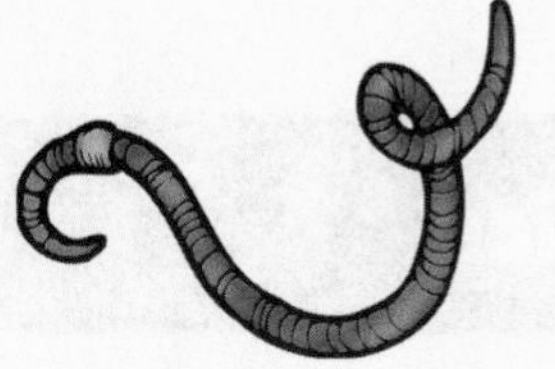

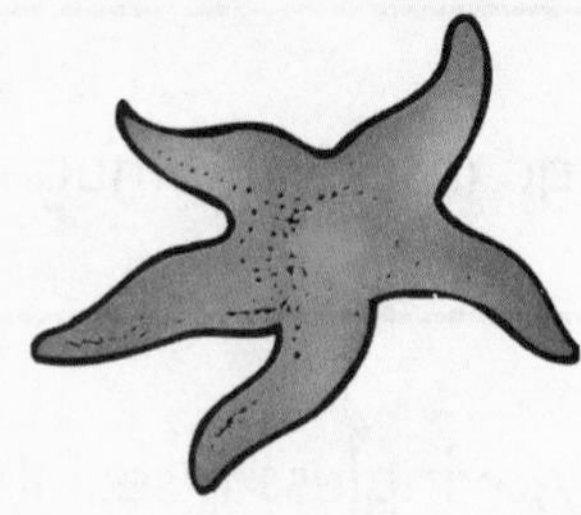

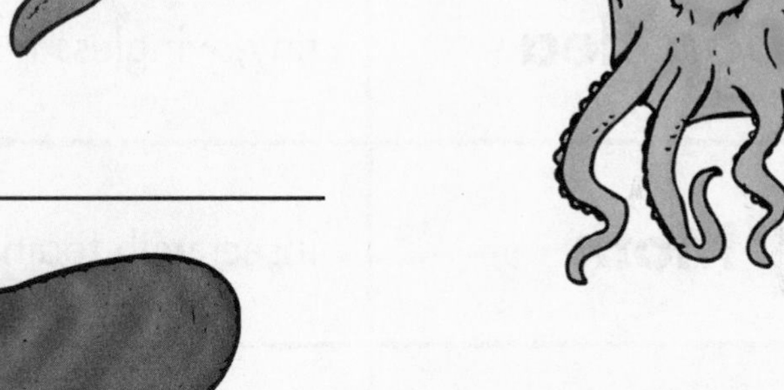

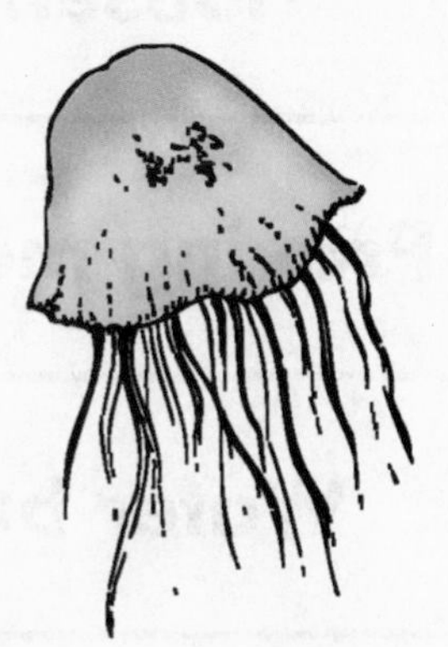

Kinds of Insects

There are many kinds of insects. This table shows some common insects that represent different insect groups.

insect	characteristics
Stag beetle	large, rounded insect with large mouth that looks like a deer's antlers
Dragonfly	large insect with huge front and back wings
Dog flea	tiny, wingless insect that sucks blood from dogs
Moth	insect with feathery antennae and broad wings
Housefly	small, two-winged insect found almost everywhere
Praying mantis	large insect with front legs that look like they are folded in prayer
Water bug	large, rounded insect with wings folded back and pierce-sucking mouths
Wasp	large, thin insect with narrow wings and a stinger at the rear

Kinds of Insects

Write the name of each insect on the line.

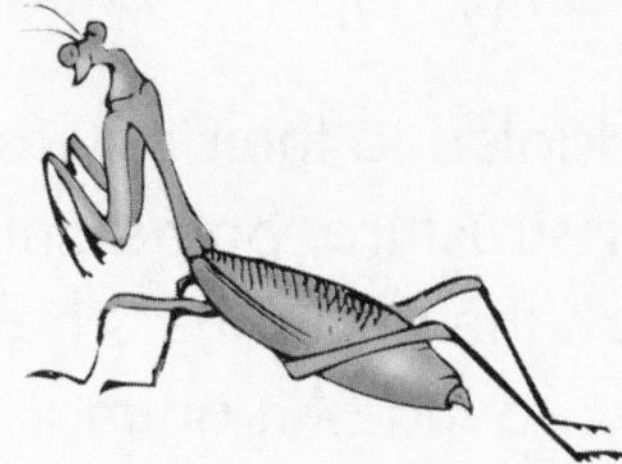

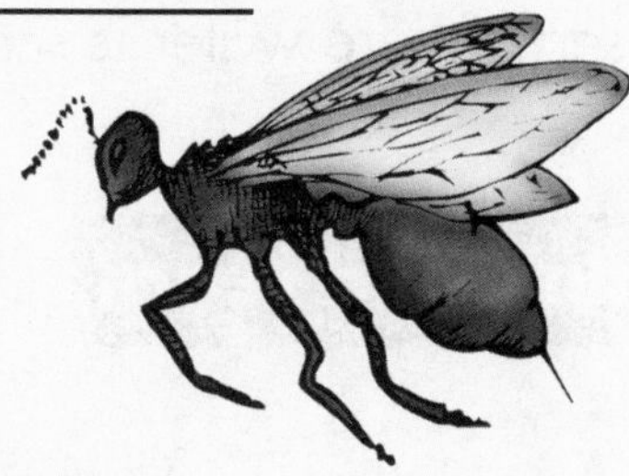

moth
praying mantis
dog flea
wasp
housefly
water bug
stag beetle
dragonfly

Animal Adaptations

Each kind of animal has characteristics that allow it to survive in its environment. For example, a fish has gills for breathing underwater. If it had lungs like mammals, a fish could not survive underwater. Any characteristic that helps an animal survive in its environment is called an *adaptation* (a dap TAY shun).

Animals are adapted to their environment through their body structure. Some animals have wings to fly through the air. Others have claws to burrow into the ground. An animal's body must fit its environment if it is to live and survive. A good example is a camel's body, which stores water. This adaptation makes the camel well-suited to live in a desert, where water is scarce.

Think and Learn

1. Any characteristic that helps an animal survive in its environment is called an

   ____.

2. A fish's ______________________ are an adaptation that allow it

   to breathe underwater.

3. A bird's ______________________ are an adaptation for flying.

Animal Adaptations

Describe an adaptation of each animal that helps it live in its environment.

Clam ______________________________

____

____

Polar Bear ______________________________

____

____

Spider ______________________________

____

____

Duck ______________________________

____

____

Animal Defenses

Each of these animals has an adaptation that helps it defend itself from enemies. For each animal, describe its adaptation.

clam ______________________

____

skunk ______________________

____

honeybee ______________________

____

porcupine ______________________

____

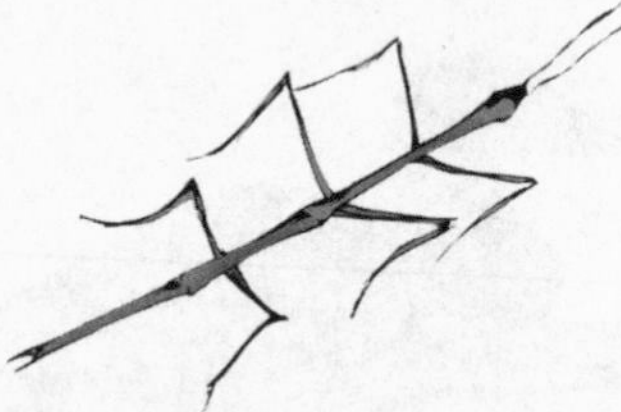

walking stick ______________________

____

pigeon ______________________

____

hard shell
stinger
pointed quills
fast flyer
bad smell
blends in with environment

Animal Locomotion

One important animal adaptation is the way in which an animal moves around in its environment. The way in which an animal moves is called *locomotion*. Complete the table by writing a one-word description of each animal's main method of locomotion. Then, name the body part used to make this movement.

Animal	Method of Locomotion	Body Part Used for Movement
rabbit		
fish		
clam		
dragonfly		

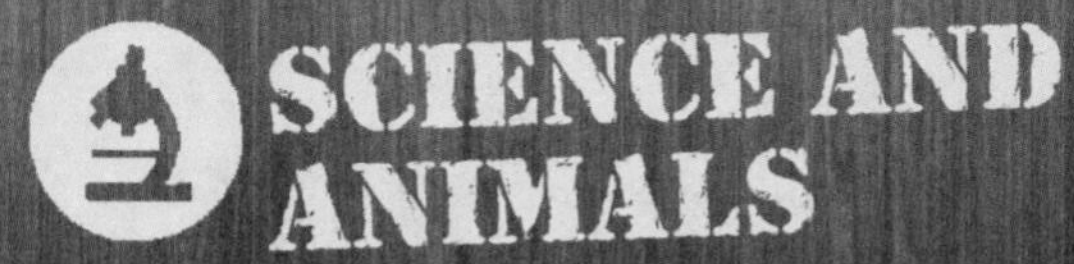

Food Chains

Animals need energy to stay alive. They get this energy by eating food. Some animals eat plants. Some eat other animals. And some eat both plants and other animals. Think of all the living things that feed on one another in an environment. This is called a *food chain*. Each living thing in a food chain is a link in the chain. The energy of food passes from one living thing to another through the food chain.

The food chain shown on this page begins with underwater plants in a pond. The plants make up the first link in the food chain. A fish eats the plants. The fish is the second link in the food chain. Finally, an eagle swoops down and catches the fish. The eagle becomes the last link in this food chain.

Think and Learn

1. What are all the living things that feed on one another in an environment called?

____

2. Each plant or animal in a food chain is one _______________________

in the chain.

3. What kind of living thing almost always begins a food chain? _______________

____

ANSWER KEY

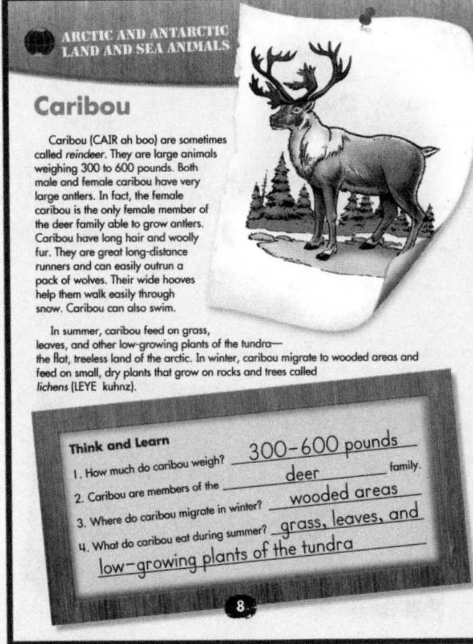

ARCTIC AND ANTARCTIC LAND AND SEA ANIMALS

Caribou

Caribou (CAIR ah boo) are sometimes called *reindeer*. They are large animals weighing 300 to 600 pounds. Both male and female caribou have very large antlers. In fact, the female caribou is the only female member of the deer family able to grow antlers. Caribou have long hair and woolly fur. They are great long-distance runners and can easily outrun a pack of wolves. Their wide hooves help them walk easily through snow. Caribou can also swim.

In summer, caribou feed on grass, leaves, and other low-growing plants of the tundra—the flat, treeless land of the arctic. In winter, caribou migrate to wooded areas and feed on small, dry plants that grow on rocks and trees called *lichens* (LEYE kuhnz).

Think and Learn

1. How much do caribou weigh? 300–600 pounds
2. Caribou are members of the deer family.
3. Where do caribou migrate in winter? wooded areas
4. What do caribou eat during summer? grass, leaves, and low-growing plants of the tundra

8

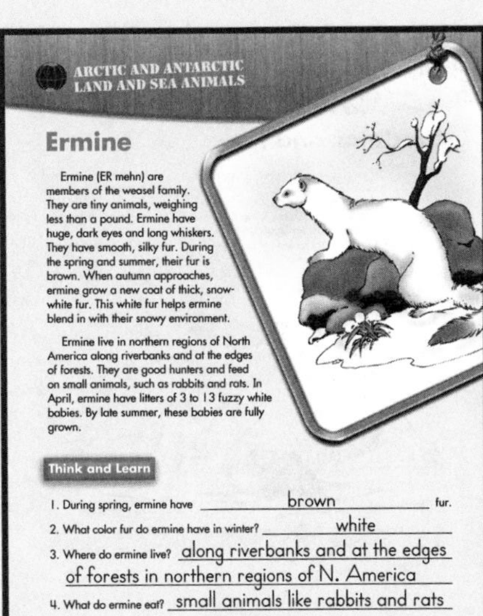

ARCTIC AND ANTARCTIC LAND AND SEA ANIMALS

Ermine

Ermine (ER mehn) are members of the weasel family. They are tiny animals, weighing less than a pound. Ermine have huge, dark eyes and long whiskers. They have smooth, silky fur. During the spring and summer, their fur is brown. When autumn approaches, ermine grow a new coat of thick, snow-white fur. This white fur helps ermine blend in with their snowy environment.

Ermine live in northern regions of North America along riverbanks and at the edges of forests. They are good hunters and feed on small animals, such as rabbits and rats. In April, ermine have litters of 3 to 13 fuzzy white babies. By late summer, these babies are fully grown.

Think and Learn

1. During spring, ermine have brown fur.
2. What color fur do ermine have in winter? white
3. Where do ermine live? along riverbanks and at the edges of forests in northern regions of N. America
4. What do ermine eat? small animals like rabbits and rats

9

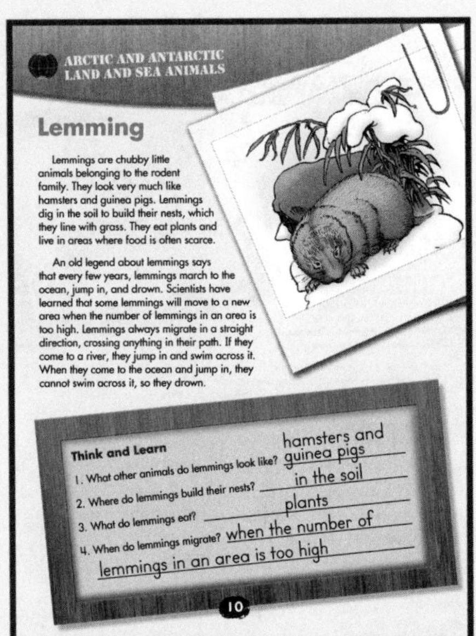

ARCTIC AND ANTARCTIC LAND AND SEA ANIMALS

Lemming

Lemmings are chubby little animals belonging to the rodent family. They look very much like hamsters and guinea pigs. Lemmings dig in the soil to build their nests, which they line with grass. They eat plants and live in areas where food is often scarce.

An old legend about lemmings says that every few years, lemmings march to the ocean, jump in, and drown. Scientists have learned that some lemmings will move to a new area when the number of lemmings in an area is too high. Lemmings always migrate in a straight direction, crossing anything in their path. If they come to a river, they jump in and swim across it. When they come to the ocean and jump in, they cannot swim across it, so they drown.

Think and Learn

1. What other animals do lemmings look like? hamsters and guinea pigs
2. Where do lemmings build their nests? in the soil
3. What do lemmings eat? plants
4. When do lemmings migrate? when the number of lemmings in an area is too high

10

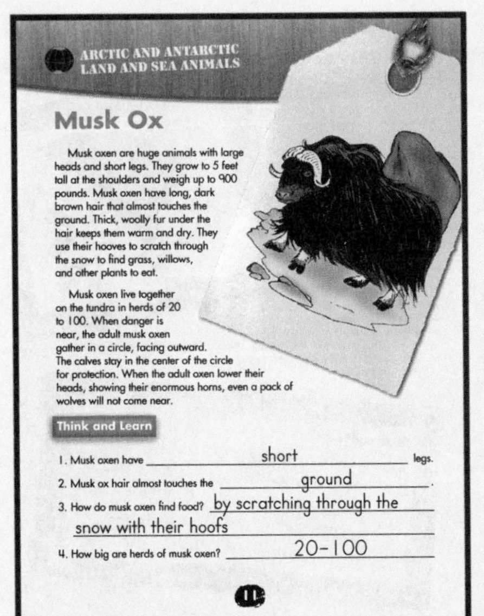

ARCTIC AND ANTARCTIC LAND AND SEA ANIMALS

Musk Ox

Musk oxen are huge animals with large heads and short legs. They grow to 5 feet tall at the shoulders and weigh up to 900 pounds. Musk oxen have long, dark brown hair that almost touches the ground. Thick, woolly fur under the hair keeps them warm and dry. They use their hooves to scratch through the snow to find grass, willows, and other plants to eat.

Musk oxen live together on the tundra in herds of 20 to 100. When danger is near, the adult musk oxen gather in a circle, facing outward. The calves stay in the center of the circle for protection. When the adult oxen lower their heads, showing their enormous horns, even a pack of wolves will not come near.

Think and Learn

1. Musk oxen have short legs.
2. Musk ox hair almost touches the ground.
3. How do musk oxen find food? by scratching through the snow with their hoofs
4. How big are herds of musk oxen? 20–100

11

ARCTIC AND ANTARCTIC LAND AND SEA ANIMALS

Orca (Killer Whale)

The black and white orca (OR kuh) is a large dolphin that is often called a *killer whale*. It grows up to 30 feet long and weighs 3 to 10 tons. The orca has 40 to 48 large pointed teeth that it uses to catch and hold its prey. It eats over 100 pounds of food every day.

Orcas live and travel in family groups called *pods*. They are affectionate animals and are often seen touching each other. Female orcas give birth to one baby every 3 to 10 years. The baby will stay with its mother for 10 years. Orcas are very intelligent animals. They communicate with each other by making sounds.

Think and Learn

1. Is an orca a dolphin or a whale? a dolphin
2. What color is an orca? black and white
3. How much food does an orca eat each day? over 100 lb
4. Orcas travel in family groups called pods.
5. Orcas communicate by making sounds.

12

ARCTIC AND ANTARCTIC LAND AND SEA ANIMALS

Polar Bear

Polar bears are the world's largest four-legged meat-eating animals—9 feet tall and 1,600 pounds! They have special features to help them live in the arctic. Their thick fur and a layer of fat keep them warm. Their small ears lose less body heat. Pads on the bottom of their feet keep them from slipping on ice. Polar bears are excellent swimmers. Webbing between their clawed toes helps them swim. Polar bears hunt seals, walruses, small whales, and fish. In the summer months, they eat berries and plants.

Female polar bears make dens in ice caves or in snow banks. They give birth to 1 to 3 cubs, weighing 1 pound. The cubs stay with their mother for 2 years.

Think and Learn

1. What features keep polar bears warm? thick fur, a layer of fat, small ears
2. Polar bears have webbed toes to help them swim.
3. What do they eat in the summer? berries and plants
4. How long do polar bear cubs stay with their mother? 2 years

23

ANSWER KEY

ARCTIC AND ANTARCTIC LAND AND SEA ANIMALS

Seal

Seals are animals with special features to live in water. Their flippers move them quickly and gracefully through water. Their bodies are covered with oily fur and a layer of blubber, or fat, to keep them warm. There are two kinds of seals—sea lions and true seals. Sea lions have ears outside their heads, but true seals have no outer ears. While sea lions can move easily on land, true seals must use their chest muscles to move on land. True seals never have to leave the water.

True seals hunt underwater for their food. They eat shrimp, crab, fish, and seabirds. Seals give birth to white baby seals, called *pups*. Their coloring helps hide them from polar bears. As the pup grows, its white fur will turn dark brown like its parents' fur.

Think and Learn

1. Seals are adapted to live in water.
2. Flippers move seals quickly through water.
3. What keeps seals warm? oily fur and a layer of blubber
4. Which kind of seal moves easily on land? sea lion
5. What color are seal pups? white

24

ARCTIC AND ANTARCTIC LAND AND SEA ANIMALS

Predator and Prey

Polar bears live along frozen shores and on ice floating in arctic waters. The polar bear is a predator (PRED uh tur) because it hunts other animals for food. The animals hunted by predators are called *prey*. When hunting for seals, polar bears like to wait by a seal's breathing hole in the ice. The seal may not see the polar bear waiting by the breathing hole. The polar bear's white fur helps it blend in with its snowy environment. When the seal comes up to breathe, the polar bear catches it. Seals are dark brown to help them blend in with their environment. When a polar bear looks down into the water, the water reflects the color of the ocean bottom, which is dark brown or black. Sometimes, the polar bear does not see the seal.

1. Color the picture to show how the animals blend into the environment.
2. Label the predator and the prey in the picture.

25

ARCTIC AND ANTARCTIC LAND AND SEA ANIMALS

Snowy Owl

The snowy owl gets its name from the snow-white feathers covering its body. It has thick feathers covering its feet and legs for warmth. Like other owls, snowy owls must turn their heads to look around because their eyes cannot move. Their ears are tiny slits on their faces. Owls raise their face feathers when they are listening.

Snowy owls hunt for rats and arctic hares, but lemmings are their main food source. If lemmings are plentiful, snowy owls will lay more eggs. When lemmings are scarce, snowy owls may not lay any eggs. Snowy owls live on the treeless tundra, so they build their nests on the ground in places where they can watch for predators.

Think and Learn

1. Snowy owls have feathers covering their feet and legs.
2. Why must owls turn their heads to look around? Their eyes cannot move.
3. What is the main food source for snowy owls? lemmings
4. Snowy owls build nests on the ground.

26

ARCTIC AND ANTARCTIC LAND AND SEA ANIMALS

Walrus

The walrus is a huge animal, weighing between 2 and 3 tons. Its thick skin and layer of blubber protect it from the cold. Both male and female walruses have ivory tusks. They use their tusks to pull themselves across ice and for protection against polar bears.

Walruses are excellent swimmers. They can stay out at sea for days. They feed on the ocean floor by using their "moustache" bristles to feel for clams. Then, they use their snouts to dig the clams out. Walruses live together in herds containing thousands of walruses. One of their favorite things to do is sleep. When one walrus is awakened, it slaps another walrus. This goes on until the whole herd is awake. In time, they will fall back to sleep.

Think and Learn

1. How much does a walrus weigh? between 2 and 3 tons
2. Why are the tusks of a walrus important? They help the walrus to move on ice and are used for protection.
3. What do walruses eat? clams
4. Walruses live together in herds.

27

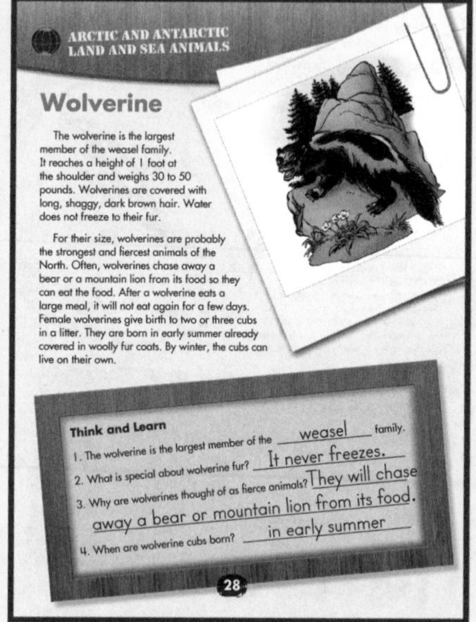

ARCTIC AND ANTARCTIC LAND AND SEA ANIMALS

Wolverine

The wolverine is the largest member of the weasel family. It reaches a height of 1 foot at the shoulder and weighs 30 to 50 pounds. Wolverines are covered with long, shaggy, dark brown hair. Water does not freeze to their fur.

For their size, wolverines are probably the strongest and fiercest animals of the North. Often, wolverines chase away a bear or a mountain lion from its food so they can eat the food. After a wolverine eats a large meal, it will not eat again for a few days. Female wolverines give birth to two or three cubs in a litter. They are born in early summer already covered in woolly fur coats. By winter, the cubs can live on their own.

Think and Learn

1. The wolverine is the largest member of the weasel family.
2. What is special about wolverine fur? It never freezes.
3. Why are wolverines thought of as fierce animals? They will chase away a bear or mountain lion from its food.
4. When are wolverine cubs born? in early summer

28

NORTH AMERICAN ANIMALS

Bald Eagle

The bald eagle is a bird of prey, or a bird that catches and eats other animals. It is a large bird, with a wingspan reaching 8 feet. The bald eagle is well-known for its white head and neck. Most bald eagles live near water because they love to eat fish. Their hooked bills and long, curved claws help them to catch fish.

Of all the eagles, bald eagles build the largest nests. Some nests have been measured at 8 feet across! Eagles lay two ivory-white eggs. The eaglets are born brown. They do not look like adults until they are 3 years old. The bald eagle has been the national bird of the United States since 1782. It is a symbol of freedom and courage.

Think and Learn

1. The bald eagle has a wingspan of 8 feet.
2. What color is the bald eagle's head? white
3. What helps bald eagles catch fish? their hooked bills and long, curved claws
4. The bald eagle is the national bird of the United States.

30

ANSWER KEY

NORTH AMERICAN ANIMALS

Beaver

The beaver is a member of the rodent family. It grows to a length of 2 feet and usually weighs 35 to 40 pounds. The beaver has dark brown fur that keeps the animal warm and dry. Its strong jaws have two cutting teeth, called *incisors*. The incisors keep growing all through a beaver's life so that these teeth are never worn down. Beavers use their incisors to cut down trees. Beavers eat twigs and bark from trees that grow near water.

Beavers are graceful swimmers. They move easily through the water with their webbed toes. Their tail helps steer them. Beavers mate for life and live in colonies. All the beavers in a colony work together and build lodges as their homes.

Think and Learn

1. What are the beaver's cutting teeth called? incisors
2. What do beavers eat? twigs and bark from trees
3. How does a beaver use its tail? for steering in water
4. What is a beaver's home called? a lodge

31

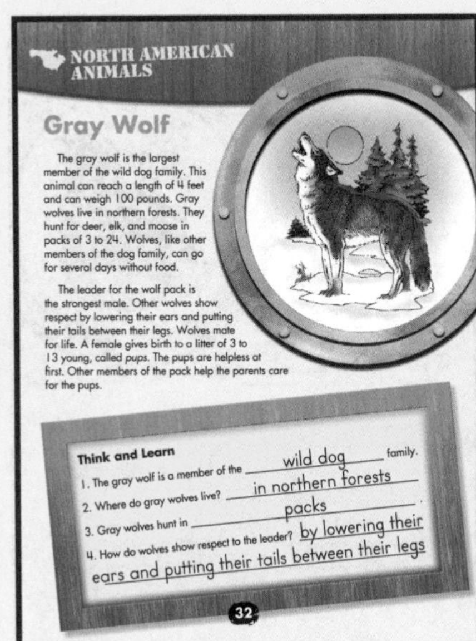

NORTH AMERICAN ANIMALS

Gray Wolf

The gray wolf is the largest member of the wild dog family. This animal can reach a length of 4 feet and can weigh 100 pounds. Gray wolves live in northern forests. They hunt for deer, elk, and moose in packs of 3 to 24. Wolves, like other members of the dog family, can go for several days without food.

The leader for the wolf pack is the strongest male. Other wolves show respect by lowering their ears and putting their tails between their legs. Wolves mate for life. A female gives birth to a litter of 3 to 13 young, called *pups*. The pups are helpless at first. Other members of the pack help the parents care for the pups.

Think and Learn

1. The gray wolf is a member of the wild dog family.
2. Where do gray wolves live? in northern forests
3. Gray wolves hunt in packs.
4. How do wolves show respect to the leader? by lowering their ears and putting their tails between their legs

32

NORTH AMERICAN ANIMALS

Grizzly Bear

Grizzly bears once lived in large numbers from Canada to Mexico. Now, most grizzly bears live in national parks. Male grizzly bears stand 8 feet tall and weigh 800 to 1,000 pounds. Grizzly bears have very good senses of smell and hearing. These senses make up for their poor eyesight.

Grizzly bears are omnivores—they eat both plants and animals. Their favorite foods are berries, leaves, fish, and small animals. In autumn, grizzly bears spend a lot of time eating. They are fattening up to get ready for their winter sleep, or hibernation. Grizzly bears hibernate differently from other animals. Their body functions do not slow down, and they are easily awakened.

Think and Learn

1. Where do most grizzly bears live today? in national parks
2. Which senses make up for the grizzly bear's poor eyesight? their good senses of smell and hearing
3. What do omnivores eat? plants and animals
4. How do grizzly bears get ready for hibernation? eat a lot of food to fatten up

43

NORTH AMERICAN ANIMALS

Moose

The largest member of the deer family is the moose. These huge animals are 10 feet long and weigh about 1,800 pounds. Male moose have very large, flattened antlers. Every year, they shed their antlers and grow a new pair in spring. Moose enjoy water and are excellent swimmers. They usually live near marshes, lakes, or in moist forests.

During the summer months, moose eat water plants, roots, leaves, and grass. In winter, moose walk easily through the deep snow. They find tree shoots and twigs to eat. Moose live alone in the summer. When winter arrives, it is common for small bands of moose to stay together in the woods for warmth and protection.

Think and Learn

1. The moose is a member of the deer family.
2. Each year, moose shed their antlers, then grow a new pair.
3. Where do moose usually live? near marshes, lakes, or in moist forests
4. Why do moose stay together in small bands in winter? for warmth and protection

44

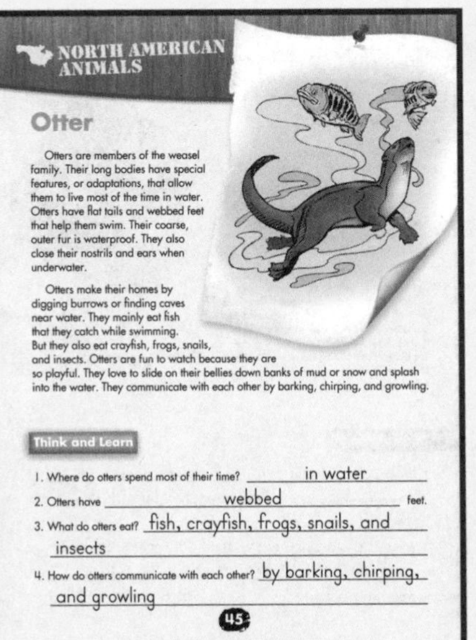

NORTH AMERICAN ANIMALS

Otter

Otters are members of the weasel family. Their long bodies have special features, or adaptations, that allow them to live most of the time in water. Otters have flat tails and webbed feet that help them swim. Their coarse, outer fur is waterproof. They also close their nostrils and ears when underwater.

Otters make their homes by digging burrows or finding caves near water. They mainly eat fish that they catch while swimming. But they also eat crayfish, frogs, snails, and insects. Otters are fun to watch because they are so playful. They love to slide on their bellies down banks of mud or snow and splash into the water. They communicate with each other by barking, chirping, and growling.

Think and Learn

1. Where do otters spend most of their time? in water
2. Otters have webbed feet.
3. What do otters eat? fish, crayfish, frogs, snails, and insects
4. How do otters communicate with each other? by barking, chirping, and growling

45

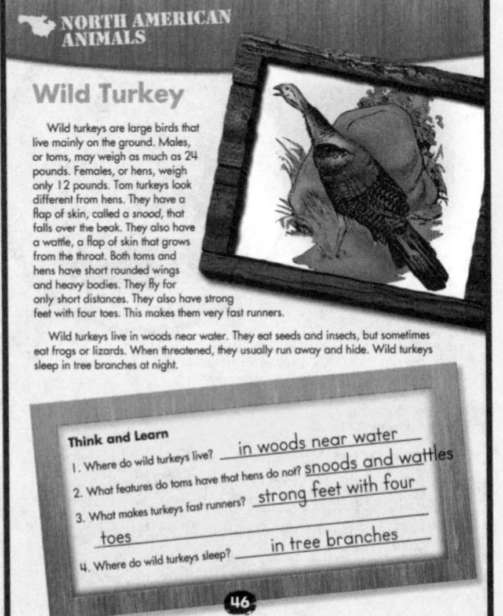

NORTH AMERICAN ANIMALS

Wild Turkey

Wild turkeys are large birds that live mainly on the ground. Males, or toms, may weigh as much as 24 pounds. Females, or hens, weigh only 12 pounds. Tom turkeys look different from hens. They have a flap of skin, called a *snood*, that falls over the beak. They also have a wattle, a flap of skin that grows from the throat. Both toms and hens have short rounded wings and heavy bodies. They fly for only short distances. They also have strong feet with four toes. This makes them very fast runners.

Wild turkeys live in woods near water. They eat seeds and insects, but sometimes eat frogs or lizards. When threatened, they usually run away and hide. Wild turkeys sleep in tree branches at night.

Think and Learn

1. Where do wild turkeys live? in woods near water
2. What features do toms have that hens do not? snoods and wattles
3. What makes turkeys fast runners? strong feet with four toes
4. Where do wild turkeys sleep? in tree branches

46

ANSWER KEY

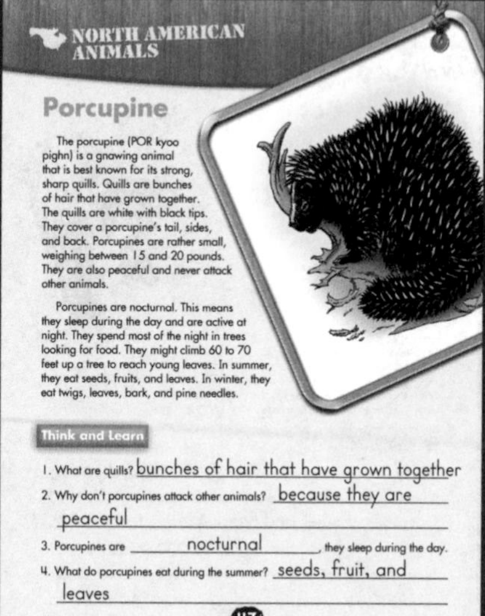

NORTH AMERICAN ANIMALS

Porcupine

The porcupine (POR kyoo pighn) is a gnawing animal that is best known for its strong, sharp quills. Quills are bunches of hair that have grown together. The quills are white with black tips. They cover a porcupine's tail, sides, and back. Porcupines are rather small, weighing between 15 and 20 pounds. They are also peaceful and never attack other animals.

Porcupines are nocturnal. This means they sleep during the day and are active at night. They spend most of the night in trees looking for food. They might climb 60 to 70 feet up a tree to reach young leaves. In summer, they eat seeds, fruits, and leaves. In winter, they eat twigs, leaves, bark, and pine needles.

Think and Learn

1. What are quills? bunches of hair that have grown together
2. Why don't porcupines attack other animals? because they are peaceful
3. Porcupines are nocturnal, they sleep during the day.
4. What do porcupines eat during the summer? seeds, fruit, and leaves

47

NORTH AMERICAN ANIMALS

Striped Skunk

The skunk is known for its black and white fur and its horrible odor. The striped skunk is the most common kind of skunk. It gets its name from the white stripes running down its back. Skunks are about the size of a small cat, measuring 15 inches long. They weigh 5 to 6 pounds. Skunks have short legs, an arched back, a long bushy tail, and a patch of white fur on their forehead.

Skunks make their dens in burrows, hollow trees, and under buildings. They are found in forests, grasslands, and in towns. Even though skunks annoy people with their odor, skunks are very helpful animals. Skunks eat harmful insects, rats, mice, and other small animals that damage crops and fields.

Think and Learn

1. What two things are skunks known for? their black and white fur and horrible odor
2. A skunk is about the same size as a small cat.
3. Where are skunks found? in forests, grasslands, and towns
4. How are skunks helpful to people? They eat harmful insects, rats, and mice.

48

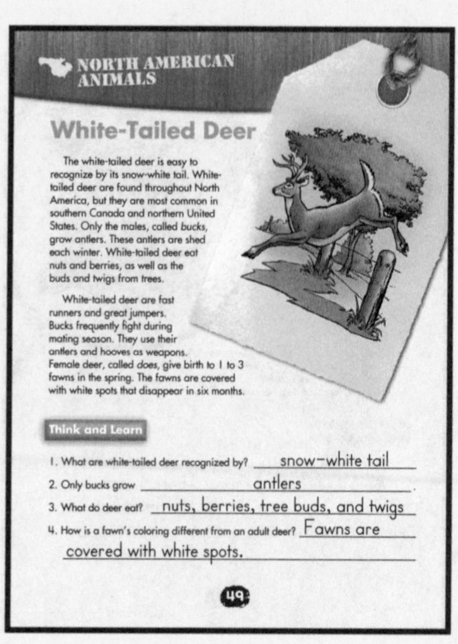

NORTH AMERICAN ANIMALS

White-Tailed Deer

The white-tailed deer is easy to recognize by its snow-white tail. White-tailed deer are found throughout North America, but they are most common in southern Canada and northern United States. Only the males, called *bucks*, grow antlers. These antlers are shed each winter. White-tailed deer eat nuts and berries, as well as the buds and twigs from trees.

White-tailed deer are fast runners and great jumpers. Bucks frequently fight during mating season. They use their antlers and hooves as weapons. Female deer, called *does*, give birth to 1 to 3 fawns in the spring. The fawns are covered with white spots that disappear in six months.

Think and Learn

1. What are white-tailed deer recognized by? snow-white tail
2. Only bucks grow antlers.
3. What do deer eat? nuts, berries, tree buds, and twigs
4. How is a fawn's coloring different from an adult deer? Fawns are covered with white spots.

49

NORTH AMERICAN ANIMALS

Pronghorn

The pronghorn is North America's fastest animal. It can run about 40 miles per hour and jump very high. The pronghorn is mostly covered with reddish-brown fur and has white fur on the lower parts of its body, including the tail. The pronghorn lifts its fur straight up to cool its body in hot weather. In cold weather, it holds its fur flat against its body for warmth. The pronghorn has long horns that it never sheds.

Pronghorn live in the grasslands of western United States and Canada. They eat shrubs, sagebrush, grass, and twigs. In the summer, they live in small groups. As winter comes, they form large herds of 100 or more.

Think and Learn

1. The pronghorn is North America's fastest animal.
2. How does a pronghorn keep cool in hot weather? It lifts its fur straight up.
3. Where do pronghorn live? in grasslands of western U.S. and Canada
4. What do pronghorn eat? shrubs, sagebush, grass, and twigs

50

ASIAN ANIMALS

Chevrotain

Chevrotains (SHEHV ruh taynz) are very small animals with cowlike hooves. They are sometimes called *mouse deer* because they look like tiny deer. Chevrotains have two long tusklike teeth and no other upper teeth. They use their long upper teeth to defend themselves from other animals.

Chevrotains live in the tropical forests of India and Southeast Asia. They eat at night, keeping hidden in the underbrush. They feed on fruit, leaves, twigs, and grass. During the day, chevrotains hide behind rocks or in the bushes. They are quiet, timid animals. Chevrotains live alone except during the mating season. A female chevrotain usually gives birth to two babies, called *fawns*.

Think and Learn

1. Chevrotains are also called mouse deer.
2. What do chevrotains use to defend themselves? two long, tusklike teeth
3. Where do chevrotains live? in the tropical forests of India and Southeast Asia
4. When do chevrotains eat? at night

52

ASIAN ANIMALS

Giant Panda

The giant panda is a very large black and white furry animal. Scientists used to classify pandas as part of the raccoon family. Now, they classify pandas as bears. The giant panda is found in bamboo forests in the mountains of west central China.

Pandas reach a height of 5 feet and weigh about 200 pounds. They easily climb trees and spend most of their time eating bamboo plants. They eat every part of the plant. Pandas have a special thumblike toe on their front feet used for holding bamboo stems. Their teeth are large and wide to help them grind up the bamboo.

Think and Learn

1. Scientists now classify the giant panda as a as bears
2. Where do giant pandas live? in bamboo forests in China
3. Pandas eat all parts of the bamboo plant.
4. How do pandas use the thumblike toe on their front feet? for holding bamboo

53

ASIAN ANIMALS

A Vanishing Act

The panda is one of many endangered animals. Endangered animals may soon disappear from Earth. That's what happened to dinosaurs, dodo birds, and passenger pigeons. They disappeared, or became extinct.

Write the letter that comes before each letter in the alphabet to decode the names of some endangered animals.

A B C D E F G H I J K L M N O P Q R S T U V W X Y Z

MOUNTAIN GORILLA
N P V O U B J O H P S J M M B

AFRICAN ELEPHANT
B G S J D B O F M F Q I B O U

WHOOPING CRANE
X I P P Q J O H D S B O F

BLACK RHINO
C M B D L S I J O P

GIANT PANDA
H J B O U Q B O E B

SEA LION
T F B M J P O

GRAY WOLF
H S B Z X P M G

CHEETAH
D I F F U B I

54

ASIAN ANIMALS

Gibbon

Gibbons (GIHB uhnz) are the smallest members of the ape family. Gibbons are built for swinging through the trees. In fact, it is awkward for them to walk on the ground. Their long arms enable them to "fly" from branch to branch, with leaps over 30 feet.

Gibbons are found in the rainforests of Southeast Asia. They live in the trees, where they get most of their food. They eat seeds, leaves, fruits, young birds, and insects. Gibbons live in family groups made up of a male, a female, and their young. Gibbons mate for life. At night, the gibbon family huddles together for safety.

Think and Learn

1. Gibbons are the smallest member of the ape family.
2. How are gibbons built for swinging through trees? They have long arms.
3. Where are gibbons found? rainforests of Southeast Asia
4. Gibbons live in family groups.

55

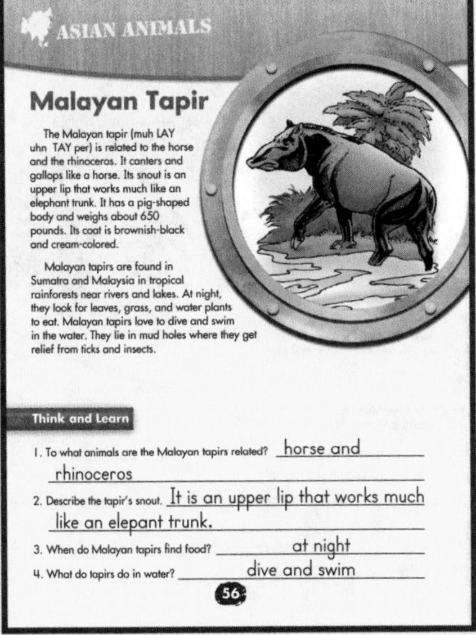

ASIAN ANIMALS

Malayan Tapir

The Malayan tapir (muh LAY uhn TAY per) is related to the horse and the rhinoceros. It canters and gallops like a horse. Its snout is an upper lip that works much like an elephant trunk. It has a pig-shaped body and weighs about 650 pounds. Its coat is brownish-black and cream-colored.

Malayan tapirs are found in Sumatra and Malaysia in tropical rainforests near rivers and lakes. At night, they look for leaves, grass, and water plants to eat. Malayan tapirs love to dive and swim in the water. They lie in mud holes where they get relief from ticks and insects.

Think and Learn

1. To what animals are the Malayan tapirs related? horse and rhinoceros
2. Describe the tapir's snout. It is an upper lip that works much like an elepant trunk.
3. When do Malayan tapirs find food? at night
4. What do tapirs do in water? dive and swim

56

ASIAN ANIMALS

Orangutan

Orangutan (oh RANG uh tan) is a Malay word that means *forest man.* Do you think an orangutan looks like a person? It is a large animal that grows to be 5 feet tall. Its arms, hands, and feet help the orangutan to live in the trees. An orangutan is easily identified by its long, shaggy, reddish-brown hair.

Orangutans are found in Borneo and Sumatra. They eat fruits, nuts, seeds, and leaves, as well as lizards, tree frogs, eggs, young birds, and insects. Orangutans build sleeping platforms in the trees. They sometimes use large leaves as blankets when it rains. Orangutans do not live in family groups like other apes.

Think and Learn

1. What does the word *orangutan* mean? forest man
2. Where do orangutans live? in trees in Borneo and Sumatara
3. What color is orangutan hair? reddish-brown
4. What do orangutans build for sleeping? platforms in trees
5. How do orangutans sometimes use leaves? as blankets

57

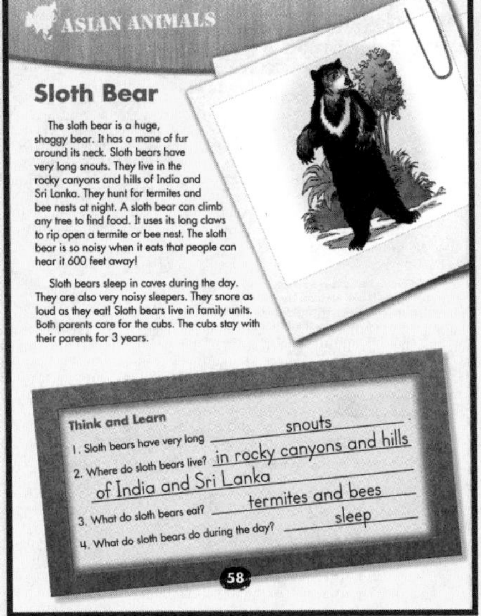

ASIAN ANIMALS

Sloth Bear

The sloth bear is a huge, shaggy bear. It has a mane of fur around its neck. Sloth bears have very long snouts. They live in the rocky canyons and hills of India and Sri Lanka. They hunt for termites and bee nests at night. A sloth bear can climb any tree to find food. It uses its long claws to rip open a termite or bee nest. The sloth bear is so noisy when it eats that people can hear it 600 feet away!

Sloth bears sleep in caves during the day. They are also very noisy sleepers. They snore as loud as they eat! Sloth bears live in family units. Both parents care for the cubs. The cubs stay with their parents for 3 years.

Think and Learn

1. Sloth bears have very long snouts.
2. Where do sloth bears live? in rocky canyons and hills of India and Sri Lanka
3. What do sloth bears eat? termites and bees
4. What do sloth bears do during the day? sleep

58

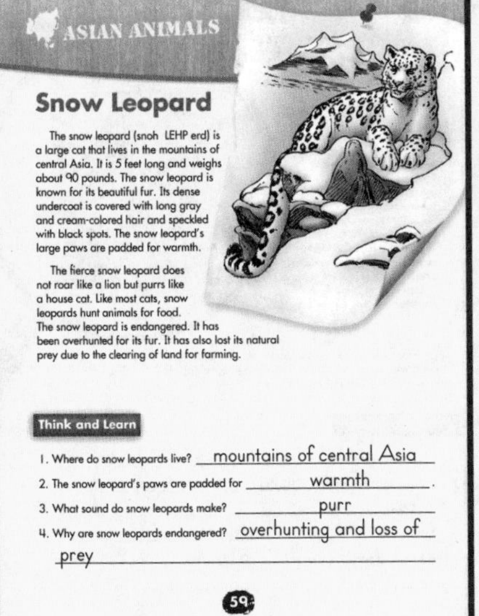

ASIAN ANIMALS

Snow Leopard

The snow leopard (snoh LEHP erd) is a large cat that lives in the mountains of central Asia. It is 5 feet long and weighs about 90 pounds. The snow leopard is known for its beautiful fur. Its dense undercoat is covered with long gray and cream-colored hair and speckled with black spots. The snow leopard's large paws are padded for warmth.

The fierce snow leopard does not roar like a lion but purrs like a house cat. Like most cats, snow leopards hunt animals for food. The snow leopard is endangered. It has been overhunted for its fur. It has also lost its natural prey due to the clearing of land for farming.

Think and Learn

1. Where do snow leopards live? mountains of central Asia
2. The snow leopard's paws are padded for warmth.
3. What sound do snow leopards make? purr
4. Why are snow leopards endangered? overhunting and loss of prey

59

ANSWER KEY

ASIAN ANIMALS

Tiger

The tiger is the largest member of the cat family. It is known by its orange and black stripes. Tigers are found only in Asia. They live in different environments—from cold regions to rainforests. Tigers live alone. Every tiger claims its own territory. Tigers, like all cats, stalk their prey and swiftly attack. Tigers hunt at night. They hunt deer, antelope, and wild pigs.

Female tigers, called *tigresses*, give birth every 2 years to a litter of 3 or 4 cubs. The tigress is a loving mother. She teaches her young how to hunt and care for themselves. The cubs stay with their mother for 2 years.

Think and Learn

1. The tiger is the largest member of the cat family.
2. Tigers are found only in Asia.
3. What animals do tigers hunt? deer, antelope, and wild pigs
4. What do tigresses teach their cubs? how to hunt and care for themselves

60

ASIAN ANIMALS

Water Buffalo

The water buffalo is a gigantic animal that is 10 feet long and 6 feet tall. It has thick, grayish-black skin. Water buffalo have large horns. The horns grow out of each side of the head and curve upward. Water buffalo love water. They are often found resting in water up to their noses. Water buffalo also roll in mud until they are covered with it. This helps protect them from insects.

Water buffalo are wild cattle. Some have been tamed and help with rice farming. Rice is grown in flooded fields. Water buffalo can easily pull a plow through water that is knee deep. Although they look like gentle animals, water buffalo can become very fierce. However, they are friendly to people they know.

Think and Learn

1. Large horns grow out of a water buffalo's head.
2. What do water buffalo like to rest in? water
3. Why do water buffalo roll in mud? to help protect themselves from insects
4. How do water buffalo help with rice farming? They pull a plow through water.

61

ASIAN ANIMALS

Wild Boar

The wild boar is a wild hog found in forests throughout Asia. It can reach a length of 4 to 5 feet and weighs an average of 300 pounds. Its long, piglike snout is used for lifting, pushing, and digging. The wild boar has two long tusks that grow out of its lower jaw. These tusks are 1 foot long. Wild boars use their tusks to protect themselves.

Wild boars like to eat almost anything. They use their snout to search for leaves, fruit, roots, worms, and insects. Wild boars can see and hear well. However, they rely mainly on their sense of smell. Male and female boars travel in separate herds. The female boars raise their young alone.

Think and Learn

1. Where are wild boars found? in forests throughout Asia
2. How do wild boars use their snouts? for lifting, pushing, and digging
3. Wild boars use their tusks for protection.
4. Which sense do wild boars rely on most? smell

62

CENTRAL AND SOUTH AMERICAN ANIMALS

Chinchilla

Chinchillas (chihn CHIHL uhz) look like large mice, but they are actually related to squirrels. They have thick, soft fur. Their blue-gray color is beautiful. In the 1500s, Spanish explorers brought chinchillas back to Europe. The demand for chinchilla fur nearly caused this animal to be killed off. Today, a small chinchilla population lives in the Andes Mountains.

Chinchillas eat roots and grass. Water is scarce high in the Andes. However, chinchillas get enough water from the plants they eat. Chinchillas are nocturnal, or active at night. They sleep during the day. At sundown, they begin looking for food.

Think and Learn

1. Chinchillas are related to squirrels.
2. Describe chinchilla fur. thick, soft, beautiful blue-gray color
3. Where do chinchillas live? in the Andes Mountains
4. How do chinchillas get water? from the plants they eat

64

CENTRAL AND SOUTH AMERICAN ANIMALS

Giant Anteater

The giant anteater is an animal that eats ants and termites. Giant anteaters have three large claws on each paw. They use their claws to rip open ant nests. Giant anteaters have a sticky tongue that is 2 feet long. They push their tongue into an anthill to get the ants. Giant anteaters cannot see well. Instead, they find ants with their sharp sense of smell.

Giant anteaters are found only in Central and South America. They never dig burrows or make homes. Instead, they wander alone looking for food until they tire. Then, they lie down in a hidden place, cover their heads with their long bushy tails, and fall asleep.

Think and Learn

1. What do giant anteaters eat? ants and termites
2. How do giant anteaters use their claws? to rip open ant nests
3. Giant anteaters have sticky tongues.
4. Where do giant anteaters sleep? in a hidden place with their heads covered by their tails

65

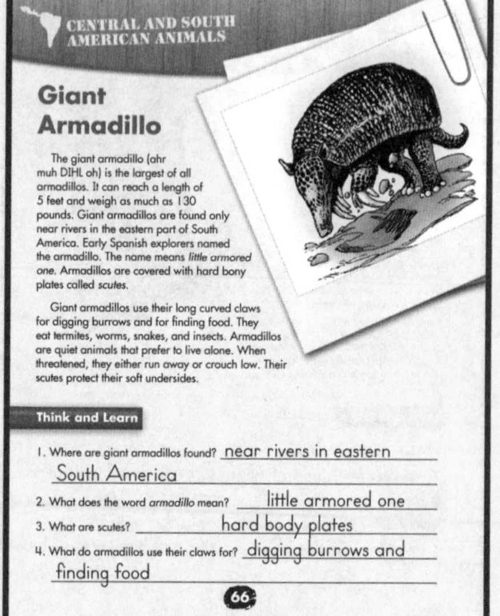

CENTRAL AND SOUTH AMERICAN ANIMALS

Giant Armadillo

The giant armadillo (ahr muh DIHL oh) is the largest of all armadillos. It can reach a length of 5 feet and weigh as much as 130 pounds. Giant armadillos are found only near rivers in the eastern part of South America. Early Spanish explorers named the armadillo. The name means *little armored one*. Armadillos are covered with hard bony plates called scutes.

Giant armadillos use their long curved claws for digging burrows and for finding food. They eat termites, worms, snakes, and insects. Armadillos are quiet animals that prefer to live alone. When threatened, they either run away or crouch low. Their scutes protect their soft undersides.

Think and Learn

1. Where are giant armadillos found? near rivers in eastern South America
2. What does the word *armadillo* mean? little armored one
3. What are scutes? hard body plates
4. What do armadillos use their claws for? digging burrows and finding food

66

ANSWER KEY

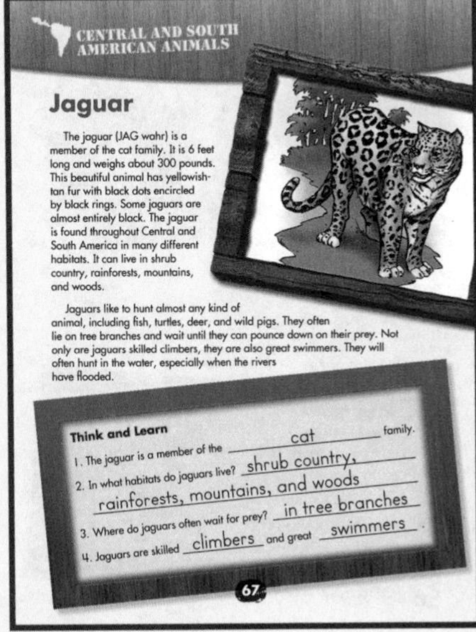

CENTRAL AND SOUTH AMERICAN ANIMALS

Jaguar

The jaguar (JAG wahr) is a member of the cat family. It is 6 feet long and weighs about 300 pounds. This beautiful animal has yellowish-tan fur with black dots encircled by black rings. Some jaguars are almost entirely black. The jaguar is found throughout Central and South America in many different habitats. It can live in shrub country, rainforests, mountains, and woods.

Jaguars like to hunt almost any kind of animal, including fish, turtles, deer, and wild pigs. They often lie on tree branches and wait until they can pounce down on their prey. Not only are jaguars skilled climbers, they are also great swimmers. They will often hunt in the water, especially when the rivers have flooded.

Think and Learn

1. The jaguar is a member of the cat family.
2. In what habitats do jaguars live? shrub country, rainforests, mountains, and woods
3. Where do jaguars often wait for prey? in tree branches
4. Jaguars are skilled climbers and great swimmers.

67

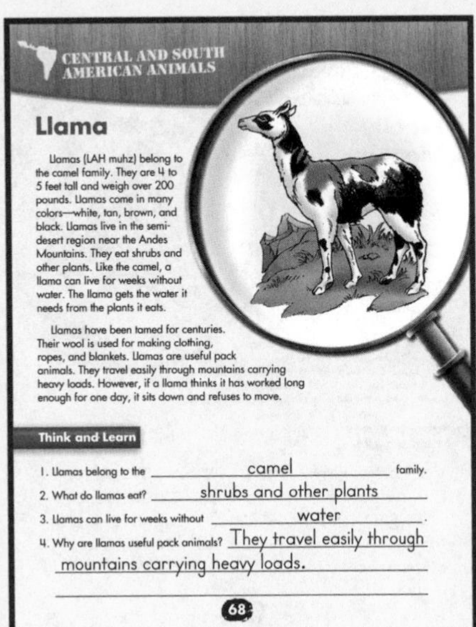

CENTRAL AND SOUTH AMERICAN ANIMALS

Llama

Llamas (LAH muhz) belong to the camel family. They are 4 to 5 feet tall and weigh over 200 pounds. Llamas come in many colors—white, tan, brown, and black. Llamas live in the semi-desert region near the Andes Mountains. They eat shrubs and other plants. Like the camel, a llama can live for weeks without water. The llama gets the water it needs from the plants it eats.

Llamas have been tamed for centuries. Their wool is used for making clothing, ropes, and blankets. Llamas are useful pack animals. They travel easily through mountains carrying heavy loads. However, if a llama thinks it has worked long enough for one day, it sits down and refuses to move.

Think and Learn

1. Llamas belong to the camel family.
2. What do llamas eat? shrubs and other plants
3. Llamas can live for weeks without water.
4. Why are llamas useful pack animals? They travel easily through mountains carrying heavy loads.

68

CENTRAL AND SOUTH AMERICAN ANIMALS

Macaw

Macaws (muh KAWZ) are the largest members of the parrot family. They come in many bright colors. All macaws have powerful hooked bills. They use their bills to help them climb and to break open nuts and seeds. Macaws have four toes on each foot. Their feet are well-suited for perching, climbing, and holding objects. Macaws are only found in rainforests. They live in holes that they make in tree trunks.

Macaws are in danger of extinction, or dying out. They are losing their homes as the rainforest is destroyed. Laws protect these birds, but people still capture them to sell as pets. Macaws are not good pets because they like to scream and bite.

Think and Learn

1. Macaws are members of the parrot family.
2. All macaws have powerful, hooked bills.
3. What do macaws use their feet for? perching, climbing, and holding objects
4. Why are macaws in danger of extinction? They are losing their homes and are captured to sell as pets.

69

CENTRAL AND SOUTH AMERICAN ANIMALS

Spider Monkey

Spider monkeys are small monkeys well-suited for living in trees. In fact, they rarely come down to the ground. These monkeys move quickly through trees by swinging and jumping from branch to branch. Spider monkeys have tails that are longer than their bodies. These tails can easily grab and pick up things.

Spider monkeys are found in rainforests from southern Mexico to the northern part of South America. They eat nuts, fruit, and sometimes eggs. Spider monkeys live in groups, or bands, of 10 to 40 monkeys. Every band of monkeys lives in its own area, or territory. One band of monkeys will not go into the territory of another band.

Think and Learn

1. How do spider monkeys move quickly through trees? by swinging and jumping from branch to branch
2. Their tails can grab and pick up things.
3. What do spider monkeys eat? nuts, fruit, and eggs
4. Spider monkeys live in groups called bands

70

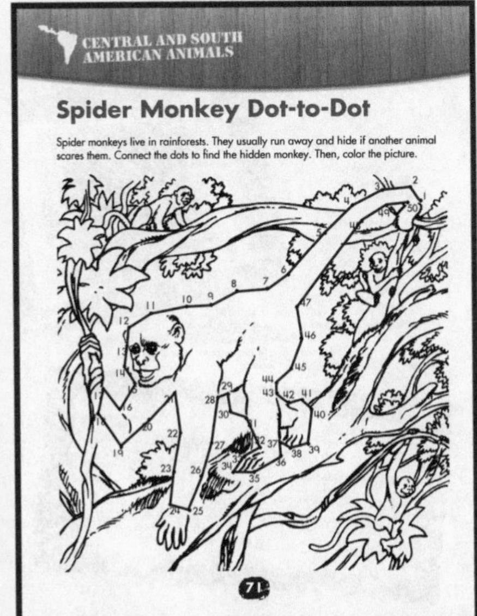

CENTRAL AND SOUTH AMERICAN ANIMALS

Spider Monkey Dot-to-Dot

Spider monkeys live in rainforests. They usually run away and hide if another animal scares them. Connect the dots to find the hidden monkey. Then, color the picture.

71

CENTRAL AND SOUTH AMERICAN ANIMALS

Toucan

Toucans (TOO kanz) are birds with large, colorful bills. Although a toucan bill looks heavy, it is really very light. The bill is hollow. It is made from a hornlike material. Toucans live in the rainforests of Central and South America. Toucans eat fruit, large insects, lizards, and young birds. A toucan sits on a branch and reaches for fruit with its long bill. The curved end of the bill helps the toucan pick the fruit and hold on to it.

Toucans make their nests in the holes of trees. Both the male and female take turns sitting on the eggs. Newly hatched toucans are blind and have no feathers. After 6 to 7 weeks, the young toucans are ready to live on their own.

Think and Learn

1. Toucans have large, colorful bills.
2. Where do toucans live? rainforests of Central and South America
3. What do they eat? fruit, large insects, lizards, young birds
4. Where do toucans make nests? in the holes of trees

72

ANSWER KEY

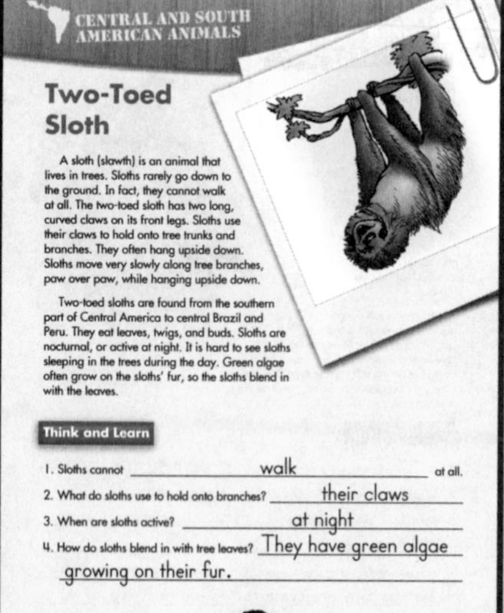
CENTRAL AND SOUTH AMERICAN ANIMALS

Two-Toed Sloth

A sloth (slawth) is an animal that lives in trees. Sloths rarely go down to the ground. In fact, they cannot walk at all. The two-toed sloth has two long, curved claws on its front legs. Sloths use their claws to hold onto tree trunks and branches. They often hang upside down. Sloths move very slowly along tree branches, paw over paw, while hanging upside down.

Two-toed sloths are found from the southern part of Central America to central Brazil and Peru. They eat leaves, twigs, and buds. Sloths are nocturnal, or active at night. It is hard to see sloths sleeping in the trees during the day. Green algae often grow on the sloths' fur, so the sloths blend in with the leaves.

Think and Learn

1. Sloths cannot walk at all.
2. What do sloths use to hold onto branches? their claws
3. When are sloths active? at night
4. How do sloths blend in with tree leaves? They have green algae growing on their fur.

73

CENTRAL AND SOUTH AMERICAN ANIMALS

Woolly Monkey

Woolly monkeys are named for their beautiful thick, woolly coats. They are found in forests along the Amazon River in Columbia, Ecuador, Peru, and Brazil. They eat fruit, flowers, and leaves. Unlike other tree-living monkeys, woolly monkeys are often found on the ground. While on the ground, they stand straight up, using their tails for support.

Woolly monkeys live in groups, or bands, of 10 to 30 monkeys. They move more slowly than other monkeys. When frightened, they swing through tree branches and hide. Woolly monkeys are friendly. They are often seen in the company of other kinds of monkeys.

Think and Learn

1. Woolly monkeys are named for their their woolly coats.
2. How do woolly monkeys stand while on the ground? straight up, using their tails for support
3. Woolly monkeys live in groups called bands.
4. Woolly monkeys move more slowly than other monkeys.

74

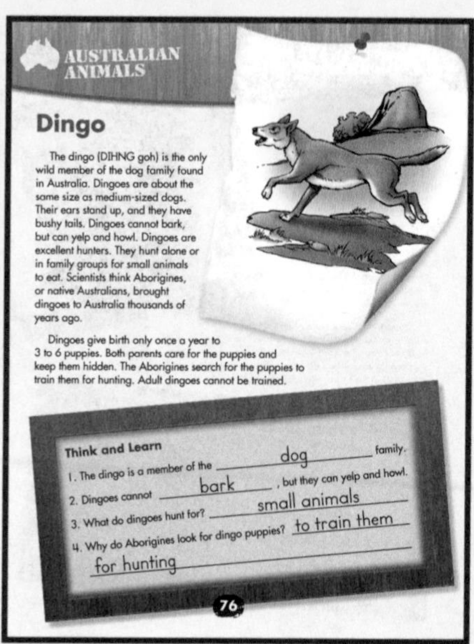
AUSTRALIAN ANIMALS

Dingo

The dingo (DIHNG goh) is the only wild member of the dog family found in Australia. Dingoes are about the same size as medium-sized dogs. Their ears stand up, and they have bushy tails. Dingoes cannot bark, but can yelp and howl. Dingoes are excellent hunters. They hunt alone or in family groups for small animals to eat. Scientists think Aborigines, or native Australians, brought dingoes to Australia thousands of years ago.

Dingoes give birth only once a year to 3 to 6 puppies. Both parents care for the puppies and keep them hidden. The Aborigines search for the puppies to train them for hunting. Adult dingoes cannot be trained.

Think and Learn

1. The dingo is a member of the dog family.
2. Dingoes cannot bark, but they can yelp and howl.
3. What do dingoes hunt for? small animals
4. Why do Aborigines look for dingo puppies? to train them for hunting

76

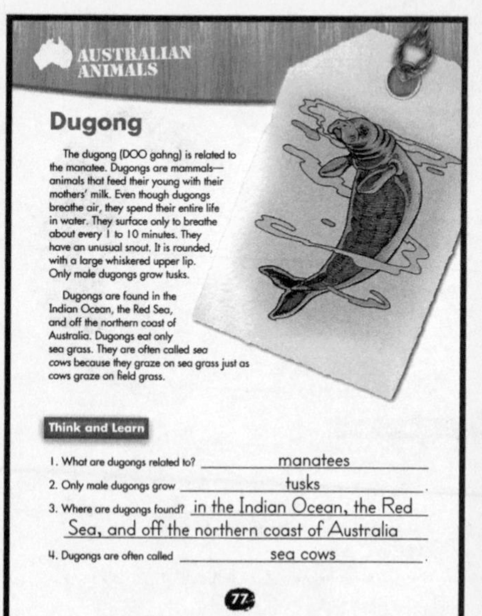
AUSTRALIAN ANIMALS

Dugong

The dugong (DOO gahng) is related to the manatee. Dugongs are mammals—animals that feed their young with their mothers' milk. Even though dugongs breathe air, they spend their entire life in water. They surface only to breathe about every 1 to 10 minutes. They have an unusual snout. It is rounded, with a large whiskered upper lip. Only male dugongs grow tusks.

Dugongs are found in the Indian Ocean, the Red Sea, and off the northern coast of Australia. Dugongs eat only sea grass. They are often called sea cows because they graze on sea grass just as cows graze on field grass.

Think and Learn

1. What are dugongs related to? manatees
2. Only male dugongs grow tusks.
3. Where are dugongs found? in the Indian Ocean, the Red Sea, and off the northern coast of Australia
4. Dugongs are often called sea cows.

77

AUSTRALIAN ANIMALS

Echidna

The echidna (ih KIHD nuh) is sometimes called a *spiny anteater*. It is found throughout Australia in open forests. The echidna's body is covered with coarse hair and pointed spines. Echidnas sleep in hollow logs during the day. At night, they use their sharp claws to scratch up insects. They eat the insects by licking them up with their long sticky tongues. Echidnas do not have teeth.

Echidnas are mammals that lay eggs. Mammals are animals whose young feed on the mother's milk. Female echidnas lay one egg each year. The mother keeps the egg in her pouch, where it hatches. The baby stays in the pouch for several weeks, drinking the mother's milk and growing.

Think and Learn

1. What is another name for an echidna? spiny anteater
2. When do echidnas sleep? during the day
3. How do echidnas eat insects? by licking them up with their long sticky tongues
4. Echidnas are mammals that lay eggs.

78

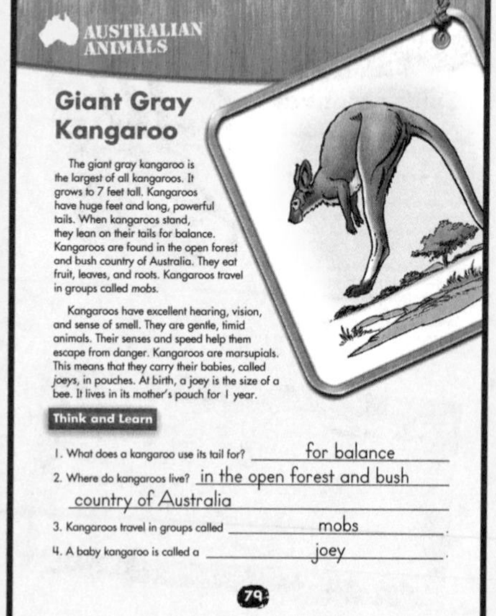
AUSTRALIAN ANIMALS

Giant Gray Kangaroo

The giant gray kangaroo is the largest of all kangaroos. It grows to 7 feet tall. Kangaroos have huge feet and long, powerful tails. When kangaroos stand, they lean on their tails for balance. Kangaroos are found in the open forest and bush country of Australia. They eat fruit, leaves, and roots. Kangaroos travel in groups called mobs.

Kangaroos have excellent hearing, vision, and sense of smell. They are gentle, timid animals. Their senses and speed help them escape from danger. Kangaroos are marsupials. This means that they carry their babies, called joeys, in pouches. At birth, a joey is the size of a bee. It lives in its mother's pouch for 1 year.

Think and Learn

1. What does a kangaroo use its tail for? for balance
2. Where do kangaroos live? in the open forest and bush country of Australia
3. Kangaroos travel in groups called mobs.
4. A baby kangaroo is called a joey.

79

ANSWER KEY

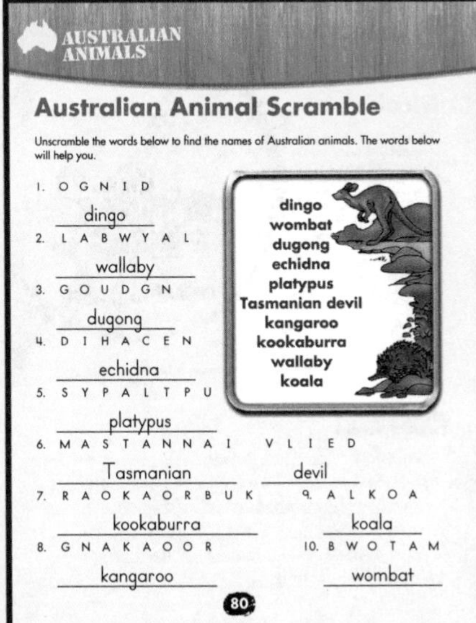

AUSTRALIAN ANIMALS

Australian Animal Scramble

Unscramble the words below to find the names of Australian animals. The words below will help you.

1. O G N I D — dingo
2. L A B W Y A L — wallaby
3. G O U D G N — dugong
4. D I H A C E N — echidna
5. S Y P A L T P U — platypus
6. M A S T A N N A I V L I E D — Tasmanian devil
7. R A O K A O R B U K — kookaburra
8. G N A K A O O R — kangaroo
9. A L K O A — koala
10. B W O T A M — wombat

dingo
wombat
dugong
echidna
platypus
Tasmanian devil
kangaroo
kookaburra
wallaby
koala

80

AUSTRALIAN ANIMALS

Koala

Although many people call the koala (koh AW luh) a *koala bear*, it is not a bear. The koala is a marsupial—a mammal with a pouch for carrying its young. The koala has beautiful gray, woolly fur. If threatened, koalas defend themselves with their sharp claws.

Koalas eat the leaves of eucalyptus trees. Koalas are found in the eucalyptus forests on the east coast of Australia. The only time a koala climbs down from a tree is to move to another tree. They get the water they need from the leaves they eat. Koalas are nocturnal and sleep 18 hours during the day. Female koalas have one baby at a time. The baby crawls into the mother's pouch, where it stays for 6 months. Then, the mother carries the baby on her back for 4 or 5 months.

Think and Learn

1. What is a marsupial? a mammal with a pouch for its young
2. What do koalas eat? eucalyptus leaves
3. When do koalas climb down a tree? to move to another tree
4. How long does a baby koala stay in its mother's pouch? for 6 months

81

AUSTRALIAN ANIMALS

Kookaburra

The kookaburra (KOOK uh ber uh) is a bird that lives in forests in the southern parts of Australia. It is best known for its loud, screaming laughter. The kookaburra screams its laughing sounds at dawn and at dusk. Kookaburras make their homes in holes in trees. They eat a wide variety of foods, such as caterpillars, fish, small mammals, frogs, and worms. Insects, however, are their favorite food.

Kookaburras usually lay 1 to 4 eggs in spring. Male kookaburras protect the nest. Young kookaburras stay in their parents' territory for up to 4 years. The young kookaburras even help to feed their parents' new babies.

Think and Learn

1. The kookaburra is known for its loud screaming laughter.
2. Where do kookaburras make their homes? in holes in trees
3. A kookaburra's favorite food is insects.
4. How do young kookaburras help their parents? by helping to feed the new babies

82

AUSTRALIAN ANIMALS

Platypus

The platypus (PLAT ih pus) is a mammal that has a bill like a duck and a flat, beaverlike tail. It is found near rivers and streams in eastern Australia and Tasmania. The platypus is awkward on land but swims gracefully. It has claws under its webbed toes. It uses its claws for digging burrows and getting food. The platypus eats large amounts of snails, worms, shrimp, and small fish.

The male platypus is poisonous. It has a poison gland attached to a hollow claw on each hind leg. A scratch from this claw can kill an animal or make a human very sick. The female platypus lays her eggs in a burrow lined with leaves. When the babies hatch, she holds them with her tail. The babies drink milk from her body.

Think and Learn

1. The platypus has a bill like a duck.
2. What does a platypus use its claws for? digging burrows and getting food
3. The male platypus is poisonous.
4. How does a mother platypus hold her babies? with her tail

83

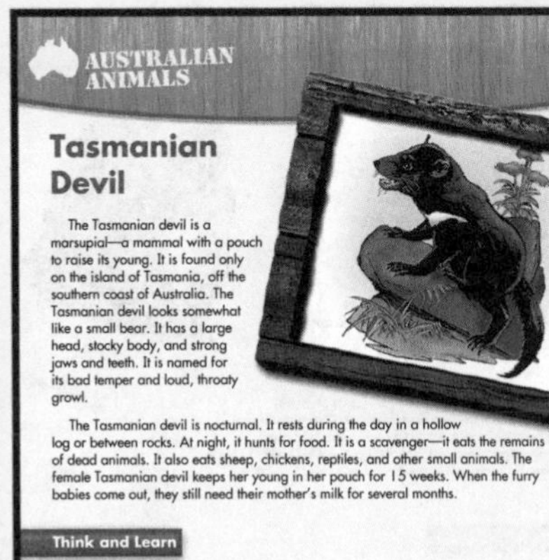

AUSTRALIAN ANIMALS

Tasmanian Devil

The Tasmanian devil is a marsupial—a mammal with a pouch to raise its young. It is found only on the island of Tasmania, off the southern coast of Australia. The Tasmanian devil looks somewhat like a small bear. It has a large head, stocky body, and strong jaws and teeth. It is named for its bad temper and loud, throaty growl.

The Tasmanian devil is nocturnal. It rests during the day in a hollow log or between rocks. At night, it hunts for food. It is a scavenger—it eats the remains of dead animals. It also eats sheep, chickens, reptiles, and other small animals. The female Tasmanian devil keeps her young in her pouch for 15 weeks. When the furry babies come out, they still need their mother's milk for several months.

Think and Learn

1. The Tasmanian devil looks like a small bear.
2. What is the Tasmanian devil named for? its bad temper and loud, throaty growl
3. What does the Tasmanian devil do at night? hunts for food
4. A scavenger eats the remains of dead animals.

84

AUSTRALIAN ANIMALS

Wallaby

Wallabies (WAHL uh beez) belong to the kangaroo family. Like kangaroos, they stand on their hind legs and use their tail for balance. Wallabies are found in Australia, New Guinea, and Tasmania. They live in grasslands or in woods. They graze on plants in the early morning and late afternoon. During the heat of the day, they rest in the shade. When the weather is very hot, wallabies lick their forearms and paws to cool themselves. Wallabies do not drink much water. They get enough water from the plants they eat.

Like other marsupials, wallabies carry their young in a pouch. The baby crawls through its mother's fur and climbs into the pouch after it is born. There, it drinks milk and grows.

Think and Learn

1. Wallabies belong to the kangaroo family.
2. During the heat of the day, wallabies rest in the shade.
3. How do wallabies cool themselves in hot weather? by licking their forearms and paws
4. Wallabies get water from the plants they eat.

85

AUSTRALIAN ANIMALS

Wombat

A wombat (WAHM bat) is a marsupial that looks like a small bear. However, it acts more like a rabbit or a mouse. Wombats have two upper and two lower front teeth that never stop growing. They use their strong legs and claws for digging and burrowing. Adult wombats weigh up to 75 pounds.

Wombats live in dry climates in southern Australia and Tasmania. They can go without water for a long time. Wombats stay in underground burrows all day. At night, they come out to eat roots and leaves. A wombat builds a nest of leaves and bark, where it gives birth to one baby. The baby spends the first part of its life in its mother's pouch. A wombat can live up to 25 years.

Think and Learn

1. What do wombats use their claws for? digging and burrowing
2. Wombats live in dry climates.
3. When do wombats eat? at night
4. How long can a wombat live? up to 25 years

86

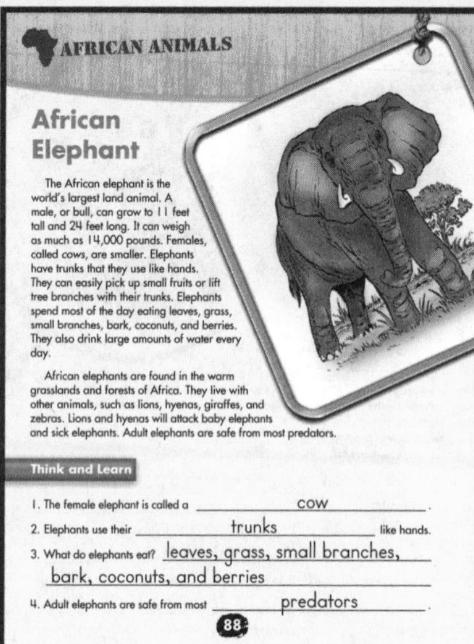

AFRICAN ANIMALS

African Elephant

The African elephant is the world's largest land animal. A male, or bull, can grow to 11 feet tall and 24 feet long. It can weigh as much as 14,000 pounds. Females, called cows, are smaller. Elephants have trunks that they use like hands. They can easily pick up small fruits or lift tree branches with their trunks. Elephants spend most of the day eating leaves, grass, small branches, bark, coconuts, and berries. They also drink large amounts of water every day.

African elephants are found in the warm grasslands and forests of Africa. They live with other animals, such as lions, hyenas, giraffes, and zebras. Lions and hyenas will attack baby elephants and sick elephants. Adult elephants are safe from most predators.

Think and Learn

1. The female elephant is called a cow.
2. Elephants use their trunks like hands.
3. What do elephants eat? leaves, grass, small branches, bark, coconuts, and berries
4. Adult elephants are safe from most predators.

88

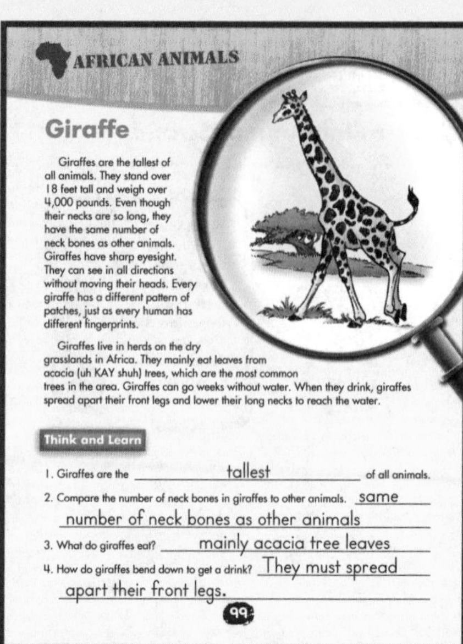

AFRICAN ANIMALS

Giraffe

Giraffes are the tallest of all animals. They stand over 18 feet tall and weigh over 4,000 pounds. Even though their necks are so long, they have the same number of neck bones as other animals. Giraffes have sharp eyesight. They can see in all directions without moving their heads. Every giraffe has a different pattern of patches, just as every human has different fingerprints.

Giraffes live in herds on the dry grasslands in Africa. They mainly eat leaves from acacia (uh KAY shuh) trees, which are the most common trees in the area. Giraffes can go weeks without water. When they drink, giraffes spread apart their front legs and lower their long necks to reach the water.

Think and Learn

1. Giraffes are the tallest of all animals.
2. Compare the number of neck bones in giraffes to other animals. same number of neck bones as other animals
3. What do giraffes eat? mainly acacia tree leaves
4. How do giraffes bend down to get a drink? They must spread apart their front legs.

99

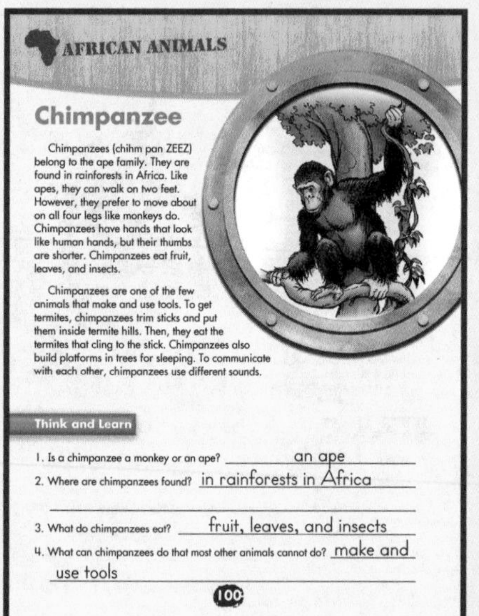

AFRICAN ANIMALS

Chimpanzee

Chimpanzees (chihm pan ZEEZ) belong to the ape family. They are found in rainforests in Africa. Like apes, they can walk on two feet. However, they prefer to move about on all four legs like monkeys do. Chimpanzees have hands that look like human hands, but their thumbs are shorter. Chimpanzees eat fruit, leaves, and insects.

Chimpanzees are one of the few animals that make and use tools. To get termites, chimpanzees trim sticks and put them inside termite hills. Then, they eat the termites that cling to the stick. Chimpanzees also build platforms in trees for sleeping. To communicate with each other, chimpanzees use different sounds.

Think and Learn

1. Is a chimpanzee a monkey or an ape? an ape
2. Where are chimpanzees found? in rainforests in Africa
3. What do chimpanzees eat? fruit, leaves, and insects
4. What can chimpanzees do that most other animals cannot do? make and use tools

100

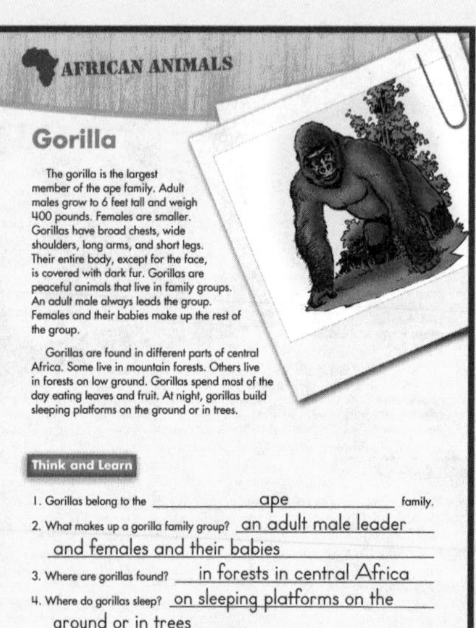

AFRICAN ANIMALS

Gorilla

The gorilla is the largest member of the ape family. Adult males grow to 6 feet tall and weigh 400 pounds. Females are smaller. Gorillas have broad chests, wide shoulders, long arms, and short legs. Their entire body, except for the face, is covered with dark fur. Gorillas are peaceful animals that live in family groups. An adult male always leads the group. Females and their babies make up the rest of the group.

Gorillas are found in different parts of central Africa. Some live in mountain forests. Others live in forests on low ground. Gorillas spend most of the day eating leaves and fruit. At night, gorillas build sleeping platforms on the ground or in trees.

Think and Learn

1. Gorillas belong to the ape family.
2. What makes up a gorilla family group? an adult male leader and females and their babies
3. Where are gorillas found? in forests in central Africa
4. Where do gorillas sleep? on sleeping platforms on the ground or in trees

101

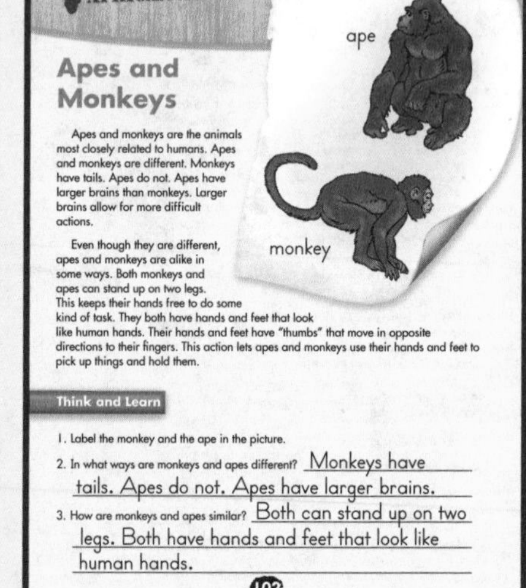

AFRICAN ANIMALS

Apes and Monkeys

Apes and monkeys are the animals most closely related to humans. Apes and monkeys are different. Monkeys have tails. Apes do not. Apes have larger brains than monkeys. Larger brains allow for more difficult actions.

Even though they are different, apes and monkeys are alike in some ways. Both monkeys and apes can stand up on two legs. This keeps their hands free to do some kind of task. They both have hands and feet that look like human hands. Their hands and feet have "thumbs" that move in opposite directions to their fingers. This action lets apes and monkeys use their hands and feet to pick up things and hold them.

Think and Learn

1. Label the monkey and the ape in the picture.
2. In what ways are monkeys and apes different? Monkeys have tails. Apes do not. Apes have larger brains.
3. How are monkeys and apes similar? Both can stand up on two legs. Both have hands and feet that look like human hands.

102

ANSWER KEY

AFRICAN ANIMALS

Hippopotamus

The hippopotamus (hihp uh PAHT uh muhs) is second only to elephants in size. Hippos are about 12 feet long and weigh up to 8,000 pounds. Hippos have very thick, bluish-gray skin. They have small eyes and ears on their large heads. Their enormous mouths can open 3 to 4 feet wide.

Hippos live by streams and marshes in many parts of Africa. During the day, they rest and sleep in the water. They keep their entire body under water, except for their eyes, ears, and nose. Hippos are very graceful swimmers. At night, they leave the water to eat grass. They spend up to 6 hours a night eating. Hippos live in herds with 15 to 30 members.

Think and Learn

1. Hippos have very thick skin.
2. Where do hippos live? by streams and marshes in Africa
3. What do hippos do during the day? rest and sleep in water
4. Hippos are very graceful swimmers.

103

AFRICAN ANIMALS

Lion

The lion is one of the largest and fiercest members of the cat family. Lions range in size from 270 to 500 pounds. Only male lions have a mane—the thick fur around the head. The mane protects lions when they fight to defend their territory, or area in which they live.

Lions sleep during the day and hunt at night. They hunt for antelope, zebras, young elephants, and other smaller animals. Lions are social animals. They live in groups called *prides*. A pride is usually made up of 1 to 6 males and 4 to 12 females with their cubs. Each pride has its own territory. The members of a pride hunt only in their territory.

Think and Learn

1. Why do male lions have manes? to protect them when they fight to defend their territory
2. When do lions hunt? at night
3. Lions live in groups called prides.
4. Each pride hunts in its own territory.

104

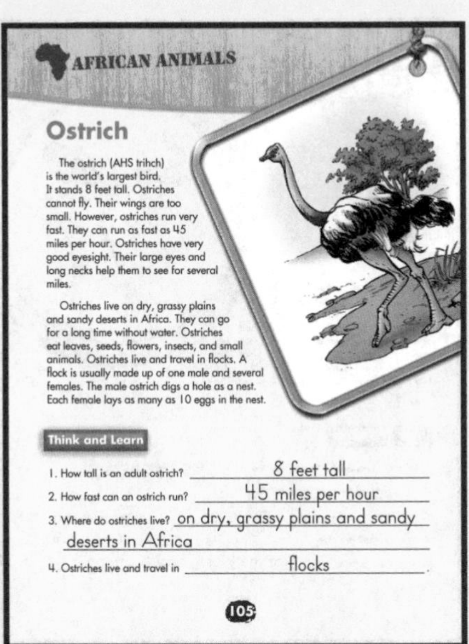

AFRICAN ANIMALS

Ostrich

The ostrich (AHS trihch) is the world's largest bird. It stands 8 feet tall. Ostriches cannot fly. Their wings are too small. However, ostriches run very fast. They can run as fast as 45 miles per hour. Ostriches have very good eyesight. Their large eyes and long necks help them to see for several miles.

Ostriches live on dry, grassy plains and sandy deserts in Africa. They can go for a long time without water. Ostriches eat leaves, seeds, flowers, insects, and small animals. Ostriches live and travel in flocks. A flock is usually made up of one male and several females. The male ostrich digs a hole as a nest. Each female lays as many as 10 eggs in the nest.

Think and Learn

1. How tall is an adult ostrich? 8 feet tall
2. How fast can an ostrich run? 45 miles per hour
3. Where do ostriches live? on dry, grassy plains and sandy deserts in Africa
4. Ostriches live and travel in flocks.

105

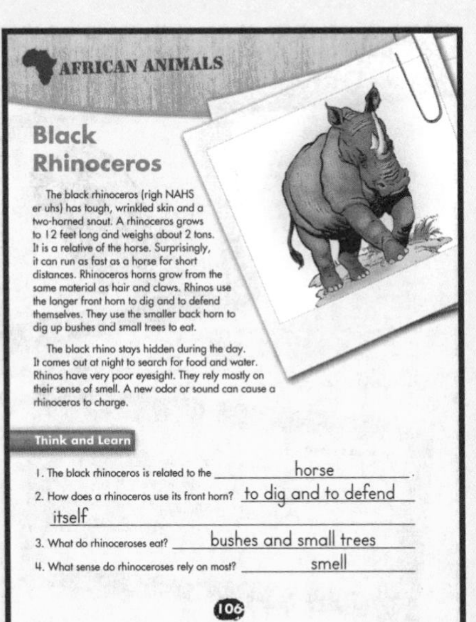

AFRICAN ANIMALS

Black Rhinoceros

The black rhinoceros (righ NAHS er uhs) has tough, wrinkled skin and a two-horned snout. A rhinoceros grows to 12 feet long and weighs about 2 tons. It is a relative of the horse. Surprisingly, it can run as fast as a horse for short distances. Rhinoceros horns grow from the same material as hair and claws. Rhinos use the longer front horn to dig and to defend themselves. They use the smaller back horn to dig up bushes and small trees to eat.

The black rhino stays hidden during the day. It comes out at night to search for food and water. Rhinos have very poor eyesight. They rely mostly on their sense of smell. A new odor or sound can cause a rhinoceros to charge.

Think and Learn

1. The black rhinoceros is related to the horse.
2. How does a rhinoceros use its front horn? to dig and to defend itself
3. What do rhinoceroses eat? bushes and small trees
4. What sense do rhinoceroses rely on most? smell

106

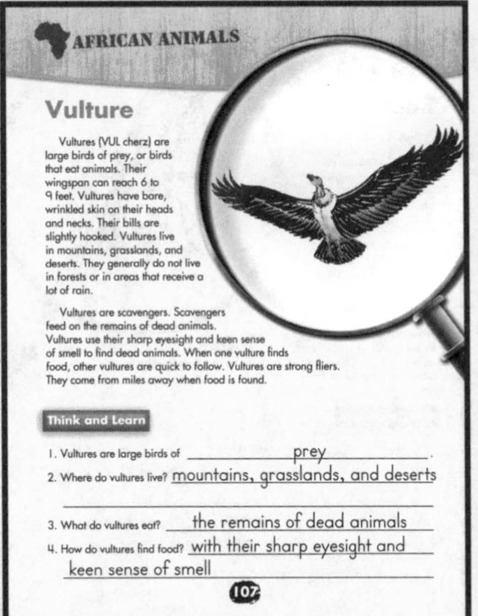

AFRICAN ANIMALS

Vulture

Vultures (VUL cherz) are large birds of prey, or birds that eat animals. Their wingspan can reach 6 to 9 feet. Vultures have bare, wrinkled skin on their heads and necks. Their bills are slightly hooked. Vultures live in mountains, grasslands, and deserts. They generally do not live in forests or in areas that receive a lot of rain.

Vultures are scavengers. Scavengers feed on the remains of dead animals. Vultures use their sharp eyesight and keen sense of smell to find dead animals. When one vulture finds food, other vultures are quick to follow. Vultures are strong fliers. They come from miles away when food is found.

Think and Learn

1. Vultures are large birds of prey.
2. Where do vultures live? mountains, grasslands, and deserts
3. What do vultures eat? the remains of dead animals
4. How do vultures find food? with their sharp eyesight and keen sense of smell

107

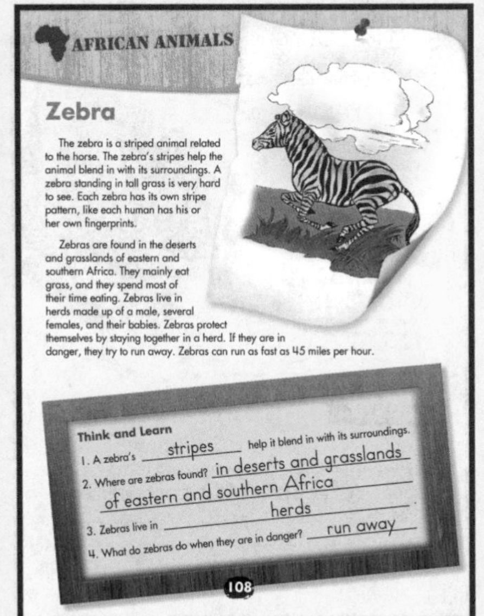

AFRICAN ANIMALS

Zebra

The zebra is a striped animal related to the horse. The zebra's stripes help the animal blend in with its surroundings. A zebra standing in tall grass is very hard to see. Each zebra has its own stripe pattern, like each human has his or her own fingerprints.

Zebras are found in the deserts and grasslands of eastern and southern Africa. They mainly eat grass, and they spend most of their time eating. Zebras live in herds made up of a male, several females, and their babies. Zebras protect themselves by staying together in a herd. If they are in danger, they try to run away. Zebras can run as fast as 45 miles per hour.

Think and Learn

1. A zebra's stripes help it blend in with its surroundings.
2. Where are zebras found? in deserts and grasslands of eastern and southern Africa
3. Zebras live in herds.
4. What do zebras do when they are in danger? run away

108

ANSWER KEY

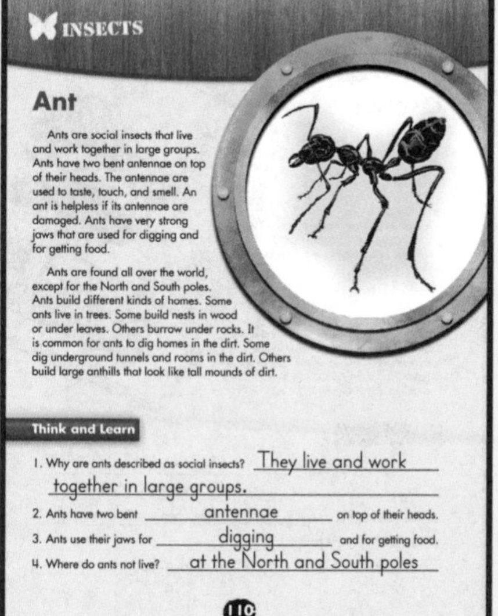

INSECTS

Ant

Ants are social insects that live and work together in large groups. Ants have two bent antennae on top of their heads. The antennae are used to taste, touch, and smell. An ant is helpless if its antennae are damaged. Ants have very strong jaws that are used for digging and for getting food.

Ants are found all over the world, except for the North and South poles. Ants build different kinds of homes. Some ants live in trees. Some build nests in wood or under leaves. Others burrow under rocks. It is common for ants to dig homes in the dirt. Some dig underground tunnels and rooms in the dirt. Others build large anthills that look like tall mounds of dirt.

Think and Learn

1. Why are ants described as social insects? They live and work together in large groups.
2. Ants have two bent antennae on top of their heads.
3. Ants use their jaws for digging and for getting food.
4. Where do ants not live? at the North and South poles

110

INSECTS

Ant Colonies

Ants live in groups called *colonies*. There are three different groups of ants in a colony—the queen ants, the workers, and the males. Each ant in the colony has a special job. The queen ants are the largest females. Their only job is to lay eggs. The worker ants are usually females that do not lay eggs. The workers have many jobs. Some workers are nursery ants who care for the eggs. Other worker ants find food and bring it back to the colony. The largest workers are soldier ants who guard the nest. Male ants live in the nest only at certain times. Their job is to mate with the queen ants. After mating, the male ants soon die.

1. Label the ant in the colony that is a nursery ant. Label the soldier ant.
2. What are the three different groups of ants living in an ant colony? queen ants, worker ants, and the males

111

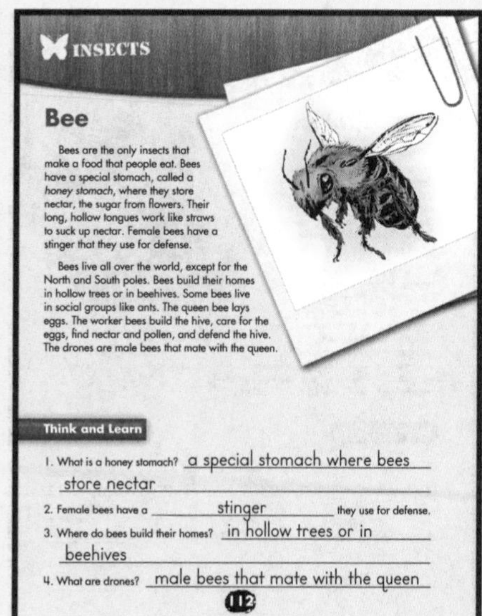

INSECTS

Bee

Bees are the only insects that make a food that people eat. Bees have a special stomach, called a *honey stomach*, where they store nectar, the sugar from flowers. Their long, hollow tongues work like straws to suck up nectar. Female bees have a stinger that they use for defense.

Bees live all over the world, except for the North and South poles. Bees build their homes in hollow trees or in beehives. Some bees live in social groups like ants. The queen bee lays eggs. The worker bees build the hive, care for the eggs, find nectar and pollen, and defend the hive. The drones are male bees that mate with the queen.

Think and Learn

1. What is a honey stomach? a special stomach where bees store nectar
2. Female bees have a stinger they use for defense.
3. Where do bees build their homes? in hollow trees or in beehives
4. What are drones? male bees that mate with the queen

112

INSECTS

Honeybees

Some farmers build wooden hives for honeybees. Then, the bees move in and make honeycombs. Honeycombs look like a wall with many six-sided rooms. Worker bees build the honeycomb out of beeswax, which they make in their stomach. The rooms in the honeycomb are used for storing eggs, young bees, and honey.

Worker bees make honey from the nectar they collect from flowers. As bees collect nectar from flowers, they spread pollen from one flower to another. Pollen grains are the male sex cells of a flowering plant. A flower needs pollen to form fruit and seeds. Farmers often keep bees to help spread the pollen on their fruit trees. Then, the fruit trees will have a lot of fruit. Farmers also collect the honey.

Think and Learn

1. What are honeycombs made of? beeswax
2. Why do farmers keep bees? They help spread pollen on the farmers' fruit trees, and the farmers collect the honey.

113

INSECTS

Beetle

Beetles are the largest group of insects and come in every color of the rainbow. All beetles have two pairs of wings. The outer wings are hard. They protect the inner, or flight, wings. The flight wings are thin and clear. They stay folded under the outer wings until needed for flight. Beetles have very strong jaws to grab and chew food.

Beetles are found all over the world. Beetles make their homes in many different places, from in water to under the ground. Beetles can be harmful or helpful to people, depending on what they eat. Some beetles damage the plants in gardens and farmers' fields. Other beetles eat harmful insects.

Think and Learn

1. Beetles are the largest group of insects.
2. Which wings do beetles use for flight? the thin, clear inner wings
3. Beetles have strong jaws to grab and chew food.
4. How are beetles helpful to people? by eating harmful insects

114

INSECTS

Butterfly

Butterflies are beautiful insects. The body of a butterfly is long and slender. They have knobs at the ends of their antennae, which are used for smelling. Their wings are covered with tiny scales that give the wings their color. All butterflies hatch as caterpillars, which look like worms. The caterpillars change to adult butterflies in a cocoon, or paperlike case.

Butterflies are found everywhere. They live on mountains and in deserts. As caterpillars, they eat leaves and fruit, often damaging crops. As butterflies, they cannot bite or chew. For food, they drink nectar, the sugary liquid, from flowers. Butterflies fly only during the day. When resting, they fold their wings straight up.

Think and Learn

1. What do butterflies use their antennae for? smelling
2. Tiny scales give butterfly wings their color.
3. What do caterpillars eat? leaves and fruit
4. When do butterflies fly? only during the day

115

ANSWER KEY

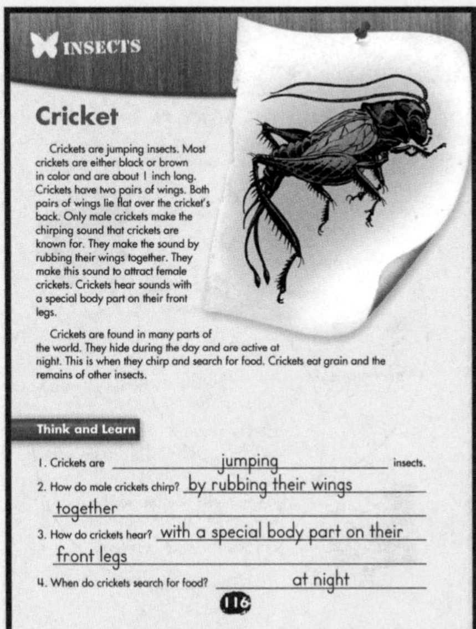
INSECTS

Cricket

Crickets are jumping insects. Most crickets are either black or brown in color and are about 1 inch long. Crickets have two pairs of wings. Both pairs of wings lie flat over the cricket's back. Only male crickets make the chirping sound that crickets are known for. They make the sound by rubbing their wings together. They make this sound to attract female crickets. Crickets hear sounds with a special body part on their front legs.

Crickets are found in many parts of the world. They hide during the day and are active at night. This is when they chirp and search for food. Crickets eat grain and the remains of other insects.

Think and Learn

1. Crickets are jumping insects.
2. How do male crickets chirp? by rubbing their wings together
3. How do crickets hear? with a special body part on their front legs
4. When do crickets search for food? at night

116

INSECTS

Fly

Flies are very common insects. People see and hear them everywhere. There are many different kinds of flies, such as house flies, fruit flies, gnats, and deer flies. Flies have only one pair of wings. The buzzing sound you hear when a fly flies by is the sound of its wings beating together. Flies use their antennae to touch and smell things. Flies have tiny, hairy pads on the bottoms of their feet. These help flies cling to walls and walk upside down on ceilings.

Although flies look harmless, they can carry and spread germs. Some flies, however, are helpful. They spread pollen from flower to flower like bees do.

Think and Learn

1. What are some kinds of flies? house flies, fruit flies, gnats, and deer flies
2. Flies have one pair of wings.
3. Flies use their antennae to touch and smell things.
4. Flies can carry and spread germs.

117

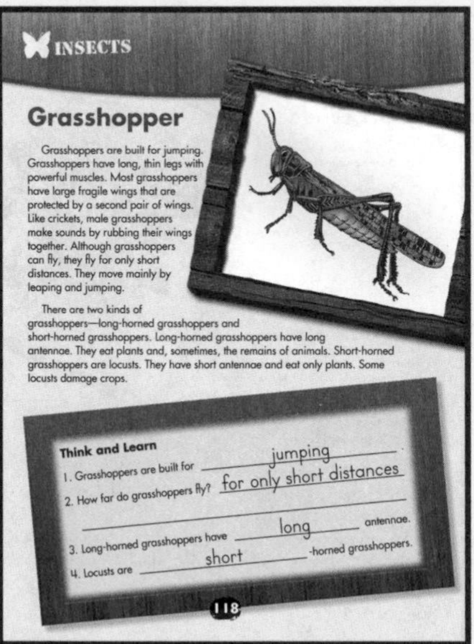
INSECTS

Grasshopper

Grasshoppers are built for jumping. Grasshoppers have long, thin legs with powerful muscles. Most grasshoppers have large fragile wings that are protected by a second pair of wings. Like crickets, male grasshoppers make sounds by rubbing their wings together. Although grasshoppers can fly, they fly for only short distances. They move mainly by leaping and jumping.

There are two kinds of grasshoppers—long-horned grasshoppers and short-horned grasshoppers. Long-horned grasshoppers have long antennae. They eat plants and, sometimes, the remains of animals. Short-horned grasshoppers are locusts. They have short antennae and eat only plants. Some locusts damage crops.

Think and Learn

1. Grasshoppers are built for jumping.
2. How far do grasshoppers fly? for only short distances
3. Long-horned grasshoppers have long antennae.
4. Locusts are short-horned grasshoppers.

118

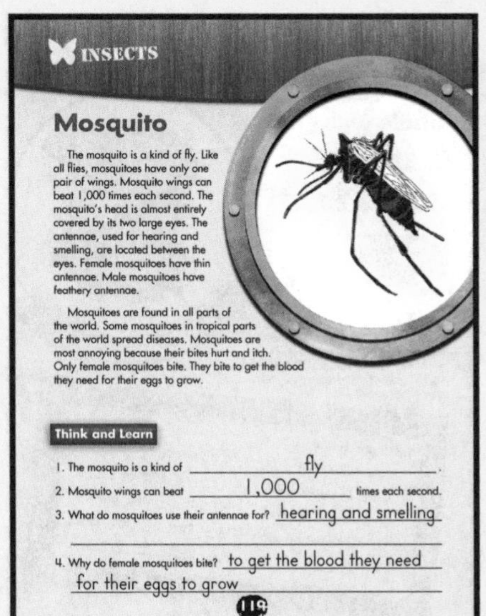
INSECTS

Mosquito

The mosquito is a kind of fly. Like all flies, mosquitoes have only one pair of wings. Mosquito wings can beat 1,000 times each second. The mosquito's head is almost entirely covered by its two large eyes. The antennae, used for hearing and smelling, are located between the eyes. Female mosquitoes have thin antennae. Male mosquitoes have feathery antennae.

Mosquitoes are found in all parts of the world. Some mosquitoes in tropical parts of the world spread diseases. Mosquitoes are most annoying because their bites hurt and itch. Only female mosquitoes bite. They bite to get the blood they need for their eggs to grow.

Think and Learn

1. The mosquito is a kind of fly.
2. Mosquito wings can beat 1,000 times each second.
3. What do mosquitoes use their antennae for? hearing and smelling
4. Why do female mosquitoes bite? to get the blood they need for their eggs to grow

119

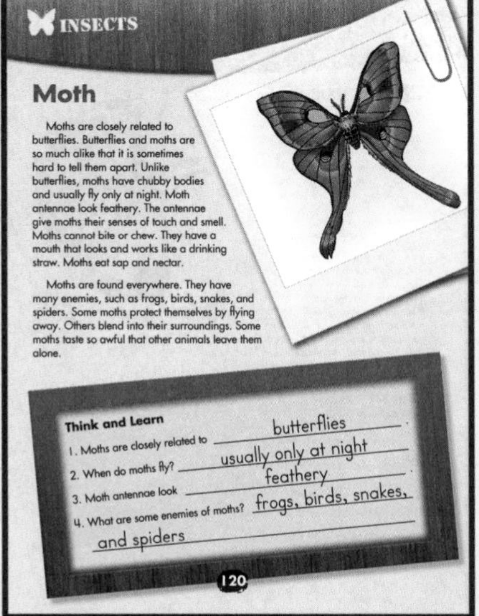
INSECTS

Moth

Moths are closely related to butterflies. Butterflies and moths are so much alike that it is sometimes hard to tell them apart. Unlike butterflies, moths have chubby bodies and usually fly only at night. Moth antennae look feathery. The antennae give moths their senses of touch and smell. Moths cannot bite or chew. They have a mouth that looks and works like a drinking straw. Moths eat sap and nectar.

Moths are found everywhere. They have many enemies, such as frogs, birds, snakes, and spiders. Some moths protect themselves by flying away. Others blend into their surroundings. Some moths taste so awful that other animals leave them alone.

Think and Learn

1. Moths are closely related to butterflies.
2. When do moths fly? usually only at night
3. Moth antennae look feathery.
4. What are some enemies of moths? frogs, birds, snakes, and spiders

120

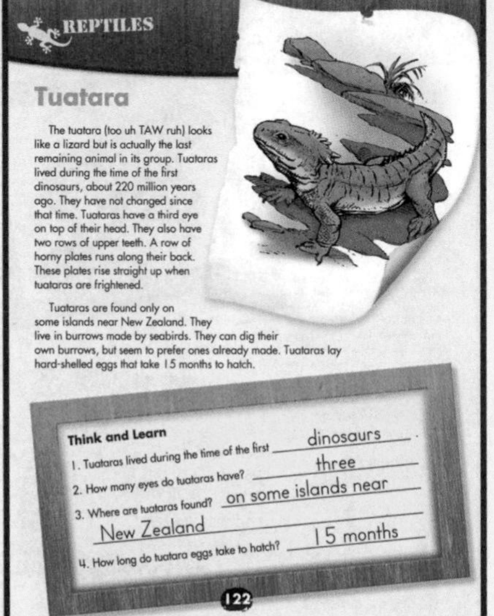
REPTILES

Tuatara

The tuatara (too uh TAW ruh) looks like a lizard but is actually the last remaining animal in its group. Tuataras lived during the time of the first dinosaurs, about 220 million years ago. They have not changed since that time. Tuataras have a third eye on top of their head. They also have two rows of upper teeth. A row of horny plates runs along their back. These plates rise straight up when tuataras are frightened.

Tuataras are found only on some islands near New Zealand. They live in burrows made by seabirds. They can dig their own burrows, but seem to prefer ones already made. Tuataras lay hard-shelled eggs that take 15 months to hatch.

Think and Learn

1. Tuataras lived during the time of the first dinosaurs.
2. How many eyes do tuataras have? three
3. Where are tuataras found? on some islands near New Zealand
4. How long do tuatara eggs take to hatch? 15 months

122

ANSWER KEY

REPTILES

Crocodile

Crocodiles (KRAHK uh dighlz) are the largest reptiles. They can reach 25 feet in length. Of all the animals belonging to the crocodile group, crocodiles are the most dangerous. Crocodiles have long narrow snouts. When their mouths are closed, their lower teeth show.

Crocodiles are found in the tropical parts of the world. They catch fish and small land animals for food. Like alligators, crocodiles, are most active at night. During the day, they rest in the sun. Often a crocodile lies with its mouth open to help cool its body. When its mouth is open, the crocodile lets birds go in it and peck out leftover pieces of food.

Think and Learn

1. Crocodiles are the largest reptiles.
2. Describe the shape of a crocodile's snout. long and narrow
3. What do crocodiles eat? fish and small land animals
4. How does a crocodile cool its body? by lying with its mouth open

123

REPTILES

Alligator

Alligators (AL ih gay terz) belong to the crocodile group of reptiles. Although they are members of this group, alligators and crocodiles are two different animals. Alligators have wide, rounded snouts. When their mouths are closed, their lower teeth are inside. Alligators are smaller than crocodiles. They grow up to 12 feet long.

Alligators are found in southeastern United States and in parts of China. They eat frogs, fish, snakes, turtles, and small mammals. Like crocodiles, alligators are good swimmers. Alligators move through the water by moving their tails from side to side. Female alligators lay as many as 50 eggs and guard the eggs until they hatch. Mother alligators care for their young for up to a year.

Think and Learn

1. Alligators belong to the crocodile group of reptiles.
2. Describe the shape of an alligator's snout. wide and rounded
3. How do alligators move through water? by moving their tails from side to side
4. Mother alligators care for their young for up to a year.

124

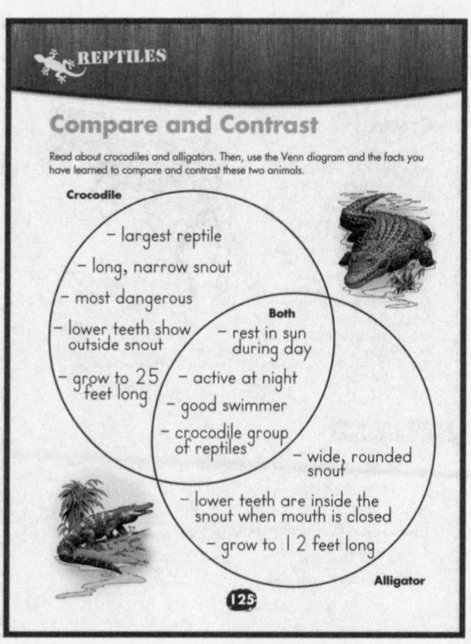

REPTILES

Compare and Contrast

Read about crocodiles and alligators. Then, use the Venn diagram and the facts you have learned to compare and contrast these two animals.

Crocodile
- largest reptile
- long, narrow snout
- most dangerous
- lower teeth show outside snout
- grow to 25 feet long

Both
- rest in sun during day
- active at night
- good swimmer
- crocodile group of reptiles

Alligator
- wide, rounded snout
- lower teeth are inside the snout when mouth is closed
- grow to 12 feet long

125

REPTILES

Lizard

Lizards and snakes make up the largest group of reptiles. Most lizards have four legs with five clawed toes on each leg. Some lizards do not have legs. Lizards have movable eyelids and good eyesight. They do not have ears, but they have ear openings on the sides of their head. Lizards use their tongue for smelling.

Lizards are found in all parts of the world, except the North and South poles. Most lizards eat insects and small mammals. Some lizards eat plants. Lizards protect themselves by blending in with their surroundings, making their bodies look bigger, or making hissing sounds. Some lizards have tails that break off and keep wiggling, while the lizard escapes. Later, it grows a new tail.

Think and Learn

1. Lizards have movable eyelids.
2. What do lizards use their tongues for? smelling
3. What do most lizards eat? Most eat insects and small mammals. Some eat plants.
4. Some lizards protect themselves by losing their tails.

126

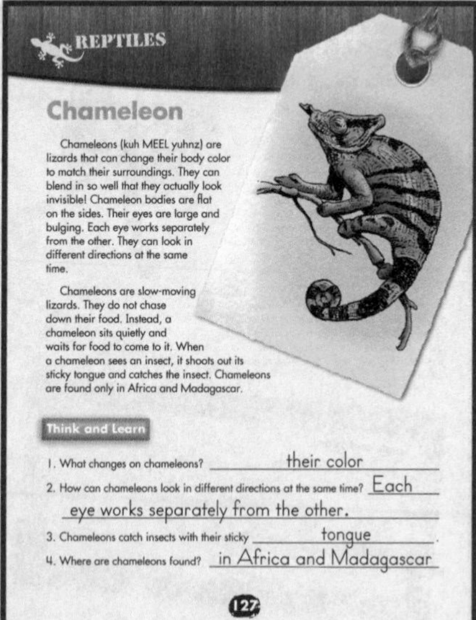

REPTILES

Chameleon

Chameleons (kuh MEEL yuhnz) are lizards that can change their body color to match their surroundings. They can blend in so well that they actually look invisible! Chameleon bodies are flat on the sides. Their eyes are large and bulging. Each eye works separately from the other. They can look in different directions at the same time.

Chameleons are slow-moving lizards. They do not chase down their food. Instead, a chameleon sits quietly and waits for food to come to it. When a chameleon sees an insect, it shoots out its sticky tongue and catches the insect. Chameleons are found only in Africa and Madagascar.

Think and Learn

1. What changes on chameleons? their color
2. How can chameleons look in different directions at the same time? Each eye works separately from the other.
3. Chameleons catch insects with their sticky tongue.
4. Where are chameleons found? in Africa and Madagascar

127

REPTILES

Snake

Snakes are reptiles that have long bodies and no legs. Snakes move by sliding on their belly. Snakes cannot shut their eyes, because they do not have eyelids. Their eyes are covered with clear scales. Snakes do not have ear slits. Instead, they hear sounds by feeling the movement of air around them. Snakes have a long, forked tongue that helps them smell.

Snakes eat other animals. The size of animal they can eat depends on the size of their mouth. A snake swallows its food whole. Snakes do not eat often. Most snakes eat only a few times a year. Snakes, like all other reptiles, lay eggs or give birth to live young. They do not take care of their young.

Think and Learn

1. How do snakes move? by sliding on their belly
2. What covers a snake's eyes? clear scales
3. Snakes use their long, forked tongue to help them smell.
4. How often do most snakes eat? only a few times a year

128

REPTILES

Garter Snake

Garter snakes are harmless snakes found in Central and North America. Female garter snakes grow 20 to 30 inches long. Males are slightly smaller. Garter snakes living in different areas look different from each other. They come in many different colors. However, most garter snakes have three stripes running along their body.

Garter snakes are most active in the spring and autumn. That is when most people see them in their yards or in parks. Garter snakes catch and eat small animals, such as frogs, salamanders, and fish. Garter snakes do not lay eggs. Instead, they give birth to live young.

Think and Learn

1. Garter snakes are harmless snakes.
2. What feature do most garter snakes have? three stripes running along their body
3. When are garter snakes most active? spring and autumn
4. Garter snakes do not lay eggs.

129

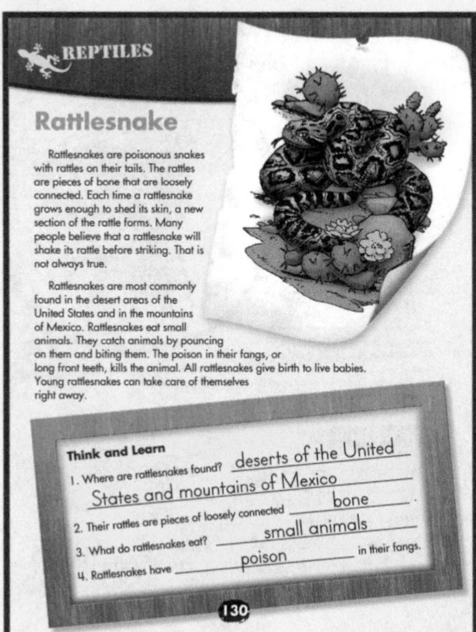

REPTILES

Rattlesnake

Rattlesnakes are poisonous snakes with rattles on their tails. The rattles are pieces of bone that are loosely connected. Each time a rattlesnake grows enough to shed its skin, a new section of the rattle forms. Many people believe that a rattlesnake will shake its rattle before striking. That is not always true.

Rattlesnakes are most commonly found in the desert areas of the United States and in the mountains of Mexico. Rattlesnakes eat small animals. They catch animals by pouncing on them and biting them. The poison in their fangs, or long front teeth, kills the animal. All rattlesnakes give birth to live babies. Young rattlesnakes can take care of themselves right away.

Think and Learn

1. Where are rattlesnakes found? deserts of the United States and mountains of Mexico
2. Their rattles are pieces of loosely connected bone.
3. What do rattlesnakes eat? small animals
4. Rattlesnakes have poison in their fangs.

130

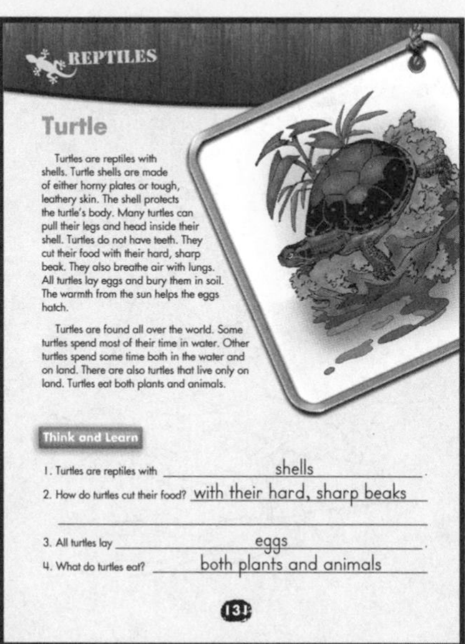

REPTILES

Turtle

Turtles are reptiles with shells. Turtle shells are made of either horny plates or tough, leathery skin. The shell protects the turtle's body. Many turtles can pull their legs and head inside their shell. Turtles do not have teeth. They cut their food with their hard, sharp beak. They also breathe air with lungs. All turtles lay eggs and bury them in soil. The warmth from the sun helps the eggs hatch.

Turtles are found all over the world. Some turtles spend most of their time in water. Other turtles spend some time both in the water and on land. There are also turtles that live only on land. Turtles eat both plants and animals.

Think and Learn

1. Turtles are reptiles with shells.
2. How do turtles cut their food? with their hard, sharp beaks
3. All turtles lay eggs.
4. What do turtles eat? both plants and animals

131

REPTILES

Sea Turtle

Sea turtles are turtles that live in the ocean. Sea turtles are very large. They range in size from 2 to 8 feet and weigh from 100 to 1,800 pounds. Instead of claws, sea turtles have flippers to help them swim easily through water. Sea turtles have flat shells instead of rounded shells like land turtles. Flat shells also help them move more easily through water.

Sea turtles are found in warm oceans throughout the world. They eat fish, shrimp, crabs, jellyfish, and plants. Sea turtles dig holes and lay their eggs on sandy beaches. The eggs lay buried in the sand for a couple of months before they hatch. When the eggs hatch, the babies dig out of the sand and head for the ocean.

Think and Learn

1. Flippers and flat shells help sea turtles move in the water.
2. Where are sea turtles found? in warm oceans
3. Sea turtles eat fish, shrimp, crabs, jellyfish, and plants.
4. Sea turtles lay their eggs on sandy beaches.

132

ANIMALS THAT LIVE IN THE WATER

Crab

A crab is a sea animal covered by a hard shell. Crabs have five pairs of jointed legs. The first pair of legs has large claws. Crabs use their claws to attract mates, defend themselves, and get food. On crabs that swim, the last pair of legs is shaped like flippers. On land, crabs often walk sideways on their last four pairs of legs. Crabs come in all sizes, from less than 1 inch long to 12 feet long.

Crabs are found in oceans all over the world. Some crabs live on land, but must lay their eggs in the sea. Their young grow in the sea until they are adults. Then, they move to the land. Crabs eat both plants and animals.

Think and Learn

1. Crabs have five pairs of jointed legs.
2. How do crabs use their claws? to attract mates, defend themselves, and get food
3. Crabs walk sideways on their last four pairs of legs.
4. What do crabs eat? plants and animals

134

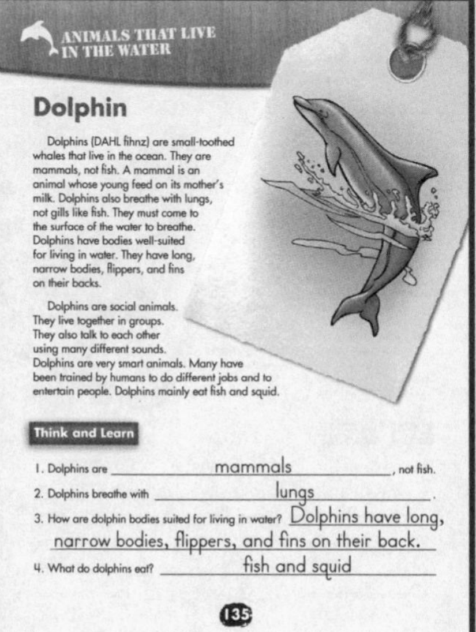

ANIMALS THAT LIVE IN THE WATER

Dolphin

Dolphins (DAHL fihnz) are small-toothed whales that live in the ocean. They are mammals, not fish. A mammal is an animal whose young feed on its mother's milk. Dolphins also breathe with lungs, not gills like fish. They must come to the surface of the water to breathe. Dolphins have bodies well-suited for living in water. They have long, narrow bodies, flippers, and fins on their backs.

Dolphins are social animals. They live together in groups. They also talk to each other using many different sounds. Dolphins are very smart animals. Many have been trained by humans to do different jobs and to entertain people. Dolphins mainly eat fish and squid.

Think and Learn

1. Dolphins are mammals, not fish.
2. Dolphins breathe with lungs.
3. How are dolphin bodies suited for living in water? Dolphins have long, narrow bodies, flippers, and fins on their back.
4. What do dolphins eat? fish and squid

135

ANSWER KEY

ANIMALS THAT LIVE IN THE WATER

Dolphin Dot-to-Dot

Connect the dots. Color the picture.

136

ANIMALS THAT LIVE IN THE WATER

Jellyfish

Jellyfish are soft-bodied animals that live in oceans. Jellyfish get their name from the stiff, jellylike material that makes up their body. Jellyfish have no bones. Their body is shaped like an open umbrella. Their mouth hangs down from the center of their body. Long tentacles hang down around the outside of their body. These tentacles are poisonous.

Jellyfish swim by opening and closing their body. This action pushes the jellyfish through the water. To get food, jellyfish first swim upward. Then, as they float down to the bottom, they catch fish and other small animals by stinging them with their poisonous tentacles.

Think and Learn

1. What are jellyfish named for? the stiff, jellylike material that makes up their body
2. What are jellyfish shaped liked? open umbrellas
3. Jellyfish have poisonous tentacles.
4. How do jellyfish swim? by opening and closing their body

147

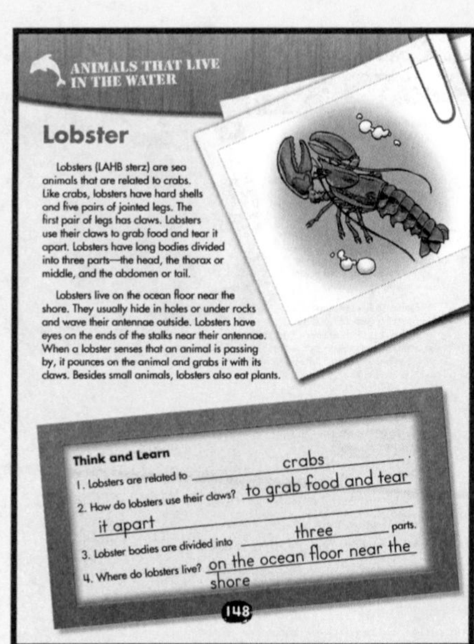

ANIMALS THAT LIVE IN THE WATER

Lobster

Lobsters (LAHB sterz) are sea animals that are related to crabs. Like crabs, lobsters have hard shells and five pairs of jointed legs. The first pair of legs has claws. Lobsters use their claws to grab food and tear it apart. Lobsters have long bodies divided into three parts—the head, the thorax or middle, and the abdomen or tail.

Lobsters live on the ocean floor near the shore. They usually hide in holes or under rocks and wave their antennae outside. Lobsters have eyes on the ends of the stalks near their antennae. When a lobster senses that an animal is passing by, it pounces on the animal and grabs it with its claws. Besides small animals, lobsters also eat plants.

Think and Learn

1. Lobsters are related to crabs.
2. How do lobsters use their claws? to grab food and tear it apart
3. Lobster bodies are divided into three parts.
4. Where do lobsters live? on the ocean floor near the shore

148

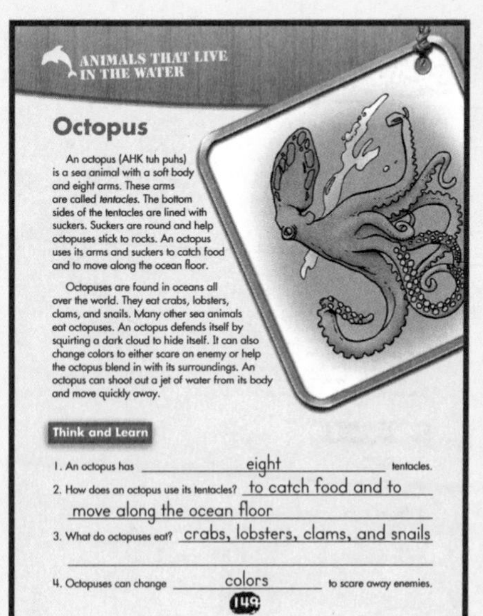

ANIMALS THAT LIVE IN THE WATER

Octopus

An octopus (AHK tuh puhs) is a sea animal with a soft body and eight arms. These arms are called *tentacles*. The bottom sides of the tentacles are lined with suckers. Suckers are round and help octopuses stick to rocks. An octopus uses its arms and suckers to catch food and to move along the ocean floor.

Octopuses are found in oceans all over the world. They eat crabs, lobsters, clams, and snails. Many other sea animals eat octopuses. An octopus defends itself by squirting a dark cloud to hide itself. It can also change colors to either scare an enemy or help the octopus blend in with its surroundings. An octopus can shoot out a jet of water from its body and move quickly away.

Think and Learn

1. An octopus has eight tentacles.
2. How does an octopus use its tentacles? to catch food and to move along the ocean floor
3. What do octopuses eat? crabs, lobsters, clams, and snails
4. Octopuses can change colors to scare away enemies.

149

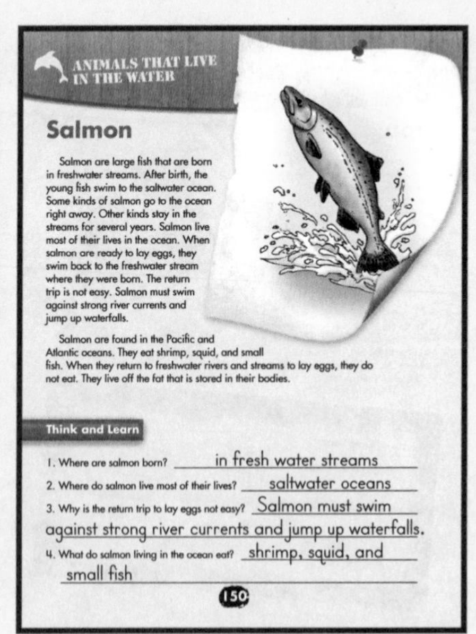

ANIMALS THAT LIVE IN THE WATER

Salmon

Salmon are large fish that are born in freshwater streams. After birth, the young fish swim to the saltwater ocean. Some kinds of salmon go to the ocean right away. Other kinds stay in the streams for several years. Salmon live most of their lives in the ocean. When salmon are ready to lay eggs, they swim back to the freshwater stream where they were born. The return trip is not easy. Salmon must swim against strong river currents and jump up waterfalls.

Salmon are found in the Pacific and Atlantic oceans. They eat shrimp, squid, and small fish. When they return to freshwater rivers and streams to lay eggs, they do not eat. They live off the fat that is stored in their bodies.

Think and Learn

1. Where are salmon born? in fresh water streams
2. Where do salmon live most of their lives? saltwater oceans
3. Why is the return trip to lay eggs not easy? Salmon must swim against strong river currents and jump up waterfalls.
4. What do salmon living in the ocean eat? shrimp, squid, and small fish

150

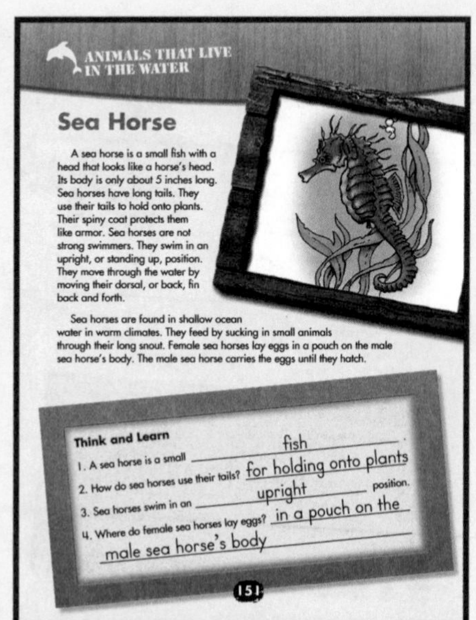

ANIMALS THAT LIVE IN THE WATER

Sea Horse

A sea horse is a small fish with a head that looks like a horse's head. Its body is only about 5 inches long. Sea horses have long tails. They use their tails to hold onto plants. Their spiny coat protects them like armor. Sea horses are not strong swimmers. They swim in an upright, or standing up, position. They move through the water by moving their dorsal, or back, fin back and forth.

Sea horses are found in shallow ocean water in warm climates. They feed by sucking in small animals through their long snout. Female sea horses lay eggs in a pouch on the male sea horse's body. The male sea horse carries the eggs until they hatch.

Think and Learn

1. A sea horse is a small fish.
2. How do sea horses use their tails? for holding onto plants
3. Sea horses swim in an upright position.
4. Where do female sea horses lay eggs? in a pouch on the male sea horse's body

151

ANIMALS THAT LIVE IN THE WATER

Shark

Sharks are fish that feed on other animals. Unlike most fish, sharks do not have bones. Instead, their bodies are supported with cartilage (KART l ij). Cartilage is a tough, bendable material. You have cartilage at the tip of your nose. Most sharks have mouths on the bottom side of their head. Some kinds of sharks have grinding teeth. Others have tearing teeth.

Sharks come in all sizes. Some are as small as 6 inches long. Others can grow to 40 feet long. Sharks are found in all parts of oceans. They are very good swimmers. Their long, narrow bodies help them move easily through water. Their curved tails help them swim fast.

Think and Learn

1. Sharks are fish that feed on other animals.
2. Sharks have cartilage instead of bones.
3. Where are sharks found? in all parts of oceans
4. How do curved tails help sharks? Curved tails help sharks swim fast.

152

ANIMALS THAT LIVE IN THE WATER

Starfish

Starfish are sea animals with spines on their skin. Starfish are sometimes called *sea stars* because they are shaped like stars. Many starfish have five arms pointing out from their body. However, some starfish have as many as 40 arms. Starfish have rows of tiny, tube-shaped feet along their arms. These tube feet help starfish move and get food.

Starfish are found in oceans all over the world. They eat animals with shells, such as clams and oysters. A starfish opens up a shell by attaching its tube feet to both halves of the shell. Then, it pulls apart the shell and pushes its stomach through the opening in the shell.

Think and Learn

1. Starfish have spines on their skin.
2. Starfish have a body shaped liked a star.
3. How do starfish use their tube feet? to move and get food
4. What do starfish eat? animals with shells, such as clams and oysters

153

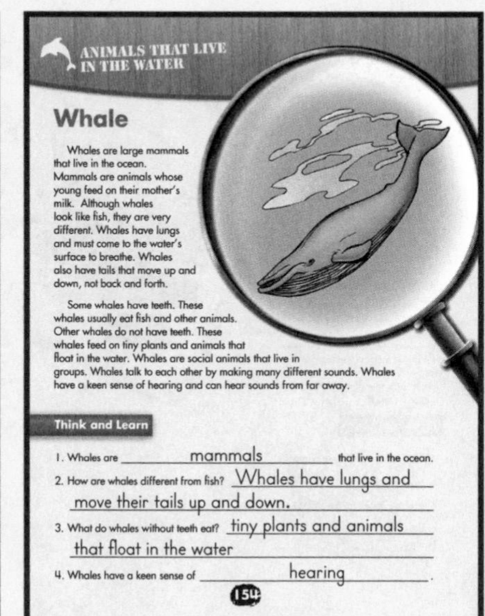

ANIMALS THAT LIVE IN THE WATER

Whale

Whales are large mammals that live in the ocean. Mammals are animals whose young feed on their mother's milk. Although whales look like fish, they are very different. Whales have lungs and must come to the water's surface to breathe. Whales also have tails that move up and down, not back and forth.

Some whales have teeth. These whales usually eat fish and other animals. Other whales do not have teeth. These whales feed on tiny plants and animals that float in the water. Whales are social animals that live in groups. Whales talk to each other by making many different sounds. Whales have a keen sense of hearing and can hear sounds from far away.

Think and Learn

1. Whales are mammals that live in the ocean.
2. How are whales different from fish? Whales have lungs and move their tails up and down.
3. What do whales without teeth eat? tiny plants and animals that float in the water
4. Whales have a keen sense of hearing.

154

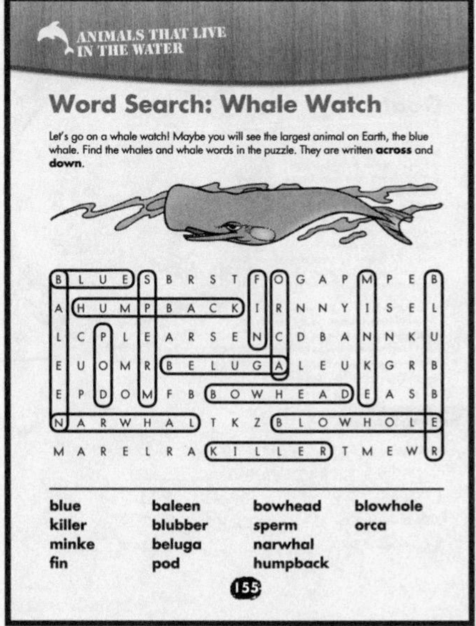

ANIMALS THAT LIVE IN THE WATER

Word Search: Whale Watch

Let's go on a whale watch! Maybe you will see the largest animal on Earth, the blue whale. Find the whales and whale words in the puzzle. They are written **across** and **down**.

B L U E S B R S T F O G A P M P E B
A H U M P B A C K I R N N Y I S E L
L C P L E A R S E N C D B A N N K U
E U O M R B E L U G A L E U K G R B
E P D O M F B B O W H E A D E A S B
N A R W H A L T K Z B L O W H O L E
M A R E L R A K I L L E R T M E W R

blue	**baleen**	**bowhead**	**blowhole**
killer	**blubber**	**sperm**	**orca**
minke	**beluga**	**narwhal**	
fin	**pod**	**humpback**	

155

ANIMALS THAT LIVE IN THE WATER

Hidden Pictures: Ocean Animals

Find the ocean animals hidden in the picture. Color the picture.

Colors will vary.

156

FARM ANIMALS

Duck

Ducks are birds that spend part of the time in water. Their webbed feet act as paddles to move them easily through the water. Most ducks get their food from water or from the areas around water. Some ducks eat fish. Others eat water plants and small water animals. Ducks keep dry by oiling their top feathers with oil from a special gland near their tail. They have a layer of soft fluffy feathers, called *down*, under the top feathers. Down keeps the duck warm.

Farmers raise ducks for their feathers, eggs, and meat. Duck feathers are used to stuff pillows and make winter coats. Ducks raised on farms do not get their food from water. The farmer feeds them a kind of food made just for ducks.

Think and Learn

1. What helps ducks move through water? webbed feet
2. Most ducks get their food from water.
3. What is down? a layer of soft, fluffy feathers under the top feathers
4. Farmers raise ducks for feathers, eggs, and meat.

158

FARM ANIMALS

Pig

Pigs are farm animals with short legs and a long, round body. Their body is covered with short bristles. Pigs cannot sweat to cool their body in hot weather. Instead, they lie in the mud during hot weather to cool off. Pigs have a sharp sense of smell but poor eyesight. The end of their flat snout is very sensitive to touch. Pigs use their snout for finding and digging up food.

Farmers all over the world raise pigs. Pigs are raised for their meat, which is called *pork*. Many other products, such as leather, glue, soap, fertilizer, and medicines, are made from other parts of the pig. Farmers feed pigs corn and other grains. Pigs also eat "pig food" made with meat scraps, milk, peanuts, soybeans, and other foods.

Think and Learn

1. How do pigs cool themselves? by lying in the mud
2. Pigs use their snout for finding and digging up food.
3. Pigs are raised for their meat, which is called pork.
4. What are some other products made from parts of the pig? leather, glue, soap, fertilizer, and medicines

159

FARM ANIMALS

Horse

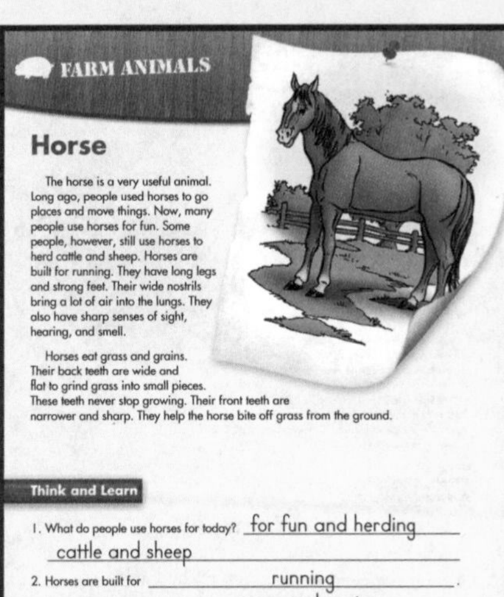

The horse is a very useful animal. Long ago, people used horses to go places and move things. Now, many people use horses for fun. Some people, however, still use horses to herd cattle and sheep. Horses are built for running. They have long legs and strong feet. Their wide nostrils bring a lot of air into the lungs. They also have sharp senses of sight, hearing, and smell.

Horses eat grass and grains. Their back teeth are wide and flat to grind grass into small pieces. These teeth never stop growing. Their front teeth are narrower and sharp. They help the horse bite off grass from the ground.

Think and Learn

1. What do people use horses for today? for fun and herding cattle and sheep
2. Horses are built for running.
3. What do horses eat? grass and grains
4. How do horses use their back teeth? for grinding grass into small pieces

160

FARM ANIMALS

Cow

Cows are large farm animals with split hooves. They have long tails that help swat insects away. Cows eat grass, hay, corn, and soybeans. They break down their food in a stomach that has four parts. When breaking down food, cows move it from the stomach back into their mouth to chew it again. The food that moves back into their mouth is called a *cud*. Cows chew the cud and swallow it again. Then, the food moves through the other parts of the stomach.

Cows are one of the most important farm animals. Farmers raise cows for their milk and their meat, called *beef*. Cow's milk is used to make cheese, butter, yogurt, and ice cream. Other parts of a cow's body are used to make leather, soap, and glue.

Think and Learn

1. What do cows eat? grass, hay, corn, and soybeans
2. Cows have a stomach that has four parts.
3. Meat from cows is called beef.
4. What foods are made from cow's milk? cheese, butter, yogurt, and ice cream

171

FARM ANIMALS

Chicken

Chickens are ground birds. They have a plump body and rounded wings. Chickens can fly but for only short distances. They fly to get away from danger. Chickens have pointed beaks and strong claws that they use to scratch in the dirt and get food. Different kinds of chickens have feathers of different colors.

Chickens are raised on farms all over the world. Farmers raise chickens for their eggs and their meat, called *poultry*. Some chickens are raised only for their meat. Other chickens are raised just to lay eggs. Some farmers raise only baby chicks. They sell the chicks to other farmers who raise them for meat or eggs. Farmers feed chickens a mixture of ground corn, wheat, and soybeans.

Think and Learn

1. Chickens fly for short distances.
2. How do chickens use their strong claws? for scratching in the dirt to get food
3. What are chickens raised for? eggs and meat
4. What do farmers feed chickens? corn, wheat, and soybeans

172

FARM ANIMALS

Sheep

Sheep are related to cows and goats. Like cows, sheep have a stomach that is divided into four parts. Sheep also have split hooves. Sheep do not need a lot of water to live. They like to eat grass and shrubs. When sheep eat, they bite off grass very close to the ground. If sheep are kept in the same pasture for a long time, they can kill all the grass.

Sheep are raised all over the world. However, the most sheep are raised in Australia and New Zealand. Sheep are very important animals because they give wool, milk, and meat, called *lamb* or *mutton*. Wool is used to make clothing, blankets, and rugs. Sheep's milk is used to make cheese.

Think and Learn

1. What other farm animals are sheep related to? cows and goats
2. Sheep do not need a lot of water to live.
3. Where are the most sheep raised? Australia and New Zealand
4. What are sheep raised for? wool, milk, and meat

173

FARM ANIMALS

Goat

Goats are related to sheep and cows. Like sheep and cows, goats have split hooves and a four-part stomach. Goats have long, shaggy hair. Most goats, both male and female, have a beard. Goats are known for eating almost anything. Because they have small mouths and flexible lips, goats can easily pick off only the healthful parts of a plant. They find food even in places where few plants can grow.

Farmers raise goats for their wool, milk, and meat. People living in rocky, mountainous areas rely on goats for meat. People in the United States use goats mainly for wool and milk. Some people even keep goats as pets. Goat's milk is used for drinking and making cheese. The wool is used to make clothing and blankets.

Think and Learn

1. How are goats like sheep and cows? They have split hooves and a four-part stomach.
2. Goats can pick off only the healthful parts of a plant.
3. Goats are raised for wool, milk, and meat.
4. Goat's milk is used for drinking and making cheese.

174

ANSWER KEY

FAVORITE PETS
Cat
Cats have been favorite pets for thousands of years. At first, people had cats to get rid of pests, such as mice and snakes. Cats are skilled hunters. They have keen senses, sharp claws, and the ability to jump and climb. Today, most people have cats to keep them company. Cats are smart but rather independent animals. They make good pets for people who are not home often.
Cats need to be fed every day. They must always have fresh water for drinking. Cats are clean animals and groom themselves often. However, cats should be brushed regularly to remove dead hair, especially if the cat has long hair. Cats must also be taken to the veterinarian for medical check-ups.
Think and Learn
1. Why did people first keep cats as pets? to get rid of pests, such as mice and snakes
2. Cats have keen senses and sharp claws.
3. Cats are clean animals and groom themselves.
4. Cats must go to the veterinarian for check-ups.
176

FAVORITE PETS
Dog
Dogs are popular pets throughout the world. Dogs have been bred through the years for certain jobs, such as guarding, hunting, and herding. Some dogs have been bred just to be pets. Dogs come in all sizes, colors, and personalities. When choosing a dog for a pet, the dog's qualities must fit in with the family's lifestyle.
Taking care of a dog is a big responsibility. Dogs need to be fed every day. They need clean, fresh water all the time and a warm, dry place to sleep. Dogs also need regular exercise, especially if they are big dogs. Dogs must be brushed and bathed regularly. Dogs also need medical check-ups every year. They must have vaccines and medicines to stay healthy.
Think and Learn
1. What jobs have dogs been bred for? guarding, hunting, and herding
2. Dogs should be fed every day.
3. Dogs need regular exercise.
4. Every year, dogs need medical check-ups.
187

FAVORITE PETS
Animal Friends
Plants, animals, and people must share our world. How can you be kind to our animal friends? Under each picture, write one way that you can be kind to that animal.
Answers will vary.
Answers will vary.
Answers will vary.
188

FAVORITE PETS
Rabbit
Rabbits are rodents with long ears and fluffy tails. Rodents are animals with front teeth that grow all the time. Pet rabbits must always have something to chew on. If not, their front teeth will grow too long for them to chew food normally.
Pet rabbits need a hutch, or a cage, to live in. They can be kept outside in a shady place during the summer. In winter, they must be kept in a heated garage or a cool basement. Rabbits eat pellets made just for them. They need fresh hay to eat every day. They also like fresh vegetables, clover, and grass. A water bottle filled with clean water should always be kept in the cage. Most rabbits do not like to be held for a long time. Never pick up a rabbit by its ears.
Think and Learn
1. A rodent has front teeth that grow all the time.
2. What do pet rabbits live in? a hutch
3. What do rabbits eat? rabbit pellets, fresh hay, fresh vegetables, clover, and grass
4. Never pick up a rabbit by its ears
189

FAVORITE PETS
Guinea Pig
A guinea pig is a small animal with a large head, short legs, and small ears. They grow to 14 inches long and weigh about 1 pound. Guinea pigs are not really pigs. They are rodents. Rodents have front teeth that never stop growing. For this reason, guinea pigs must always have a piece of wood to gnaw on.
Guinea pigs make good classroom pets. They are easy to care for, and they don't often bite. Guinea pigs need a cage through which air can easily move. They should have food and fresh water in their cage at all times. Guinea pigs eat grain, fresh vegetables, and hay. Guinea pigs are most active at night. They are quiet during the day and sleep in a burrow they make in their cage.
Think and Learn
1. Guinea pigs are not pigs; they are rodents.
2. What is the length of a guinea pig? 14 inches long
3. Why do guinea pigs make good classroom pets? They are easy to care for, and they don't often bite.
4. Guinea pigs are most active at night.
190

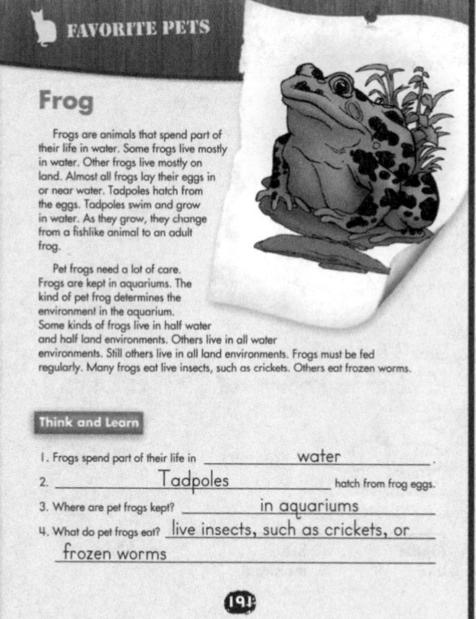

FAVORITE PETS
Frog
Frogs are animals that spend part of their life in water. Some frogs live mostly in water. Other frogs live mostly on land. Almost all frogs lay their eggs in or near water. Tadpoles hatch from the eggs. Tadpoles swim and grow in water. As they grow, they change from a fishlike animal to an adult frog.
Pet frogs need a lot of care. Frogs are kept in aquariums. The kind of pet frog determines the environment in the aquarium. Some kinds of frogs live in half water and half land environments. Others live in all water environments. Still others live in all land environments. Frogs must be fed regularly. Many frogs eat live insects, such as crickets. Others eat frozen worms.
Think and Learn
1. Frogs spend part of their life in water.
2. Tadpoles hatch from frog eggs.
3. Where are pet frogs kept? in aquariums
4. What do pet frogs eat? live insects, such as crickets, or frozen worms
191

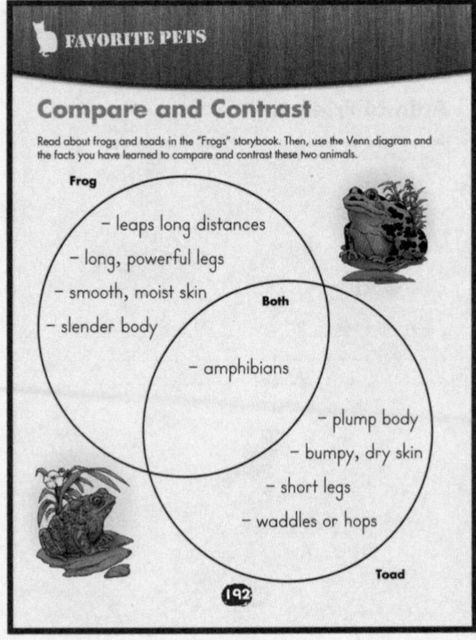

FAVORITE PETS

Compare and Contrast

Read about frogs and toads in the "Frogs" storybook. Then, use the Venn diagram and the facts you have learned to compare and contrast these two animals.

Frog
- leaps long distances
- long, powerful legs
- smooth, moist skin
- slender body

Both
- amphibians

Toad
- plump body
- bumpy, dry skin
- short legs
- waddles or hops

192

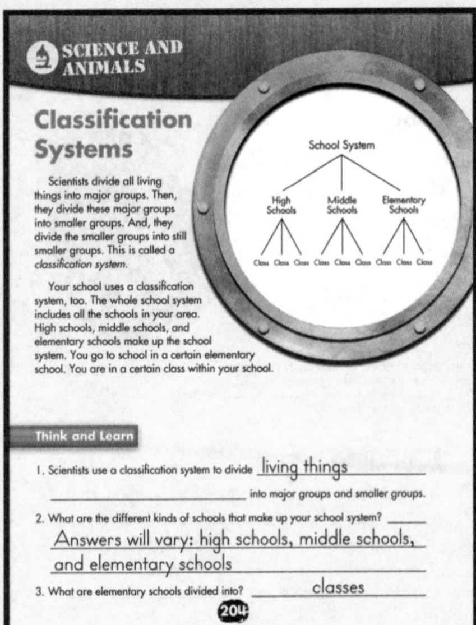

SCIENCE AND ANIMALS

Classification Systems

Scientists divide all living things into major groups. Then, they divide these major groups into smaller groups. And, they divide the smaller groups into still smaller groups. This is called a *classification system.*

Your school uses a classification system, too. The whole school system includes all the schools in your area. High schools, middle schools, and elementary schools make up the school system. You go to school in a certain elementary school. You are in a certain class within your school.

Think and Learn

1. Scientists use a classification system to divide living things into major groups and smaller groups.
2. What are the different kinds of schools that make up your school system? Answers will vary: high schools, middle schools, and elementary schools
3. What are elementary schools divided into? classes

204

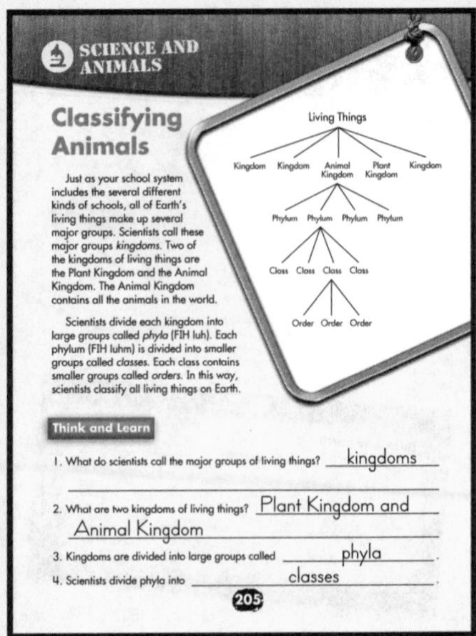

SCIENCE AND ANIMALS

Classifying Animals

Just as your school system includes the several different kinds of schools, all of Earth's living things make up several major groups. Scientists call these major groups *kingdoms.* Two of the kingdoms of living things are the Plant Kingdom and the Animal Kingdom. The Animal Kingdom contains all the animals in the world.

Scientists divide each kingdom into large groups called *phyla* (FIH luh). Each phylum (FIH luhm) is divided into smaller groups called classes. Each class contains smaller groups called orders. In this way, scientists classify all living things on Earth.

Think and Learn

1. What do scientists call the major groups of living things? kingdoms
2. What are two kingdoms of living things? Plant Kingdom and Animal Kingdom
3. Kingdoms are divided into large groups called phyla.
4. Scientists divide phyla into classes.

205

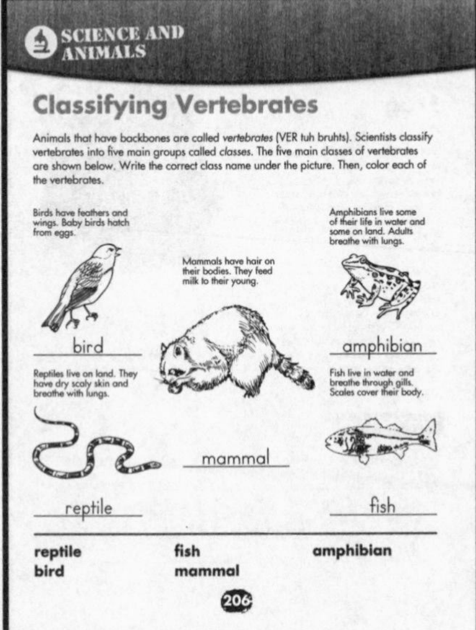

SCIENCE AND ANIMALS

Classifying Vertebrates

Animals that have backbones are called *vertebrates* (VER tuh bruhts). Scientists classify vertebrates into five main groups called classes. The five main classes of vertebrates are shown below. Write the correct class name under the picture. Then, color each of the vertebrates.

Birds have feathers and wings. Baby birds hatch from eggs. — bird

Mammals have hair on their bodies. They feed milk to their young. — mammal

Amphibians live some of their life in water and some on land. Adults breathe with lungs. — amphibian

Reptiles live on land. They have dry scaly skin and breathe with lungs. — reptile

Fish live in water and breathe through gills. Scales cover their body. — fish

reptile **fish** **amphibian** **bird** **mammal**

206

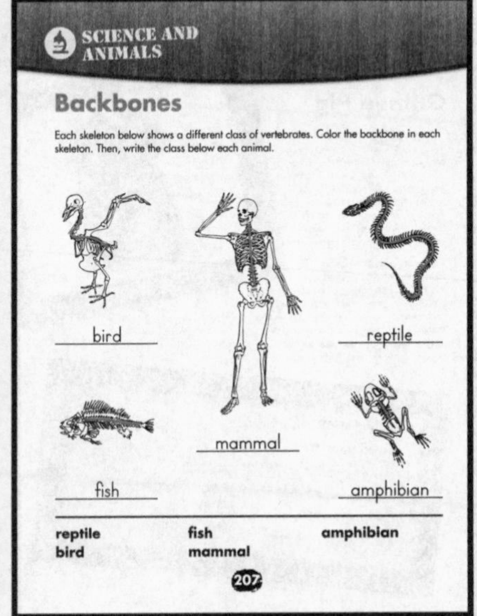

SCIENCE AND ANIMALS

Backbones

Each skeleton below shows a different class of vertebrates. Color the backbone in each skeleton. Then, write the class below each animal.

bird, mammal, reptile, fish, amphibian

reptile **fish** **amphibian** **bird** **mammal**

207

SCIENCE AND ANIMALS

Classy Vertebrates

Scientists group the vertebrates into five main classes. Write the name of the vertebrate class for each picture.

reptile	amphibian	fish	mammal
reptile	bird	mammal	amphibian
mammal	bird	fish	bird

reptile **fish** **amphibian** **bird** **mammal**

208

ANSWER KEY

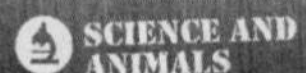

Animals With Backbones

Vertebrates are animals that have backbones. There are five main classes of vertebrates. Read the characteristics listed in the second column. Then, write the name of the class in the first column. Write an example of each class in the third column.

class	characteristics	example
fish	• live in water • breathe with gills	trout
amphibians	• live partly in water and partly on land • breathe with lungs as adults	toad
reptiles	• have dry, scaly skin • breathe with lungs	turtle
birds	• have feathers and wings • breathe with lungs	hawk
mammals	• body covered with hair • feed young with milk	bear

reptiles **birds** **toad** **fish** **mammals** **turtle** **trout** **bear** **amphibians** **hawk**

209

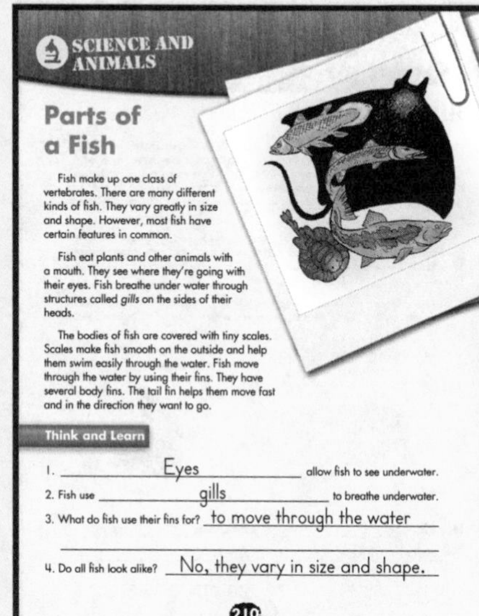

SCIENCE AND ANIMALS

Parts of a Fish

Fish make up one class of vertebrates. There are many different kinds of fish. They vary greatly in size and shape. However, most fish have certain features in common.

Fish eat plants and other animals with a mouth. They see where they're going with their eyes. Fish breathe under water through structures called *gills* on the sides of their heads.

The bodies of fish are covered with tiny scales. Scales make fish smooth on the outside and help them swim easily through the water. Fish move through the water by using their fins. They have several body fins. The tail fin helps them move fast and in the direction they want to go.

Think and Learn

1. Eyes allow fish to see underwater.
2. Fish use gills to breathe underwater.
3. What do fish use their fins for? to move through the water
4. Do all fish look alike? No, they vary in size and shape.

210

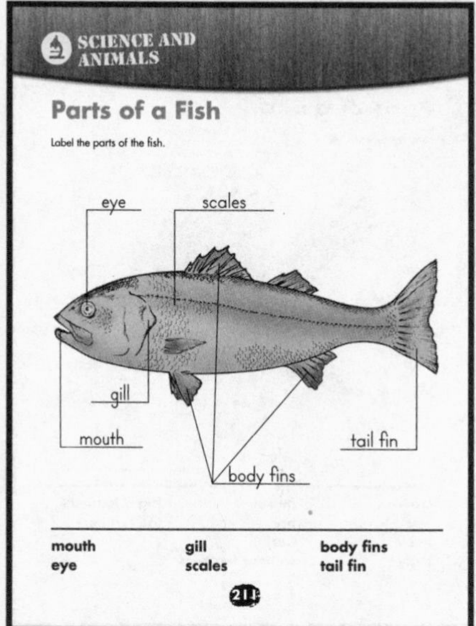

SCIENCE AND ANIMALS

Parts of a Fish

Label the parts of the fish.

mouth **eye** **gill** **scales** **body fins** **tail fin**

211

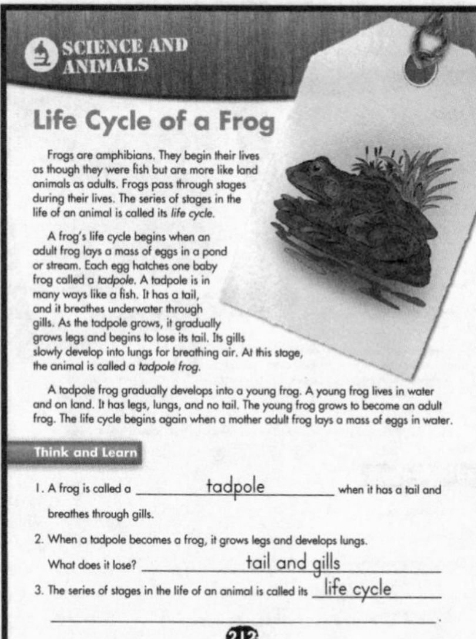

SCIENCE AND ANIMALS

Life Cycle of a Frog

Frogs are amphibians. They begin their lives as though they were fish but are more like land animals as adults. Frogs pass through stages during their lives. The series of stages in the life of an animal is called its *life cycle*.

A frog's life cycle begins when an adult frog lays a mass of eggs in a pond or stream. Each egg hatches one baby frog called a *tadpole*. A tadpole is in many ways like a fish. It has a tail, and it breathes underwater through gills. As the tadpole grows, it gradually grows legs and begins to lose its tail. Its gills slowly develop into lungs for breathing air. At this stage, the animal is called a *tadpole frog*.

A tadpole frog gradually develops into a young frog. A young frog lives in water and on land. It has legs, lungs, and no tail. The young frog grows to become an adult frog. The life cycle begins again when a mother adult frog lays a mass of eggs in water.

Think and Learn

1. A frog is called a tadpole when it has a tail and breathes through gills.
2. When a tadpole becomes a frog, it grows legs and develops lungs. What does it lose? tail and gills
3. The series of stages in the life of an animal is called its life cycle

212

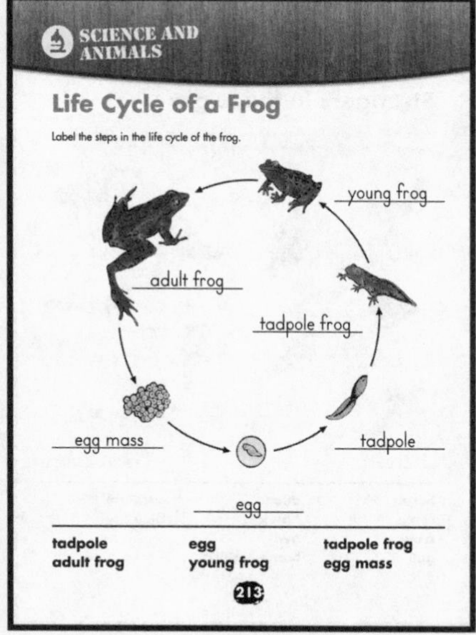

SCIENCE AND ANIMALS

Life Cycle of a Frog

Label the steps in the life cycle of the frog.

tadpole **adult frog** **egg** **young frog** **tadpole frog** **egg mass**

213

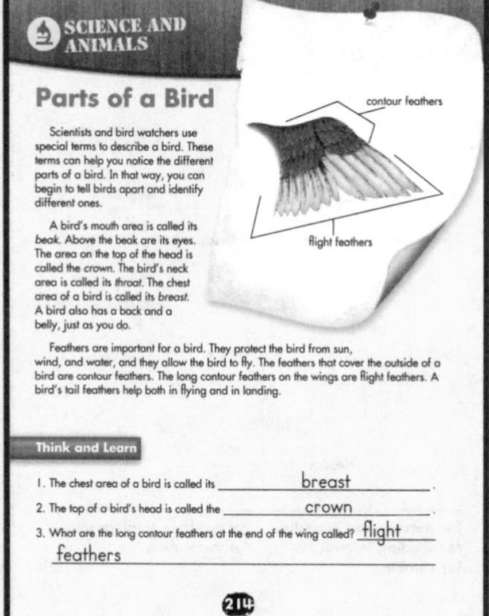

SCIENCE AND ANIMALS

Parts of a Bird

Scientists and bird watchers use special terms to describe a bird. These terms can help you notice the different parts of a bird. In that way, you can begin to tell birds apart and identify different ones.

A bird's mouth area is called its *beak*. Above the beak are its eyes. The area on the top of the head is called the *crown*. The bird's neck area is called its *throat*. The chest area of a bird is called its *breast*. A bird also has a back and a belly, just as you do.

Feathers are important for a bird. They protect the bird from sun, wind, and water, and they allow the bird to fly. The feathers that cover the outside of a bird are contour feathers. The long contour feathers on the wings are flight feathers. A bird's tail feathers help both in flying and in landing.

Think and Learn

1. The chest area of a bird is called its breast.
2. The top of a bird's head is called the crown.
3. What are the long contour feathers at the end of the wing called? flight feathers

214

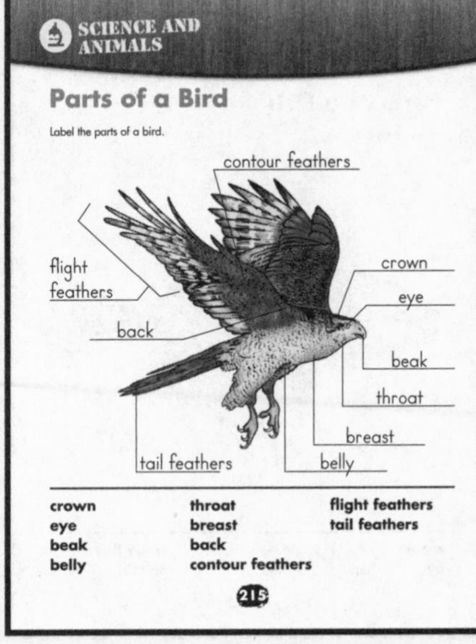
SCIENCE AND ANIMALS
Parts of a Bird
Label the parts of a bird.
contour feathers
flight feathers
crown
eye
back
beak
throat
breast
tail feathers
belly
crown
eye
beak
belly
throat
breast
back
contour feathers
flight feathers
tail feathers
215

SCIENCE AND ANIMALS
Bird Beaks
Bird beaks vary greatly in both shape and size. By looking closely at a bird's beak, you can often tell what kind of food that bird eats. Some birds feed on small animals, while other birds eat seeds. Their beaks are different, because they are used differently. Hawks, for example, have a beak made for tearing the meat of small animals, such as mice. The tiny hummingbird has a beak made for sucking liquid from flowers.
Cardinals have a strong beak good for cracking seeds. Fast-flying swallows have small beaks made for catching insects. Robins have pointed beaks for stabbing worms. Woodpeckers have strong beaks just right for pounding holes in wood as they look for insects.
Many water birds also have different kinds of beaks. A pelican has a large beak made for scooping up fishes. An anhinga has a sharp beak good for stabbing fish that swim by.
Write how each bird uses its beak.
Hawk tears the meat of small animals
Cardinal cracks open seeds
216

SCIENCE AND ANIMALS
Bird Beaks
Write how each bird uses its beak.
Hummingbird sucks liquid from flowers
Pelican scoops up fish
Swallow catches flying insects
Robin stabs worms in ground
Anhinga stabs fish in water
Woodpecker pounds holes in trees to find insects
217

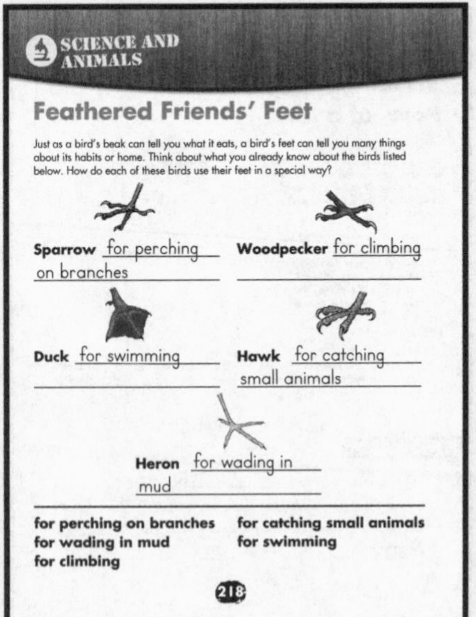
SCIENCE AND ANIMALS
Feathered Friends' Feet
Just as a bird's beak can tell you what it eats, a bird's feet can tell you many things about its habits or home. Think about what you already know about the birds listed below. How do each of these birds use their feet in a special way?
Sparrow for perching on branches
Woodpecker for climbing
Duck for swimming
Hawk for catching small animals
Heron for wading in mud
for perching on branches
for wading in mud
for climbing
for catching small animals
for swimming
218

SCIENCE AND ANIMALS
Strangers in the Night
It's much easier to identify a bird when you can see its color, size, and shape. At night, however, it is difficult to see. Identify these birds just by their shapes, or silhouettes.
blue jay
owl
robin
heron
duck
cardinal
crow
hawk
gull
hummingbird
heron
robin
crow
gull
duck
hawk
owl
hummingbird
cardinal
blue jay
219

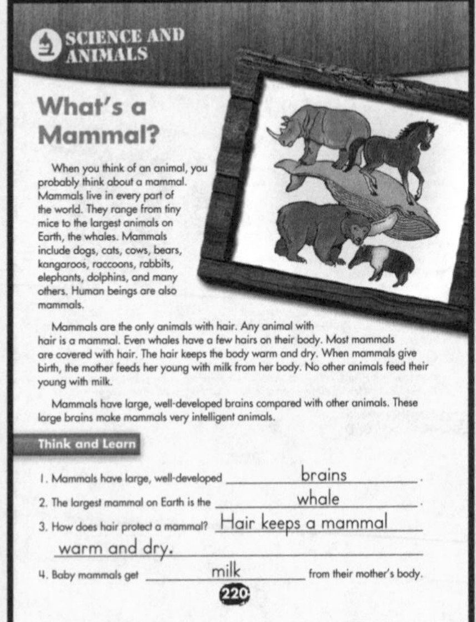
SCIENCE AND ANIMALS
What's a Mammal?
When you think of an animal, you probably think about a mammal. Mammals live in every part of the world. They range from tiny mice to the largest animals on Earth, the whales. Mammals include dogs, cats, cows, bears, kangaroos, raccoons, rabbits, elephants, dolphins, and many others. Human beings are also mammals.
Mammals are the only animals with hair. Any animal with hair is a mammal. Even whales have a few hairs on their body. Most mammals are covered with hair. The hair keeps the body warm and dry. When mammals give birth, the mother feeds her young with milk from her body. No other animals feed their young with milk.
Mammals have large, well-developed brains compared with other animals. These large brains make mammals very intelligent animals.
Think and Learn
1. Mammals have large, well-developed brains.
2. The largest mammal on Earth is the whale.
3. How does hair protect a mammal? Hair keeps a mammal warm and dry.
4. Baby mammals get milk from their mother's body.
220

ANSWER KEY

SCIENCE AND ANIMALS

What's a Mammal?

Think and Learn

1. Look at the picture above. How do you know the mother is a mammal? It has hair on its body.
2. In the picture above, what are the babies doing that only young mammals do? They are drinking milk from their mother.

221

SCIENCE AND ANIMALS

The Mammal With Wings

Bats are the only mammals that can fly. Some squirrels can glide, but bats really fly like birds. They can fly because they have wings.

A bat wing is made of a thin layer of skin called a *wing membrane*. This skin stretches between the long fingers on a bat's hands. The thumb is the only finger not attached to the wing membrane. On most bats, the wing membrane also stretches between the hands and the legs. It even stretches across the tail between the legs. When bats flap their wings, they can fly.

Bats fly mainly at night, when they hunt flying insects. They can find insects in the dark by using their large sensitive ears. During the day, most bats sleep by hanging upside down.

Think and Learn

1. Bats are the only mammals that can fly.
2. A wing membrane stretches between a bat's fingers.
3. When do bats hunt for food? at night
4. Bats sense where insects are flying with their ears.

222

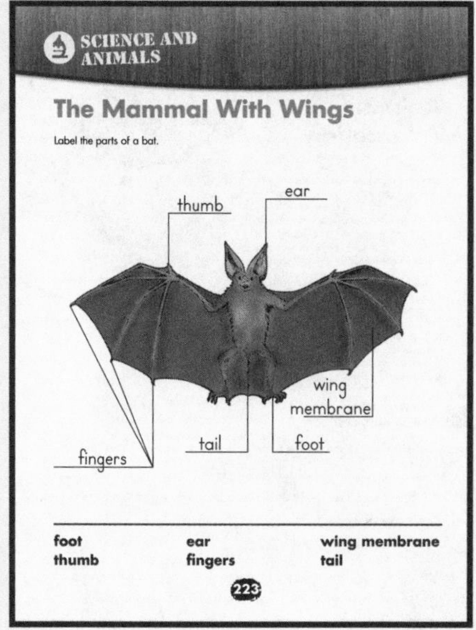
SCIENCE AND ANIMALS

The Mammal With Wings

Label the parts of a bat.

foot	ear	wing membrane
thumb	fingers	tail

223

SCIENCE AND ANIMALS

Animals Without Backbones

Animals that have a backbone are called *vertebrates*. Animals without a backbone are called *invertebrates*. There are many more invertebrates than vertebrates. More than 9 out of 10 animals on Earth are invertebrates.

The many different kinds of invertebrates vary greatly in shape and structure. They have only one thing in common. None have a backbone. Some, such as insects and lobsters, have a hard covering on the outside called an *exoskeleton*. Clams and snails have shells around their soft bodies. Other invertebrates, such as sponges and jellyfish, have no hard covering or shell.

What are some invertebrates you have seen? Sponges, jellyfish, earthworms, clams, snails, octopuses, starfishes, spiders, lobsters, and insects are all invertebrates.

Think and Learn

1. Animals without a backbone are called invertebrates.
2. Insects have an exoskeleton on the outside of their body.
3. What are two invertebrates that have no outer covering or shell? sponges and jellyfish

224

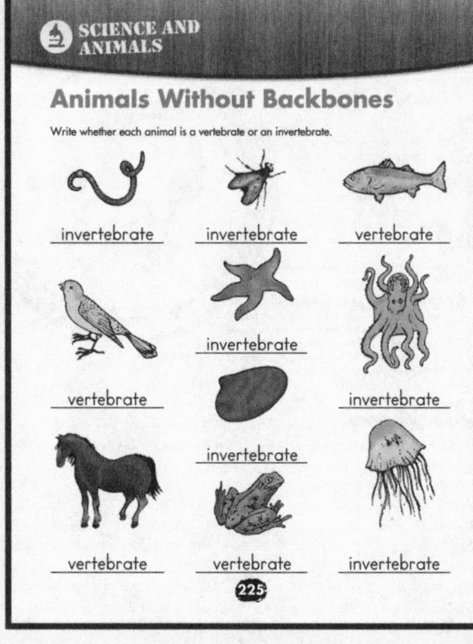
SCIENCE AND ANIMALS

Animals Without Backbones

Write whether each animal is a vertebrate or an invertebrate.

225

SCIENCE AND ANIMALS

Kinds of Insects

Write the name of each insect on the line.

moth	wasp	stag beetle
praying mantis	housefly	dragonfly
dog flea	water bug	

227

ANSWER KEY

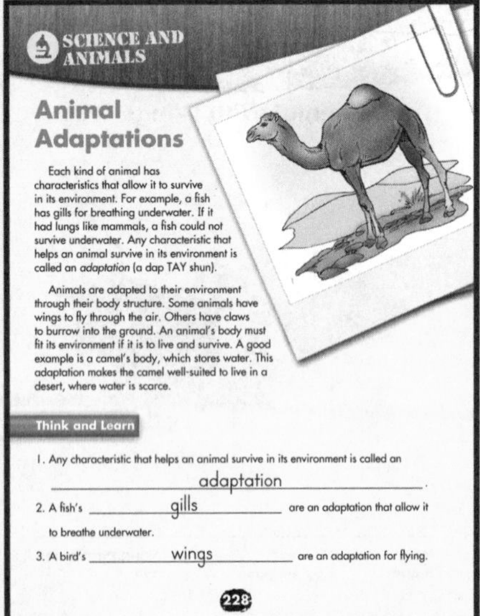

SCIENCE AND ANIMALS

Animal Adaptations

Each kind of animal has characteristics that allow it to survive in its environment. For example, a fish has gills for breathing underwater. If it had lungs like mammals, a fish could not survive underwater. Any characteristic that helps an animal survive in its environment is called an *adaptation* (a dap TAY shun).

Animals are adapted to their environment through their body structure. Some animals have wings to fly through the air. Others have claws to burrow into the ground. An animal's body must fit its environment if it is to live and survive. A good example is a camel's body, which stores water. This adaptation makes the camel well-suited to live in a desert, where water is scarce.

Think and Learn

1. Any characteristic that helps an animal survive in its environment is called an adaptation.
2. A fish's gills are an adaptation that allow it to breathe underwater.
3. A bird's wings are an adaptation for flying.

228

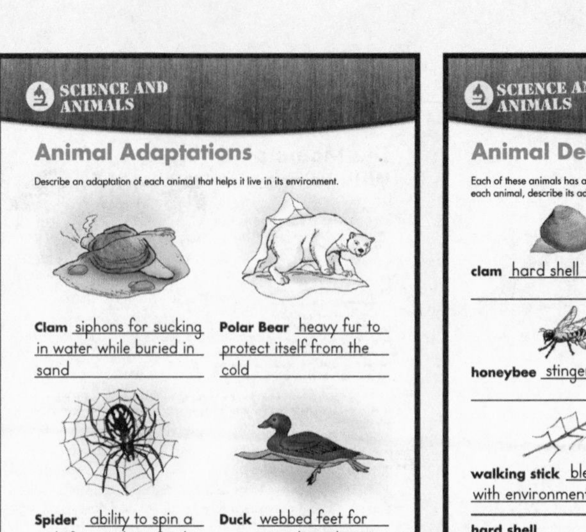

SCIENCE AND ANIMALS

Animal Adaptations

Describe an adaptation of each animal that helps it live in its environment.

Clam siphons for sucking in water while buried in sand

Polar Bear heavy fur to protect itself from the cold

Spider ability to spin a web for catching food

Duck webbed feet for swimming through water

229

SCIENCE AND ANIMALS

Animal Defenses

Each of these animals has an adaptation that helps it defend itself from enemies. For each animal, describe its adaptation.

clam hard shell

skunk bad smell

honeybee stinger

porcupine pointed quills

walking stick blends in with environment

pigeon fast flyer

hard shell **fast flyer** **blends in with environment**
stinger **bad smell**
pointed quills

230

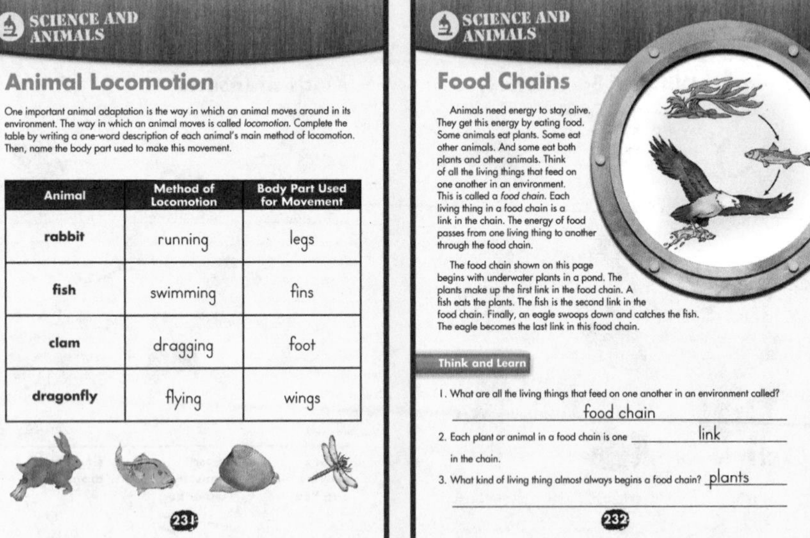

SCIENCE AND ANIMALS

Animal Locomotion

One important animal adaptation is the way in which an animal moves around in its environment. The way in which an animal moves is called *locomotion*. Complete the table by writing a one-word description of each animal's main method of locomotion. Then, name the body part used to make this movement.

Animal	Method of Locomotion	Body Part Used for Movement
rabbit	running	legs
fish	swimming	fins
clam	dragging	foot
dragonfly	flying	wings

231

SCIENCE AND ANIMALS

Food Chains

Animals need energy to stay alive. They get this energy by eating food. Some animals eat plants. Some eat other animals. And some eat both plants and other animals. Think of all the living things that feed on one another in an environment. This is called a *food chain*. Each living thing in a food chain is a link in the chain. The energy of food passes from one living thing to another through the food chain.

The food chain shown on this page begins with underwater plants in a pond. The plants make up the first link in the food chain. A fish eats the plants. The fish is the second link in the food chain. Finally, an eagle swoops down and catches the fish. The eagle becomes the last link in this food chain.

Think and Learn

1. What are all the living things that feed on one another in an environment called? food chain
2. Each plant or animal in a food chain is one link in the chain.
3. What kind of living thing almost always begins a food chain? plants

232